# Alternative Femininities

# Dress, Body, Culture

Books in this provocative series seek to articulate the connections between culture and dress, which is defined here in its broadest possible sense as any modification or supplement to the body. Interdisciplinary in approach, the series highlights the dialogue between identity and dress, cosmetics, coiffure and body alterations as manifested in practices as varied as plastic surgery, tattooing and ritual scarification. The series aims, in particular, to analyse the meaning of dress in relation to popular culture and gender issues and will included works grounded in anthropology, sociology, history, art history, literature and folklore.

ISSN: 1360–466X

Previously published in the Series

**Helen Bradley Foster**, 'New Raiments of Self': African American Clothing in the Antebellum South
**Claudine Griggs**, S/he: Changing Sex and Changing Clothes
**Michaele Thurgood Haynes**, Dressing Up Debutantes: Pageantry and Glitz in Texas
**Anne Brydon and Sandra Niessen**, Consuming Fashion: Adorning the Transnational Body
**Dani Cavallaro and Alexandra Warwick**, Fashioning the Frame: Boundaries, Dress and the Body
**Judith Perani and Norma H. Wolff**, Cloth, Dress and Art Patronage in Africa
**Linda B. Arthur**, Religion, Dress and the Body
**Paul Jobling**, Fashion Spreads: Word and Image in Fashion Photography
**Fadwa El Guindi**, Veil: Modesty, Privacy and Resistance
**Thomas S. Abler**, Hinterland Warriors and Military Dress: European Empires and Exotic Uniforms
**Linda Welters**, Folk Dress in Europe and Anatolia: Beliefs about Protection and Fertility
**Kim K.P. Johnson and Sharron J. Lennon**, Appearance and Power
**Barbara Burman**, The Culture of Sewing
**Annette Lynch**, Dress, Gender and Cultural Change
**Antonia Young**, Women Who Become Men
**David Muggleton**, Inside Subculture: The Postmodern Meaning of Style
**Nicola White**, Reconstructing Italian Fashion: America and the Development of the Italian Fashion Industry
**Brian J. McVeigh**, Wearing Ideology: The Uniformity of Self-presentation in Japan
**Shaun Cole**, Don We Now Our Gay Apparel: Gay Men's Dress in the Twentieth Century
**Kate Ince**, Orlan: Millennial Female
**Nicola White and Ian Griffiths**, The Fashion Business: Theory, Practice, Image
**Ali Guy, Eileen Green and Maura Banim**, **Through the Wardrobe: Women's Relationships with their Clothes**
**Linda B. Arthur**, Undressing Religion: Commitment and Conversion from a Cross-cultural Perspective
**William J.F. Keenan**, Dressed to Impress: Looking the Part
**Joanne Entwistle and Elizabeth Wilson**, Body Dressing
**Leigh Summers**, Bound to Please: A History of the Victorian Corset
**Paul Hodkinson**, Goth: Identity, Style and Subculture
**Michael Carter**, Fashion Classics from Carlyle to Barthes
**Sandra Niessen, Ann Marie Leshkowich and Carla Jones**, Re-Orienting Fashion: The Globalization of Asian Dress
**Kim K.P. Johnson, Susan J.Torntore and Joanne B. Eicher**, Fashion Foundations: Early Writings on Fashion and Dress
**Helen Bradley Foster and Donald Clay Johnson**, Wedding Dress Across Cultures
**Charlotte Suthrell**, Unzipping Gender: Sex, Cross-Dressing and Culture
**Yuniya Kawamura**, The Japanese Revolution in Paris Fashion
**Ruth Barcan**, Nudity: A Cultural Anatomy

# *Alternative Femininities*

## Body, Age and Identity

*Samantha Holland*

*Oxford • New York*

First published in 2004 by
Berg
Editorial offices:
1st Floor, Angel Court, 81 St Clements Street, Oxford, OX4 1AW, UK
175 Fifth Avenue, New York NY10010 USA

Berg is the imprint of Oxford International Publishers Ltd.

**Library of Congress Cataloguing-in-Publication Data**
A catalogue record for this book is available from the Library of Congress.


**British Library Cataloguing-in-Publication Data**
A catalogue record for this book is available from the British Library.


ISBN 1 85973 803 6 (Cloth)
1 85973 808 7 (Paper)


Typeset by Avocet Typeset, Chilton, Aylesbury, Bucks
Printed in the United Kingdom by Biddles Ltd, King's Lynn


**www.bergpublishers.com**

B+t

# Contents

# Acknowledgements

First, my thanks to women who allowed me to interview them about what were often very personal thoughts and feelings. I enjoyed meeting every one of the participants of this research.

I am very grateful to those people who gave general encouragement in different ways, in different amounts, and at different times (particularly when I was writing my PhD, from which this book is adapted). They are: Rik Brydson, Sally Byers, Jo Hammond, Harbie Holland, Andy Horne, Kim Pattison, and Carole Wafer.

Thanks to the following for advice at various stages and/or on various drafts: Feona Attwood, Jenni Craik, Sharon MacDonald, Diane Richardson, Cilla Ross, and Tracey Warren. I also appreciate the help and input of Ian, Kathryn and Caroline at Berg.

I would particularly like to thank Jill LeBihan, punctuation whiz and Izzard-fan, who inspired me to finish what had become a rather protracted activity!

# Growing Up but Staying 'Freaky': An Introduction

This book is centrally concerned with a particular group of women. Once, long ago, my original interest lay in researching the friendships of adolescent girls within subcultures but, at a very early stage of reviewing the literature, I was intrigued to discover what seemed to me to be a glaring omission. Recent work in subcultural studies and in fashion theory has concentrated on issues such as spectacular subcultures or the fashion industry, but there has been a notable silence on the experiences of adult women who continue to negotiate a path between being 'alternative' and being feminine. Empirical studies (such as Thornton, 1995; Muggleton, 2000; Williamson, 2001; and Hodkinson, 2002) have attempted to be more inclusive of women's experiences but have so far failed to adequately address the fact that women do not always 'grow out of' the appearance they adopted as teenagers. The interest in, and acceptability of, 'alternative' styles has become greater in the last few years, with such styles becoming more visible (for example, from an eco-warrior hippy doll called Feral Cheryl[1], to scholarly tomes on the meanings of body modifications) and yet still the voices of the women who had long been involved in this kind of lifestyle remained silent. For this reason, this research investigates the personal and complex meanings of 'femininities' through 'alternative' style and clothing, connecting work on subcultures, the body and fashion, and situated in feminist qualitative methodologies. The book theorises 'different', oppositional identities and looks, and examines the particular meanings these hold for the participants, asking if appearance is used as a site for critique and challenge, and drawing out tensions, conflicts and pleasures experienced by the participants.

Whenever a researcher embarks on a project there is usually, in the researcher's head, a list of aims. These aims, which may be modest, supply an important 'map' via which to find one's way into the research. My aims, then, were: to find out through their own narratives how, and particularly why, the participants construct their appearance as they do; and to explore existing work about 'femininities', appearance and gender. In this light I aimed to analyse themes which emerged from the interviews. My intention was to explore how a particular group of women experienced, rationalised and understood their appearance (which so clearly resisted many elements of a traditionally 'feminine' appearance), articulating and constructing their own narratives about being both 'alternative' and women. As a feminist I often despair at the rift between academic feminism and 'grass-roots' feminism and I also aimed for this book to remain accessible to a general audience as well as, at the least, of interest to the academic reader. Subcultural groups are studied, yes, but how often do they read the end-product? How often is the end-product written in a way that a general reader, even if the book is 'about you', would want to read it? This is a trend I hope not to follow.

My interviewees drew on a variety of discourses such as ageing and body image, placing themselves ambiguously both within and outside dominant ideologies of femininity. But why did I choose to focus particularly on appearance? Although appearance can be seen to be a 'slippery' matter to try to pin down, it hasn't stopped people from trying it. 'Clothing in Western society is paradoxical ... Clothes socialise our bodies ... Our dress constitutes our "appearance": the "vestimentary envelope" produces us as social beings' (Ash and Wilson, 1992: 6). As Craik has argued, women wear their bodies through their clothes (1994: 2) and one of the key ways that gender is perpetuated is through the embodiment of males and females as 'men' and 'women'. Because of this, as Evans and Thornton argue, 'the practice which a culture insists are meaningless or trivial, the places where ideology has succeeded in becoming invisible, are practices in need of investigating' (1991: 15). Such places and practices are what are investigated in this book.

## Methodological Framework

I collected the data through semi-structured interviews because I wished to be able to encourage the women I interviewed to speak to me at length, and in detailed and subjective ways. I recognise that there are particular problems with the participants telling me about how their appearance is maintained through practice as they are more likely to be talking about those practices which are engaged in self-consciously. However, as Bourdieu argues, much of practice is not engaged in consciously: 'what is learned by the body is not something that one has, like knowledge that can be brandished, but something that one is' (1990: 73). Therefore, habits, perceptions and behaviours were internalised historically so that people act, think and feel in particular ways (socially acquired, embodied systems) without necessarily being aware that they are doing them. In this way, the narratives of the participants are the conscious result of the practices they undertake and, perhaps, their anxieties about being 'feminine enough' are the unconscious results of 'habitus'. However, this is not to say that everything they say is inaccurate or not of value. It remains of value because of the reasons, outlined above, that I chose to focus on appearance in the first place.

Feminist researchers have long argued the value of empirical research and, bearing this in mind, I include a complete 'methods' chapter in Appendix 1 (Gregson and Crewe, 2003, also include a full account of their own methods, including different ways they approached research design and analysis). It contains a discussion about the methods employed, examining what I call the 'nuts and bolts' of the research: the interview process including interview schedule and timetable, and some reflections on my own place in (and outside) the research. It also introduces the women who took part. Feminism has been the inspiration for my own (late) academic progress and provided both method and motivation for my work, so it is vital to acknowledge the importance of its stress on methodologies and hearing individual voices. Muggleton is also among those who have lamented the lack of empirical work which provides 'an analysis at the levels of structure, culture and biography [which] would demonstrate how individual pathways are carved out within common cultural responses to shared structural conditions' (2000: 11). For these reasons I suggest that the reader turns to Appendix 1 before they begin reading the empirical Chapters 3 to 8.

## Theoretical Position

In Chapter 2 I provide an account of the literature read in preparation for and during the course of this research. It is not, of course, either definitive or exhaustive. Some books read will not appear in Chapter 2 and yet will be listed in the Bibliography.

The contradiction between conformity and resistance is discussed throughout the following chapters and is central to any understanding of femininity. The research explores a notion of femininity based on the contradictions that my participants displayed: the tensions that they negotiated between finding a path of 'traditional' femininity that was acceptable to them and remaining comfortably 'alternative'. My theoretical position is that of a feminist ethnographer. Therefore, feminist research methodologies and the rationale for them are the guiding features of this book. Coates defines this position as one which aims to

> put women at the centre of my work. Secondly, it means that I do not pretend to be 'objective' but acknowledge from the beginning where I am coming from ... I believe that all research is subjective and political. I would argue that being 'interested' rather than 'disinterested' is a strength, not a weakness: it means that I am engaged in what I do. (1996: 14)

This approach is borne out by the ways in which I chose to allow a certain degree of autonomy for the participants in their interviews; although I had an interview schedule there was also the possibility of each interviewee leading the interview into what was most important and relevant for her. By engaging with both the participants and their narratives each interview could become more flexible and personalised. In the same way I was willing to disclose things about myself if appropriate or if asked, which has become an accepted response in feminist interview methodology (as discussed in Appendix 1). My distance from the participants may not have been sufficient for many more traditional sociological research studies, where the researcher strives for objectivity. Again, as Coates states, 'I want to be explicit about my relationship to those who participated in my research' (1996: 14) and my relationship with my participants was that I was similar to them in that they saw me as another 'freak' woman, who was familiar with many of the same shops, clubs and pubs and the terminology of being 'alternative'. Obviously, and equally, there were also many differences between myself and the participants and it is these similarities and differences which informed and enriched the interviews and, ultimately, the research findings.

The use of the term 'participants' was used to contest the objectification of the women I interviewed. As Furman (1997), Reinharz (1992) and others have argued, allowing participants to 'speak for themselves' is a way for the feminist researcher to enable the participants' subjectivity as much as possible in a context which otherwise provides little scope for their voices to emerge clearly. The very term reflects and acknowledges their input. I wished to 'situate' their experiences within a time and a place, to move beyond the universal or the abstract, to the personal and the particular. Whilst doing this I was aware of Rowbotham's assertion that theory "doesn't mean a fixed and removed body of 'truth' which has universal validity" but, instead, should be a 'map' for feminist research, providing paths and footholds (Stanley and Wise, 1993: 71). Thus feminist methodological theory provided footholds as I sought to discover what was of central importance to each woman I interviewed.

How is it possible as a researcher to deal with contradiction and subjectivity? Coates expresses her research position as one which seeks to "validate women's everyday experience" (1996: 15). I sought to deal with conflicts by working with contradictions rather than seeing them as troubling for the research, so the many sets of themes and tensions that arose in the interviews became the focus of the research. Originality in the data is achieved through the ages of the participants and their reflections on ageing. Originality in the theory is in bringing together various theoretical fields, in particular, in giving a sociological dimension, informed by feminist methodologies, to what is essentially a piece of cultural studies research (more on this in Chapter 2). Identifying and talking to this particular group of people, who were absent from current theory, extends our ideas about femininity and the contradictions inherent in it. In this case, these ideas are extended by presenting femininity and ageing in a framework of a history of 'resisting' women.

## A Brief Overview of the Empirical Chapters

The empirical chapters focus on the contradictions and tensions experienced and negotiated by the participants in relation to their appearance, and how this affects the choices available to them. There are five empirical chapters, which I outline below. The structure of the empirical chapters partially follows a 'life-course' pattern: in the first and second empirical chapters the participants discuss their childhoods, in the third and fourth they talk about themselves only as adult women, and in the fifth chapter they reflect on their ageing. Although the interviews themselves did not necessarily adopt the pattern of chronologically following a woman from childhood to the present, the interview data did arrange themselves naturally to follow this pattern.

In Chapter 3, Negotiating Fluffy Femininities, I begin to discuss the research findings and ask 'What is femininity?' Here the focus is on individual definitions and descriptions of traditional femininity in order to ascertain how femininity as a discourse is viewed, and how it is constructed as something which women are and do.

Chapter 4, How To Be a Fairy Princess, builds on these themes with more specific examples of how the interviewees chose to render their own versions of femininity and what was important to them. I examine the subject of the fairy princess and how it sits uncomfortably with the interviewees' resistance to other equally traditional images of femininity. Hair (styles and dressing) and clothes (buying and making) are both key preoccupations and both are discussed in relation to how the former imbues many participants with a feeling of 'being feminine' (often serving as a way to confirm a femininity that other aspects of appearance may erode), and the latter represent a major commitment to constructing the finished product of being 'alternative': the appearance.

Chapter 5, Categories of Unconventional, investigates the interplay between the participants' insistence on their own femininity and on their unconventionality, and the apparent contradictions which result. The focus is on how they articulate their resistance and how this contradicts many of the statements they made about their femininity. There are descriptions and definitions of 'unconventional' women to compare with those of traditional women, and an overview of 'bohemian' dress in order to place the interviewees in some sort of historical framework of 'resisting' women.

Chapter 6, 'More Like Torture than love'?, explores how 'difference' is embodied and asks how 'alternative' women signal their difference through their body modifications. Wider issues about body image are also discussed in relation to the interviewees' perceptions of themselves as feminine women and whether their 'difference' impacts on these perceptions.

Chapter 7, Defying the Crone?, focuses on the social constraints and choices available to women as they grow older, particularly the negative aspects of ageing, and how they responded to these anxieties and fears. I attempt to unpick some of the boundaries of unconventionality, asking how much they can 'get away with' as they get older. Although they challenge some gendered norms of appearance, they are still bound by, and extremely aware of, age categories: categories they fear as more able to define them and bind them to a place or a role than gender itself.

Chapter 8 is the conclusion.

# *Background Reading*

Several main fields of theory were drawn upon as a lack of literature in the specific area of the research necessitated the use of broad fields of work. Much of the work in subcultural theory has concentrated on subculture and alternative styles being the province of youth (for example, Frith, 1984; Davis, 1992; and Borden discusses how a skateboarder of twenty years old can be considered elderly (2001: 140)!) whereas the women I interviewed would refute that their appearance or lifestyle was only suitable for the 'young'. Similarly, fashion theorists consider that women prefer to be categorised within mainstream fashion, with a few exceptions, such as Keenan (2001). For this reason, this literature review is a thematic one; dominant themes and corresponding literature are discussed in 'clusters', examining how definitions and concepts have developed over time, leading up to current theoretical perspectives. In this way I hope to unfold an historical account which considers how perceptions and approaches to the dominant themes have evolved. There are five main themes. The first theme is femininity, followed by fashion theory and then subcultural theory. Identity and the body are the final two themes.

## Femininity

Since the key overall theme of the research is femininity (how it is rendered, played out, resisted and understood), here I review ideas about and definitions of femininity and how these definitions do (or do not) link to the research. 'What is femininity?' is a question which has exercised feminist writers for decades and many feminist writers have attempted to pin down the elusive concept of femininity. For example, Brownmiller asserts that 'femininity, in essence, is a romantic sentiment, a nostalgic tradition of imposed limitations' (1984: 2); Wolf argues that 'femininity is code for femaleness plus whatever a society happens to be selling. If "femininity" means female sexuality ... women never lost it and do not need to buy it back' (1990: 177); and Smith comments that 'the notion of femininity does not define a determinate and unitary phenomenon' (1988: 36). Early accounts, such as Millett (1977) appear to skate close to placing sex and gender as the equivalent categories to nature and culture, which created difficulties as women were already aligned closely to nature (thus actually concurring with essentialist notions of women being emotional and unpredictable). A consensus was reached on the difference between sex and gender which helpfully repositioned gender as a general category which applied equally to men or women: for example, Scott provides an explanation that gender (that is, femininities and masculinities) is a 'social category imposed upon a sexed body' (1988) and Furman explains that her 'assumption is that a woman's sex – her femaleness – is biologically based, whereas her gender – her femininity – is socially constructed' (1997: 192). However, pithy definitions aside, femininity often continues to elude analysis. 'Femininity increasingly became an exasperation, a brilliant, subtle aesthetic that was bafflingly inconsistent at the same time it was minutely, demandingly concrete, a rigid code of appearance and behaviour defined by do's and don't-do's' (Brownmiller, 1984: 2).

The difficulties lie primarily in the fact that the term 'femininity' is a concept which refers to a set of gendered behaviours and practices, and yet which is fluid and not fixed, and can mean as many different things as there are women (just as there are as many 'masculinities' as there are men). As Butler argues, it is 'a stylized repetition of acts' and is fragile, shifting, contextual and never complete (1990: 140). Glover and Kaplan concur with the idea of masculinity and femininity as contextual and unfinished, referring to historical differences in gender ideals and especially when 'one considers the range of competing definitions of what it has meant to be a man or a woman' (2000: xxvii). For these reasons, there are a variety of accounts of what femininity is and how is it 'done': for example, femininity has been seen variously as a normative order, that is, a set of psychological traits (such as that women are considered to be more nurturing than men, be less aggressive and have fewer spatial skills); it has been seen as a performance; and it has been seen as a process of interaction. Crucially, various theorists have addressed the issue of how gender serves to normalise heterosexuality (for example, see Richardson, 1996, 2000) and is 'much more than just an annoyingly arbitrary and socially constructed classification system ... gender dynamically empowers heterosexuality' (Jeffreys, 1996: 75). From butch/femme lesbian relationships to transsexuals and transgender activists, Jeffreys illustrates the 'flexibility and artificiality' (1996: 84) of gender and sexuality. However, she also warns that, despite being exhorted by lesbian and gay theorists to play with gender, it is more than 'simply harmless costumes to be exhumed from mother's trunks in the attic and tried on for size' (1996: 75) and has more far-reaching results. For example, Mirza argues that 'post-modernism has allowed the celebration of difference, the recognition of otherness, the presence of multiple and changeable subjectivities' (1997: 19). Some feminist theorists have challenged the idea of sex and gender as definite categories as unworkable (as not all sex/gender categories necessarily work: for example, not all women are able to become pregnant). 'Post-modernist arguments ... suggest not only that gender identity is commonly much more fluid than commonly supposed, but also that the sex/gender distinction is untenable, because biological differences are not significant in themselves, but only if society makes them so' (Bryson, 1999: 49; see also, perhaps most notably, Butler, 1990). The main problem is avoiding notions of essentialism: ideas that femininity equates with young, white, slim, heterosexual, able-bodied women have been refuted by a number of theorists who point out that femininity should never be simply a singular descriptive term, but instead should always be femininities (Connell, 1987; Glover and Kaplan, 2000: 4) and genders (Bryson, 1999: 50). Therefore, because of these pluralities, theorists need to always take account of the differences between women, differences of ethnicities, class, age, body size (Wolf, 1990: 12–13), as well as celebrate and challenge (rather than bemoan) the differences between men and women (Bryson, 1999: 48).

A central question to this research is how the interviewees understand traditional femininities and, as a result, place themselves in opposition to them. Smith argues that femininity involves 'assembling a miscellaneous collection of instances apparently lacking coherence ... Its descriptive use relies on our background and ordinary knowledge of everyday practices, which are the source and origin of these instances' (1988: 36); so, in other words, we 'just know' what femininity means, what it is and how it is done – except, when asked to explain it, it becomes much more difficult. Smith criticises Brownmiller for collecting (into topics), but not analysing, the phenomena of femininity, 'thus enacting the indeterminacy of the concept' (1988: 36). As Smith explains, 'we can produce examples' but they will not have a pattern or even rationality so 'inquiry ... has to begin with the ordinary and unanalysed ways in which we know what we are talking about when we use the concept' (1988: 36), which is exactly what my own research sets out to do. One of the key ways that femininity has come to be understood and learnt is through what Furman calls 'the traditional practices of femininity and beautification' (1997: 2), the 'actual practices, actual activities' (Smith, 1988: 37), which construct the phenomena. The way that we learn the current practices is, to a large part, through the visual images of mass media. The rules for femininity have come to be culturally transmitted more and more through the deployment of what Bordo calls standardized visual images. As a result, femininity itself has come to be largely a matter of constructing, in the manner described by Erving Goffman, the appropriate surface presentation of the self. We no longer are told what 'a lady' is or of what femininity consists. Rather, we learn the rules directly through bodily discourse: through images which tell us what clothes, body shape, facial expression, movements and behavior is required. (1989: 17)

Smith notes that femininity is created as a 'distinctively textual phenomenon' (1988: 37). By this she means,

> to address femininity is to address a textual discourse vested in women's magazines and television, advertisements, the appearance of cosmetic counters, fashion displays, and to a lesser extent, books ... Discourse also involves the talk women do in relation to such texts, the work of producing oneself to realise the textual images, the skills involved in going shopping, making and choosing clothes, making decisions about colours, styles, make-up. (1988: 40)

This relation to the texts of femininity is particularly relevant to this research (and the gaps it seeks to fill) as the women involved both do and do not join in the sort of talk Smith describes, and both do and do not engage with many of the textual elements of femininity. For example, of course they do watch television but they criticise fashion magazines and, while they do wear make-up and buy or make clothes, they seek to exist outside the 'fashion displays'. Craik calls these textual activities a 'recipe for femininity', which implies that all of the ingredients must be included in a particular way to guarantee success. She argues, quoting Walkerdine, that

> the assumption of femininity is 'at best shaky and partial' (Walkerdine, 1984: 163). The ideals and fantasies offered to women are points of orientation for the realisation of a gendered self ... To this end, the media have provided the means for promoting desirable images and icons of femininity, because they can be endlessly reproduced and widely consumed (1994: 73).

This type of analysis (rules, requirements, orientation) seems to place women as mindless consumers, in thrall to the power of media images. However, Smith refutes the idea of femininity as only an effect of patriarchy or that women are merely the passive dupes of either mass media or male power. She argues that it is important to avoid the 'treatment of women as passive victims ... to recognise women's active and creative part in its social organisation ... They are active, they create themselves' (1988: 38). This statement echoes many of the findings of this research in that

many of the interviewees were concerned with the creation and maintenance of themselves as 'alternative' women. At the same time they challenge Smith's assertion that 'a woman active in the discourse works within
its interpretive circles, attempting to create in her own body the displays
which appeal to the public textual images as their authority and depend
upon the doctrines of femininity for their interpretation' (1988: 43). They
consume only some of the discourses of femininity so are able to move
away from them, in a limited way. Additionally, they cannot be said to be
entirely active in the discourse: although they count themselves as 'feminine', their appearance critiques the 'public textual images' and does not
look to the 'doctrines' of traditional femininity for their interpretation.

Girls learn early the standardised images through a variety of texts, for
example, from magazines (see Winship, 1987; Smith, 1988: 45; Wolf,
1990: 61–85; Macdonald, 1995: 194–7). Other studies highlight how fairy
tales create doctrines of femininity (Rowe, 1986; Zipes, 1986) or how play
(Davies, 1989, on how play is gendered; Marsh, 2000, on 'superhero' play;
Rogers, 1999, and Urla and Swedlund, 2000, both on Barbie) creates powerful images which remain one of our 'yardsticks' for femininity as adults
(more discussion about childhood can be found in Chapters 3 and 4). Both
Lees (1993) and Sharpe (1994) have studied how femininity is learnt, rendered and resisted by girls and young women at school and home. As
Gaines argues, 'from the mid-teens ... [there is] a close link between
dressing the part and playing the part' (1990: 181), the part being to fulfil
the requirements of modern femininity. This is a difficult task for, as Wolf
argues, 'young women have been doubly weakened: raised to compete like
men in rigid male-model institutions, they must also maintain to the last
detail an impeccable femininity' (1990: 211). Wolf's polemic focuses on
what Smith later called the textual discourse of femininity, including
women's magazines, beauty culture and dieting and eating disorders, highlighting how a range of institutions (from work practices to religion and
media images) serve to perpetuate the ideologies about femininity and how
women suffer through them. 'These negative associations of inferiority and
worse, which so stubbornly cling to the subjective and objective representations of woman, have been one of feminism's strongest *raisons d'être*'
and continue to divide feminist theorists about what is 'natural' and what
is cultural (Glover and Kaplan, 2000: 5). To describe the negative feelings
which women still feel and witness about themselves as women, some feminists have adopted the term 'abjection', its usual meaning being to feel
inferior, to attempt to theorise 'the interaction between the ways in which
societies and women themselves too often conceive of femininity' (ibid.,
2000: 7). Abjection, although not a term used in the empirical chapters, is

a relevant concept in that many of my interviewees were indeed negative about femininity.

There are other, more positive ways to resist the negative connotations of femininity. Glover and Kaplan outline an important concept for this research, the concept of the paradox. They argue that 'the mix of abjection and euphoria that is the psychic condition of modern femininity ... can be thought of as a creative paradox rather than as pure contradiction or simple complement, for the tension between these opposed psychic states has been productive rather than otherwise' (2000: 8). They draw on the work of Scott (1996), who explains that a paradox can be both true and false at the same time, as well as something which is resistant to dominant ideas. Therefore the term is 'an immensely suggestive way of posing the "riddle" or the "problem" of femininity' (Glover and Kaplan, 2000: 8) and is of particular use to this research as many of the accounts of my interviewees are contradictory (for example, placing themselves in relation to, and yet simultaneously resistant to, the idea of femininity) and therefore paradoxical in nature. However, girls (and women) often find ways to resist the restrictions of femininity, which were echoed by many of the accounts of my interviewees. As McRobbie (1989a) found, girls used fashion as a counter-discourse to resist the anti-feminine doctrines of school, and Blackman (1998), similarly, found that a group of 'New Wave' girls made themselves highly visible through their appearance. This type of resistance, which subverts feminine qualities while working within a general framework of femininity (for example, using fashion as the tool to resist other doctrines), is relevant to this research in that my interviewees exhibited a very similar attitude to resistance.

Ussher (1997) discusses the difference between women who were apparently traditionally (and knowingly) feminine and those who resist many aspects of traditional femininity. Although both categories entail some elements of resistance or subversion, Ussher draws a distinction between the former ('doing girl') and the latter ('resisting girl'). The former is when a woman uses feminine masquerade (using all the trappings of traditional femininity). The latter is when 'that which is traditionally signified by "femininity" is invariably ignored or denied (often derided) – the necessity for body discipline, the inevitability of the adoption of the mask of beauty and the adoption of coquettish feminine wiles' (Ussher, 1997: 455). This type of resistance highlights the elements of masquerade present in femininity. 'Feminists have more recently turned to masquerade as a theoretical paradigm, as a supplement to, as well as a reaction against, theories of voyeurism and fetishism which posit a generic male spectator' (Gaines, 1990: 24). This works (not necessarily consciously) by distancing the woman from her rendition of femininity – Barbara Cartland was a good example. Studlar notes that masquerade often involves a type of 'excess femininity' in which (as Doane argues) to 'construct a distance between the woman and her public assumption of excessive feminine accoutrements' (Studlar, 1990: 244). Tseëlon's account of masquerade was most helpful in that I was able to draw a parallel between her definition of masquerade and the actions of some of my interviewees:

> Some professional women ... flash their femininity to signal that they are not really so threatening, and to reassure that their power is just a charade. Femininity is thus a disarming disguise: it is donned, like masquerade, to disguise the female's desire ... [for] power ... The woman deflects attention from her desire for power through its opposite: constructing a very feminine, non-threatening image of herself. (1995: 39)

In this way masquerade relies entirely on an oppositional masculinity against which to define itself. Tseëlon argues that, from a feminist perspective, the 'concept of masquerade is double-edged. It implies the instability of the feminine position' (1995: 37) defining subjectivity through distance, denial and defence. However, it can also be empowering: it 'simultaneously disguises and calls attention to what it tries to hide, in the process of hiding it' (1995: 39).[1]

Yet still sexualised femininity becomes less associated with women as they age, making clear the link between femininity as a cultural phenomenon inscribed upon the bodies of young women. There is a difference between 'popular' and academic constructions of age in that cultural representations (what Smith (1988) calls texts) offer more polarised, and not necessarily more positive, images whereas academic constructions (such as Fairhurst, 1998; Gannon, 1999) tend to concentrate on the reality for 'real' women. For example, Bordo argues that actresses for whom

> face-lifts are virtually routine ... are changing cultural expectations of what a woman 'should' look like at forty-five and fifty. This is touted in popular culture as a liberating development for older women ... [where] fifty is still sexy. But in fact ... [they] have not made the aging female body sexually more acceptable. They have established a new norm – achievable only through continual cosmetic surgery – in which the surface of the female body ceases to age physically as the body grows chronologically older. (1993: 25–6)

There is nothing liberating about not being able to age; Wolf calls it 'the cult of the fear of age' (1990: 106). To scratch the surface of this ostensibly liberating development reveals stereotypes and unpalatable truths about the longevity of femininity having nothing to do with the lifespan of the woman associated with it, evading the truth of academic accounts which reveal facts such as, 'Because women form the largest proportion of the very old, where the most severe problems of care are concentrated, the notion of elderly women as problematic becomes even more pronounced and generalised' (Ford and Sinclair, 1987: 5).

Further discussion about ageing women, and their relation to femininity, can be found in Chapter 7.

## Fashion Theory

Until relatively recently, fashion held the place as the 'the F-Word' in academia; it was 'widely regarded as frivolous, sexist, bourgeois, "material" (not intellectual), and, therefore, beneath contempt' (Steele, 1997a: 1). The history of dress and fashion has developed from being located primarily in the fields of fashion history (such as Thesander, 1997; Lehnert, 1999) and anthropology (for example, see Cordwell and Schwartz, 1979; El Guindi, 1999) and now encompasses work in cultural studies (Craik, 1994); subcultural theory (Hebdige, 1979; McRobbie, 1989a, b; Muggleton, 2000); sociology (Kaiser, 1990; Keenan, 2001); geography (Gregson et al., 2001; Gregson and Crewe, 2003); and gender studies (Tseëlon, 1995; Guy et al, 2001). One of the earliest influential accounts of fashion was Veblen's (1899) examination of how women's dress was used, through the 'wasteful consumption' (1994: 104) of seasonal fashions, to signal that the wearer 'can afford to consume freely and uneconomically ... [and is] not under the necessity of earning a livelihood' (1994: 105). The 'wearer' in this case was women in their elaborate fashions of the late nineteenth century. For example, Veblen rails against particular aspects of feminine attire such as shoes, bonnets and skirts. 'The substantial reason for our tenacious attachment to the skirt is just this: it is expensive and it hampers the wearer at every turn and incapacitates her for all useful exertion' (1994: 105). Although referring to middle- and upper-class women who could afford to buy and wear clothes that 'disabled' (1994: 111) them, Veblen argues that a woman's function in this respect came to be 'to consume vicariously for the head of the household' (1994: 110), that is, to signal the status of the family on behalf of the man (see also Taylor, 1983: 120–1; Davis, 1992: 41–2; Craik, 1994: 49). Therefore, the main point of Veblen's argument is that not only do women's clothes (of that time) denote a 'general disregard of the wearer's comfort' but also they indicate that a woman is still 'the man's chattel' (1994: 111). Many of Veblen's points are relevant to this research, particularly as many of my interviewees echoed his sentiments, just as second-wave feminists did in the 1960s and 1970s.

However, Crane (1999) examines the two types of women's dress at the very time that Veblen was writing which reveals that he described only one of two prevalent and distinct styles – although he was clearly aware of class distinction in dress. In fact, Davis has criticised Veblen for placing '*too* exclusive an emphasis on social class differentiation' (original emphasis, 1992: 9). Crane points out that the fashionable styles (that is, the ones which Veblen referred to) were 'exceptionally restrictive and ornamental' (1999: 241) whereas

> co-existing with this style was an alternative style that incorporated items from men's clothing ... sometimes singly, sometimes in combination with one another, but always associated with items of fashionable female clothing. Trousers were not part of this alternative style, probably because trousers, when worn by women, constituted a greater symbolic challenge to the system than most middle-class women were prepared to make. (1999: 242)

Women's clothes symbolised a great deal about her person: 'her social role, social standing, and personal character' (Crane, 1999: 242; see also Thesander, 1997: 96; Lehnert, 1999: 100, 105–7) and as women were 'effectively denied anything but very limited participation in the public sphere, [they] were frequently identified in terms of their clothing. Political cartoons, satire, and commentary tended to refer to women as "petticoats"' (Crane, 1999: 242, and until relatively recently women could still be referred to as 'skirt').[2] Gaines has argued that this association of women with their clothes functions to perpetuate the gendered distinctions between men and women:

> Costume delivers gender as self-evident or natural then recedes as clothing, leaving the connotation 'femininity'. In popular discourse, there is often no distinction made between a woman and her attire. She is what she wears. This continuity between woman and dress works especially well to keep women in their traditional 'place', especially during epochs when styles which accentuate the 'natural' contours of woman's body are favoured. (1990: 1)[3]

The alternative style was 'a form of resistance to the dominant style of dress' although it 'was worn by many women who had no connection with the feminist movement' (Crane, 1999: 261). I also found that many of my interviewees were disinterested in, or hostile to, feminism and the adoption of alternative dress cannot be automatically equated with a woman's desire to further women's equality. Similarly, Crane notes that alternative women dressed 'not to express their rebellion against the dominant culture, but to facilitate certain types of activities, either work or pleasure' (1999: 263). This resembles the findings of my research (in that many of my interviewees claimed their style of dress was less for resistance than for comfort), as does Crane's comment that the alternative style 'appears frequently in photographs of the period, but is virtually ignored in fashion histories' (1999: 242). In the same way, although there are numerous studies of modern oppositional and anti-fashion styles, there is less written about older women who continue to dress in this way and do not 'grow out of it'.

Several studies of mainstream fashion include a chapter or section on anti-fashion or oppositional dress (Evans and Thornton, 1989; Barnard, 1996; Steele, 1997b; Pierce, 1999; Keenan, 2001). Suggesting several 'types' of anti-fashion, Davis argues that anti-fashion, in whatever form, 'must via some symbolic device of opposition, rejection, studied neglect, parody, satirization, etc., address itself to the ascendant or "in" fashion of the time' (1992: 161). Further, he refutes Polhemus and Proctor's (1978) assertion that anti-fashion can include all types of dress that fall outside the fashion system, including folk or traditional dress.[4] Instead, he suggests that, because of its relation to the 'in' fashion, it is 'more felicitous to restrict the term anti-fashion to oppositional dress [that is] that which takes place in response to the currents of fashion change and does not lie outside them' (1992: 161). Certainly, I found in my interviews that resistance to mainstream fashions cannot take place if the person in question has no idea what those fashions are (although I found that the term anti-fashion was not in usage among my participants and was therefore of little or no use for this study). Davis (like Crane, above) points out that people assume 'that anti-fashion as a kind of self-conscious, even organized, oppositional stance towards prevailing fashions is of relatively recent origin. Actually, anti-fashion themes and motifs in dress ... stretch back far in European history and appear to have served the same function as they do now: to dissent, protest, ridicule and outrage' (1992: 162). Davis cites several examples of historical anti-fashion including the 'milkmaid-attired court ladies in Marie Antoinette's *bergerie* ... the London dandies of Brummel's time ... [and] the demimonde of Lautrec's Paris and Malcolm Cowley's Greenwich Village'. But, as he later observes, 'anti-fashion presumes a certain democracy of taste and display. It is hard to conceive of anti-fashion, except perhaps through some underground manifestation, in strongly authoritarian or totalitarian societies' (1992: 165) and yet, as El Guindi argues, context is vital: Western feminists argue that the veil cannot be liberating and is 'dangerous' so the 'protest quality in veiling', in that context, is lost (1999: 163). But she also argues that the movement (or anti-fashion) of veiling is not 'simply a dress code ... By dressing this way in public these young women translated their vision of Islamic ideals ... Encoded in the dress style is a new public appearance and demeanour that reaffirms an Islamic identity and morality and rejects Western materialism, consumerism, commercialism, and values' (1999: 145). So, although the adoption of the veil is voluntary and is not seen to be particularly outrageous, and although it is seen as an aspect of Islam by outsiders, it does serve the same functions of dissent and protest to varying degrees, depending on the type of veil worn.[5]

Davis describes various types of anti-fashion groups, of which the one relevant to my research is the 'counter-cultural' and is 'the most potent' because 'it most directly confronts and challenges the symbolic hegemony of the reigning fashion' (1992: 183). He claims that anti-fashion originates from 'those whose location in the social structure permits a measure of irresponsibility and some temporary suspension of major institutional commitments. Youth, especially teenagers not yet embarked on careers or family building, constitutes a prime example of this sort of structurally based exemption' (1992: 167).

Davis is, of course, correct that many counter-cultural styles and movements originate from youth. Yet he (like others: see subcultural theory section below) assumes that people 'grow out of it'. The women in my study were aware of, and complained about, this type of assumption (and many of them had created or found jobs which allowed them to continue their lifestyle and had careers and families). Davis does, however, point out that 'in surrendering their symbols to fashion, antifashion groupings are made to search for new, more subtle, and, perhaps, harder to purloin symbols of group differentiation' (1992: 167), for example, 'Modifications of certain punk modes (e.g., men's earrings, dishevelled and spiked hair, "black everything") have already made their way into mainstream fashions ... Counterculture "purists" are likely to look askance at these borrowings and at those from within their own ranks who cater to this sort of "bourgeois frivolity"; charges of "selling out" and "commercialism" are promptly levelled' (1992: 184). In my research the mainstream fashion for facial piercing prompted many of my interviewees to have more piercings in order to differentiate themselves from people who were merely fashionable rather than alternative.

A parallel study to my own is Williamson's examination of the female 'vampire fan'. She points out that accounts of the vampire 'can only speculate on what the figure says to women who identify themselves as vampire fans and indeed ignores what these women are saying about themselves in their construction of vampiric sartorial identities' (2001: 141). My research aims to examine just such an omission – in Williamson's study the omission is the meanings of 'vampire fandom' to women; in my own, it is the meanings of 'alternative' for women who are 'getting older'. There are several instances where Williamson's findings are very similar to my own. For example, Williamson's interviewees identified traditional femininity as 'pink' femininity (2001: 144, whereas my interviewees defined it as 'fluffy'): 'looking "good" means looking different to others by rejecting pink, frilly femininity. The women vampire fans' sense of self is thus contextualized, but not immobilized by the paradox of femininity and results in an active construction of their appearance and self-presentation' (2001: 145). Again, my own research echoes Williamson's in that the women 'nevertheless continue to embrace notions of femininity by looking to the past for sartorial inspiration' (1999: 150). However, overall the two studies are quite different in that Williamson interviewed only goth women and her central focus is the vampire and its significance to the narratives of the women she interviewed.

Feminism offered one of the most enduring challenges to modes of dress (Wilson, 1992: 5; Steele, 1997b: 282–3) but in the process became associated with the policing of women and a frumpy, 'un-sexy', unadorned style of dungarees; 'the mass media promoted a caricature of feminists – the bra-burning "women's libbers" who hated men but were dressed just like them; a caricature that was virtually unchanged from nineteenth-century *Punch*' (Wilson, 1985: 230). The arguments were mainly that 'first, fashion is enslavement; women are bound by the drudgery of keeping up their appearance and by the impediments of the styles which prohibit them from acting in the world. Second, costume may "disguise the body", deform it, or follow its curves, but ultimately "puts it on display" ' (Gaines, 1990: 3). However, Wilson argues that there were two main (and opposing) approaches to fashion and appearance rather than only one which disapproved: 'a whole-hearted condemnation of every aspect of culture that reproduced sexist ideas of women and femininity, all of which came to seem in some sense "violent" and "pornographic"; the other, by contrast, was a populist liberalism which argued that that it would be élitist to criticize any popular pastime which the majority of women enjoyed, (1985: 230).

Although early feminist accounts of dress concentrated on the way that fashion reinforced the 'sexual objectification of women', feminists have now 'begun to explore the meanings of fashionable and other kinds of dress. This exploration has gone against the grain of a traditional feminist suspicion of fashionable dress' (Wilson, 1992: 5). Most work assumes a level of mainstream 'fashionability' in the women they study which is not directly relevant although could be adapted none the less. Guy and Banim's (2000) exploration of the identities women adopted in relation to their clothes is discussed further in Chapter 5. Their later study of why women keep clothes they do not wear was interesting in that several of my inter-viewees kept clothes which had gone past the point of being thrown out and now served as 'memory joggers'; additionally, the clothes had become too precious to throw away in that they evoke memories (Banim and Guy, 2001: 206). These memories can be 'like keeping an old photograph' or because 'this item makes me feel a way I want to remember' or 'I want to remember the things that were happening when I wore this' (2001: 207). They argue that kept clothes 'help women establish a personal history across their changing images' (2001: 207) which, again, was something evidenced in many of the interviews I carried out, with the women I inter-viewed able to name outfits which represented a particular time of their lives. However, Banim and Guy's analysis assumes that the women were moving with the flow of fashion changes rather than attempting to dress in ways which challenged mainstream fashion. Additionally, the women they interviewed talked about not wearing something they had worn years before whereas the women in my study were likely to retain various styles for years if they had found something they felt reflected their alternative persona.

## Subcultural Theory

There have been a number of main issues in subcultural theory, of which the two most relevant to this study are those of gender and age. The study of subcultures has been a focus of sociological, ethnographic research since the 1920s. In Chicago in the 1940s and 1950s the study of street gangs and street culture became an influential field of enquiry. The Chicago School, as it became known, was a group of male academics who, individually, went out into the streets of Chicago to study how boys lived within gangs (see, for example, Foote Whyte, 1943). The preoccu-pation with studying 'youth' and 'subculture' began in Britain in the 1950s, when there was growing interest in the new concept of 'teenager'. Previously there had been no intermediate period between being a child at school to being an adult at work. This new category, sandwiched between the two, was an unwelcome shock to many. 'The very idea of the "teenager" was, for many British adults, an alien, American idea, involved American myths, American idols, fantasies of American life'

(Frith, 1984: 11) and the category 'teenager', imported from the USA, was primarily a marketing and advertising invention and a response to the growing numbers of affluent young people. These teenagers, children during the war years in Britain, were now finally freed from rationing and had money to spend. As a result a whole new market opened up specifically designed to appeal to (and shape) their tastes. There were clothes aimed specifically at the young, music, cars – in short, a new way of life that differed from, and often was in opposition to, that which their parents and grandparents had experienced. Abrams (1959) defined 'youth' as any age between leaving school (which at this time could have been fourteen or fifteen) up to the age of twenty-five or the age when married. Abrams looked at 'youth' as a group of male consumers, rather than as a group of delinquents. However, this array of youthful display supplied material for concerned debate about delinquency, violence and morals, fuelled by media hysteria. The teenager became a 'folk devil' (Cohen, 1979) and, in varying degrees, remained one for years afterwards.

The Centre for Contemporary Cultural Studies (CCCS) in Birmingham became the successor to the Chicago School and produced a significant body of work. The CCCS produced work from the 1970s studying the phenomenon of 'youth' and youth culture. Writers such as Hall and Jefferson (1976), Willis (1977, 1978), Corrigan (1979) and Frith (1984) established a body of literature which was influenced by the ideas of class conflict and resistance, drawing upon the work of Marx, and theories of deviancy. 'A more celebratory tone entered the texts ... which constructed white working-class male "delinquency" as a form of creative culture resistance to oppressive economic and social conditions, turning the tables on mainstream arguments through the discourse of resistance' (Griffin, 1993: 108).

The CCCS's work focused primarily on boys and 'converged on the question of how young [male] people, including delinquents, football hooligans, drug-takers, music fans, or simply young stylists, "made sense" of the situation within which they found themselves' (McRobbie, 1991: 1). Sexuality did not feature in the work of the CCCS, and rarely did ethnicity or studies about specific geographical locations. Although some CCCS work was empirical, much of it was not, and their assertion that subcultures represented only cohesive, group identities has been successfully refuted by later work (such as Muggleton, 2000). The CCCS looked at friendships, beliefs, behaviours, clothes and other material objects, and how these added up to 'maps of meaning' which shaped the subcultures and its members. However, as Roman and Christian-Smith point out, the male theorists colluded, albeit unintentionally, with the sexism of their subjects (1988: 40) and this was the crux of later critiques. 'With only a few exceptions, delinquency research and most youth subcultural studies have been based on a "gang of lads" model or involved a male-specific perspective' (Griffin, 1993: 109). Brake also acknowledges that 'on the whole youth cultures and subcultures tend to be some form of exploration of masculinity' (1985: ix).

Theory at this time argued that the media and commerce were in opposition to subcultures and created hysteria about them out of a reactionary, generational, class divide. They also argued that media and commerce are 'after the fact', that is, did not affect or influence what was happening on the 'street', that there was no 'trickle-down' effect, only 'trickle-up'. For example, Hebdige's (1979) textual analysis of youth styles argues that the media and commerce draw subcultures into the mainstream of popular ideas, bestowing on them an acceptability which negates their original roots of resistance, thus making them no longer a 'danger'. This creates the need for subcultural styles to be constantly reinvented as 'dangerous' (challenging, shocking) since, he asserts, style and appearance are central to subcultural activity: the styles were a crucial element of playing the part of the unruly youth.

The fascination with male subcultures and gangs led McRobbie and Garber (1991) to examine the ways in which male researchers identified with their male subjects, adopting their attitudes and colluding with them to exclude girls. They question the absence, or marginalisation, of girls in subcultural literature and suggest a rereading of the 'classic' texts: a new analysis of subcultures to find out where the girls were. They sought to understand whether the invisibility of girls meant that they were not active in subcultures, or whether the ways in which the research had been done and where it was done had rendered them invisible. For example, they quote Willis's attitude to single girls in *Profane Culture* (1978): ' "[single girls] tended to be scruffier and less attractive than the attached girls" ' (McRobbie and Garber, 1991: 2), and question whose opinion this was: who was setting the standards of 'attractive' and what gave them the right to do so? McRobbie and Garber challenge the underlying belief that the readers (as well as the researcher and the participants) were all male. 'Girls and Subcultures' offers a feminist reappraisal of established methods of researching youth. It highlights the 'double standards' of patriarchal society, which discourages girls from being sexually adventurous whilst allowing young men to both 'sow wild oats' and then later to 'turn over a new leaf': 'For girls, the consequences of getting known in the neighbourhood as one of the "wild oats" to be "sown" were drastic and irreversible'

(1991: 213). There were also other reasons why girls could not participate as fully as boys: their earnings were likely to be less than those of their male counterparts, girls were more tied to the home by household duties so were less free to 'hang about' on street corners, girls were encouraged to save for marriage and a home of their own and to do this she had to 'catch' a man. Girls with reputations of being 'slags' were very unlikely to be able to fulfil this expectation. Brake points out that 'girls have, because of the patriarchal nature of male subcultures, been seen as the possessions of their boyfriends. They are on sexual display, never allowed sexual independence' (1985: 164). McRobbie and Garber sought to illustrate how these differences in ways of participation did not necessarily mean that girls were automatically not participants in subcultures but instead that they participated in other ways than boys were able to do, for example, through their 'conspicuous consumption' of teeny-bopper records and magazines (1991: 13). Brake echoes McRobbie and Garber, suggesting that 'one distinct sign of the emancipation of young girls from the cult of romance, and marriage as their true vocation, will be the development of subcultures exploring a new form of femininity' (1985: ix).

During the 1980s more feminist studies were produced, for example, about girls' magazines (McRobbie, 1991) and dance (McRobbie and Nava, 1989) and Winship's (1987) study of women's magazines. 'Feminist youth researchers and criminologists had a powerful impact throughout the 1980s, both on the patronizing complacency of traditional "malestream" youth research, and on the tendency to romanticize the macho sexism and racism of "the lads" ' (Griffin, 1993: 128). Ultimately, though, what was missing was an examination of more complex reactions to girls' and mixed-sex subcultures, studies about tomboys, or other girls or women who did *not* subscribe to the traditional feminine models which these studies now focused on. Early subcultural theory has since been problematised, not least because of its focus on male gangs, delinquency, and stereotypes of masculinity and poverty. As Roman and Christian-Smith (1988) point out, the studies privileged domestic life as the only source of a girl's oppression, neglecting to adequately study other forms of oppression but also of pleasures. However, later studies of girls' subcultures repeated the mistake and studied only females, tending to romanticise and inadequately interrogate girls' subcultures, or by writing as if girls had *no* interaction with boys. Roman and Christian-Smith argue that the cultural products popularly consumed by women (such as magazines and soap operas) entailed the act of consumption rather than production, leading to a static view of how women read and respond to texts, and they call for a merging of the empirical studies of subcultural groups with textual analyses of cultural products (such as music, clothes, television). Skelton and Valentine also outline areas of subcultural enquiry that they feel have been neglected. One is how subcultures are involved in 'production and marketing for consumption'. Another is that 'the emphasis on resistance and spectacular forms of youth cultures has led to a neglect of the young people who *conform* in many ways to social expectations' (1997: 24).

Another concern was the unchallenged assumption that subcultures involved only teenagers. As Griffin argues, 'this places those who are not in a "normal" heterosexual marriage, or outside full-time permanent employment, for whatever reason, in a difficult position: they are effectively denied access to "mature" adult status' (1993: 20). Similarly, Brake argues that the study of youth subcultures should not be approached as researching 'some vague structural monolith appealing to those roughly under thirty' but, rather as 'a complex kaleidoscope of several subcultures, of different age groups' (1985: ix). However, a gap in theory about older subcultural participation persists (perhaps since those in their twenties and older would often no longer define themselves as being in a subculture), which is one of the primary reasons I sought a sample of participants who were over twenty-five years old.

Evans and Thornton (1989) re-evaluate several of the recurring concerns about girls and women in subcultures. For example, they (like Brake and McRobbie) point out that although girls do participate in subcultures they are 'contained' there rather than shaping the subcultures or using them to shape new forms of femininities, and this reflects women's position in wider society. However, they also argue that 'with punk, women were able to negotiate a social and ideological space for themselves through the deployment of oppositional dress. Unlike their male counterparts, women in youth subcultures have to contend not only with the dominant culture, but also with the patriarchal structures that are almost invariably replicated within the subculture itself' (1989: 17).

As Wilson (1990b) and others (for example, Thornton, 1995; Leonard, 1998; Garrison, 2000; Borden, 2001) argue, women do not usually find (nor are they allotted) a space within which to revolt and, in fact, (white male) postwar commentators have concentrated on white male forms of resistance. Wilson comments on this omission: 'Many questions remain unanswered ... *What has been their meaning for young women?* [my emphasis] Punk alone was a style equally for both sexes; for although Mod girls, teddy girls, and others did have special ways of dressing their styles were distinct from and parasitical upon those of their boyfriends' (1990b: 32).

Wilson's question is central to this study: what is the meaning of adopting this appearance for women? Although the work of feminist writers, such as McRobbie (1991, 1994a), Sharpe (1994), McRobbie and Nava (1989), Lees (1993) and Thornton (1995), has to some extent redressed the balance by focusing on the participation of girls in subcultures, there still remains a lack of work regarding the continuing participation of adult women. Several studies have successfully highlighted how women continue to participate via music (for example, see Ross and Rose, 1994, on youth music and youth culture; Raphael, 1995, with interviews with female music artists of the 1990s; Reynolds and Press, 1995, on gender, rebellion and rock 'n' roll; Whiteley, 1997, on gender and pop music); although there remains a reliance on a handful of out-dated 'staples', such as Kate Bush, other acts are increasingly being included. Gottlieb and Wald (1994) argue that whilst the emergence of all-female pop and rock bands is in many ways a positive progression, there are also more negative considerations, such as the continued sexism of the music industry. This presents women with the problem of how they are treated by men in other bands, fans and men in the music industry. If women are 'scared off', it then creates the problem of setting no 'tradition' which other women can follow and inherit. Gottlieb and Wald also point out that girls and women are less able to participate in youth cultures (so, by extension, in band rehearsals or performances), since their lives are more strictly monitored and they are kept closer to the home than their male counterparts, and that new ways have been found to participate in subcultures, which are not as visible because they are conducted in the private sphere (1994: 252) – echoing McRobbie and Garber twenty years previously. For example, they cite the rise of fanzines:; specialist magazines, which can be produced at home. Since the article was published, the internet has become vastly more accessible, assisting a wide cross-section of people to produce their own on-line fanzines on websites. Women in bands and women producing fanzines or websites have, amongst other things, 'open[ed] a fertile space both for women's feminist interventions and for the politicization of sexuality and female identity' (Gottlieb and Wald, 1994: 253).

Although this by no means indicates the establishment of subculture/s which exclusively celebrate new forms of femininity, such as Brake advocates, it does bode well for the active and continuing participation of adult women in subcultures. Several studies (for example, see Leonard, 1997, 1998; Garrison, 2000), Gottlieb and Wald among them, examine the brief but highly visible rise of the 'riot grrl' in the 1990s, arguably a 'new form of femininity'. Riot grrls were a direct descendant of punk women, influenced by feminism and grunge/guitar underground rock music, in all-female bands (Gottlieb and Wald, 1994: 250). These developments offer situations which can encourage continuing or increased participation and, to some extent, map out for us some of the contexts and situations which may make it possible for girls to continue being 'alternative' into womanhood. For example, the recent growth of skate culture into the mainstream means that carefully produced (some might say packaged) acts like Avril Lavigne (in her late teens) and Pink (in her twenties) can incorporate 'alternative' elements into what is, basically, a career as a singer of pop songs.

McRobbie revisits subcultural theory and 'changing modes of femininity' to assess what, if any, advances have occurred for the girls within subcultures. She asks whether girls are more visible in subcultures, more involved in the creative practices (so, for example, are they the ones now making music as well as buying it?), and notes that, again, a new approach to subcultures is needed because changes in society since the 1970s have affected cultural production (1994b: 156). She cites two examples of these changes. One is that, due to the 'intensity of the subcultural activity', its effects now also reach and influence popular culture, meaning that subcultures 'no longer occupy ... only a "folk devil" position in society' (1994b: 161) – hence the acceptability of Pink's tattoos and bright pink hair. Generally they are more visible and, to a certain fluctuating extent, more accepted. The second reason that a new approach to subcultures was needed was that feminism had had an impact at all levels of society, including girls' magazines and television dramas, allowing space for more positive and varied portrayals of girls and women. McRobbie agrees neither with the notion of 'backlash' (that as women's achievements continue apace they are systematically eroded in other ways) nor that girls have 'progressed' in leaps and bounds (for example, girls and women are still judged by their appearance more than their abilities). McRobbie points out that, despite subcultural style's influence over popular culture, 'there still remains an ideology of authenticity which provides young people in youth subcultures with a way of achieving social subjectivity and therefore identity, through the subcultural experience' (1994b: 168). She 'places' girls in subcultures, using a contemporary and very visible subculture (rave) as her example. The girls in her study participated only partially, or not at all, in the production processes of the subculture, proving that girls continue to be invisible or only semi-visible in subcultures, no matter how visible the subculture itself becomes. McRobbie suggests instead that theory recognises what she called a 'dramatic "unfixing"' and explained that the "state of flux in relation to what now constitutes feminine identity" offered girls more opportunities and choices' (1994b: 168).

McRobbie's argument that subcultures provide social subjectivity, and therefore then provide identity, underlines the difference between the two terms: that they overlap and affect each other but are not quite the same. Subjectivity includes our 'sense of self', our innermost feelings and sense of who, and what, we are. Identity is the persona we adopt in response to our subjectivity when we are in a social context. 'The positions which we take up and identify with constitute our identities. Subjectivity includes unconscious dimensions of the self and implies contradiction and change' (Woodward, 1997: 39).[6]

Thornton (1995) expands on McRobbie's arguments about the peripheral roles of girls through her examination of the hierarchies within rave culture. Using Bourdieu's ideas about 'cultural capital or knowledge that is accumulated ... which confers social status' (1997: 202), she found that girls often remain at the bottom of the ladder in terms of 'capital' (that is, being 'hip'), and that they often are not as active as the boys and men in terms of organising raves (events). (In the same way, Borden found that 'while female skaters are not explicitly discouraged, their relative absence is only occasionally noted and implicitly condoned' (2001: 144).) Using 'guides' (for example, found through a letter in *The Face* magazine), Thornton visited many rave and mainstream nightclubs around the country, and completed a comparative study of the two: 'As forms of objectified subcultural and economic capital, clothes frequently act as metonyms for larger social strata. "Blue collar" and "white collar" are euphemisms for class, just as references to stilettos and handbags are roundabout ways of saying that a social group lacks subcultural capital' (1995: 114).

Thornton argues that the 'mainstream' popular culture, for example, pop music and fashion, is both derided and feminised, is seen to be '... commercial ... conformist ... [of the] family ... [is] classed', whereas subcultures see themselves as 'alternative ... cool ... independent ... [of] youth ... classless' (1995: 115) (again, equating subcultures with youth). This feminisation of the mainstream accounts, in many ways, for its denigration – and for the marginalisation of women themselves within subcultures. There has been little theoretical analysis of the use of the word 'townie', which illustrates Thornton's argument. This is a slang term for the groups of people who are diametrically opposite to those in subcultures. 'Townies' (also known as 'straight' – although not referring to sexuality) are the men and women who occupy town centres on a Saturday night and keep closely to more traditional, mainstream culture in their dress and music tastes.[7] Muggleton provides what may be the only definition of the use of the word (2000: 104), with even Thornton referring to them as 'mainstreams' or

'Sharon and Tracy' (1994: 101). And yet 'townie' remains in common usage amongst, at the very least, the women in this study.

There has been some debate over the usefulness of the term resistance. For example, 'some feminist researchers have also argued that the concept of cultural resistance is too narrow and gender specific, since young women might adopt less "visible" forms of resistance or negotiation such as silence or giggling' (Griffin, 1993: 210). However, for this research, resistance serves as an adequate term not least because many of my participants identified themselves as resisting some aspects of traditional femininity. As Griffin also argues: 'In the radical perspective, discourses of resistance and survival challenged ... negative definition[s] of youthful deviance and ... reinforced the notion that subcultures call into question the adequacy of the dominant cultural ideology' (1993: 125). Since my participants were questioning and criticising the dominant ideology about what constituted traditional or ideal femininities, Griffin's definition of resistance is the most relevant to this study. Another term, often confusingly used interchangeably with the term resistance, is transgression. On the term 'transgression' Wilson refers to it as 'the crossing of a boundary ... [which] then sets up a new boundary which was in its turn to be transgressed ... Transgression can define no final goal ... it is rather a process of continuously shifting boundaries.' She stresses that 'the desire to shock ... has always been seen as central to a deliberately transgressive act' (1994: 110). The main difference, then, between resistance and transgression is that resistance can be seen to be in itself a goal, the final stage (acting against something). If transgression can have no ultimate goals, the act of transgression is only the first stage of many; there is arguably no endpoint. 'In throwing down the gauntlet of transgression "we" – whoever the "we" is ... – are saying: ... we do not want to be like you. It defines a difference, and a separation' (Wilson, 1994: 110). In many ways transgression is similar to Okely's definition of resistance as an 'isolated act' (1996) and Garrison's assertion that resistance is everywhere (2000). But transgression is something more. 'Transgression is ... a shifting and ambiguous concept ... emphasising the single, fragmented act of defiance, unencumbered by any overarching theory or coherent world view' (Wilson, 1994: 114).

The term 'freak' is a potentially shocking term due to its history, when it was applied to a person considered 'abnormally formed' and seen to be a curiosity or monstrosity (for example, in Victorian 'freak shows') (Russo, 1995; Mifflin, 2001). Despite possibly negative meanings, the term is used here in a more positive way to mean a nonconformist person, especially a member of a subculture.[8] 'Freak' is a term used by most of the participants and the history of its usage lies in the North American counter-culture of the 1960s: hippies would also call themselves 'freaks' to reclaim the word from the people who used it as an insult. The term is used by participants in much the same way they use 'alternative': that is, as an umbrella term for a wide crossover of styles and beliefs, the only criterion being some kind of oppositional 'like-mindedness': someone who is not mainstream and so not a 'townie'. There are many overlaps, resulting in some difficulties in defining particular groupings of subcultures (Polhemus, 1994, 1996; Muggleton, 2000), and 'alternative' can cover these overlaps and re/groupings. Daly and Wice define 'alternative' as the 'Nineties term for counter-culture ... The word "alternative" came to denote any lifestyle outside the mainstream' (1995: 15).[9]

To summarise, the trouble with subcultural theory became its focus on just particular groupings of youths and their activities, privileging and prioritising these groups as if no other groups were equally worthy of study and tending to concentrate only 'on the final signifying product' (McRobbie, 1994b: 163) instead of the processes that went into creating the 'product' (that is, the product being the finished 'look'). This necessarily led to many gaps in knowledge about groups who may have described themselves as, or who may be definable as, subcultures but who were overlooked by theorists because something about their age, sex, class or activities did not 'fit' with the often narrow limits of subcultural theory. This particular study would not 'fit' into early subcultural theory in that its focus is on a group of adult women and many of their allegiances or practices do fit into ideas about what constitutes someone participating in a subculture (young men acting out the activities of the subculture in public places). The term 'youth culture' is not an appropriate one for this study, although many studies have focused on it (for example, from the same year, Hollands, 1995; Irwin, 1995; Widdicombe and Wooffitt, 1995). Leonard argues that the subculture of 'riotgrrrl', because of its feminist nature, gave 'good grounds for rethinking the associations of masculinity and deviancy brought to the term youth subculture' (1998: 102) but female participation in subcultures even before riot grrl arguably challenged the idea that subcultures equated primarily with young, white males. But, similarly, this study avoids the use of the term youth culture, as this assumes both an age bracket and masculinity. Nor would my research fulfil later definitions, again because of the age of the participants, but also because many of their concerns and preoccupations were extremely traditional.

## Identity and 'Self'

Although earlier academics had studied the 'self' (for example, Goffman, 1972; Mead, 1964), a new interest in the subject was ignited as a result of social movements in the 1960s and 1970s, movements based on a range of political issues and academic debates such as feminism, 'race' and ethnicity, sexuality and class. The new discourses about self were informed by an awareness of the issue of 'difference' (for example, see Woodward, 1997) and diverged along two paths, which can be described, for the sake of definition, as a 'social theory' approach (for example, Giddens, 1991; Jenkins, 1994; Kellner, 1995) and a 'cultural theory approach' (for example, Butler, 1990, 1993; Hall and du Gay, 1996). The two differ in the following ways. The 'cultural theory' approach is more concerned with the problematic and fragmented aspects of identity, with a focus on power and opposition (for example, woman versus man, black versus white). Hall and du Gay argue that identities are nothing more than 'points of temporary attachment to the subject positions which discursive practices construct for us' (1996: 6). 'Poststructuralist theories emphasize the instability, fluidity, fragmentary and processual character of identities, to a greater extent perhaps than the social theorists of identity' (Roseneil and Seymour, 1999: 4).

In contrast, the 'social theory' approach highlights the fact that the 'self' is not fixed and unchangeable and is in an ongoing process of refinement (Giddens, 1991) and that is only possible due to societal shifts which have occurred in modernity and late modernity. However, an identity is often thought of as being something people can simply choose and work towards (what Giddens (1991) calls 'the trajectory of the self'), especially in the last half of the twentieth century. As Roseneil and Seymour point out, 'questions of identity, individual and collective, confront us at every turn ... We are interpellated and interrogated by a multiplicity of voices to consider and reconsider our identities. How we think of ourselves ... is up for grabs, open to negotiation, subject to choice to an unprecedented extent. Or so the story goes' (1999: 1). Yet of course this is not entirely the case and

> the range of identity options available to any individual is limited, the act of choosing circumscribed by a wide range of social constraints ... it is easier to be a Spice Girl than a riot grrrl in school, a new lad rather than a new man in most workplaces, straight rather than queer, British rather than Black British in rural England. (1999: 2)

So, although the persona of 'alternative woman' is a difficult one, and undoubtedly more difficult than following a path of more traditional femininity, my interviewees were still working within a range of social constraints (a key constraint being that they were getting older).

Social theories of identity have an emphasis on reflexivity and focus on the 'active, creative, conscious practices of identity construction' (Roseneil and Seymour, 1999: 5) so, in any discussion of identity, one must consider a person's subjectivity, since, as Berger and Luckmann argue, identity is 'a key element of a subjective reality' (1966: 174) where '*any* body of [subjective] "knowledge" comes to be socially established as reality' (1966: 15). 'Life stories are a way of fashioning identity ... Individuals do not merely regale themselves with their personal narratives, they put their lives on public display' (Lieblich and Josselson, 1993: 137), and empirical studies have been an effective way of collecting narratives. For example, Roseneil, in her study of women at Greenham Common, explains subjectivity as a cross between consciousness and identity; consciousness is the way that people understand their relation to the world around them and identity refers to their sense of self within that world. She notes that to define one's identity as an oppositional one (in this case, feminist) depends on the development (or the 'consciousness raising') of an oppositional consciousness (1996: 87). Identity, consciousness and subjectivity are linked terms (Carver and Moltier, 1998: 19). Although subjectivity is seen to be a socially constructed concept (in that people exist as particular embodied identities, such as feminine or disabled), this doesn't mean that 'subjects are ... passive dupes of the discourses which shape them'. For example, Foucault argues that a subject, although socially constituted, could be a permanent provocation to the discourse that defines her subjectivity (cited in Hekman, 1990: 73). Several feminist studies of 'subjectivity' remain divided on the issue of how much a person can discursively construct their subjectivity, and how much or little human action can influence its formation (for example, see Butler, 1990; McNay, 1992; Weeks, 1998). The term 'agency' is itself often little more than a synonym for action, emphasising the voluntary actions of individuals and the value that they ascribe to those actions. Agency and identity are necessarily embodied, an idea central to this study, in that people occupy particular subjectivities within wider discourses (Mansfield and Maguire, 1999; Parkins, 2000), but this does not automatically mean that people cannot use agency to resist the 'power of discourse'.

## The Body

In recent years, 'the body' and embodiment have become the subject of academic attention (for example, see Scott and Morgan, 1993; Turner, 1996;

Price and Shildrick, 1999), whereas previous studies had underestimated the role of the body in everyday life, overlooking it in favour of identity, rendering it to what Shilling (1993) calls an 'absent presence'. Giddens (1991) has highlighted how the body can now be used to further a person's passage into the sort of life they desire (for example, through clothes and exercise), making the body part of an ongoing 'identity project' rather than just something which is made to fit into classed social structures. But all stages of life have been examined. As Davis argues, 'interest in the body also goes hand in hand with recent medical advances and improved sanitation. Life expectancy is greater than in previous centuries and the result in most Western societies is a rapidly greying population' (1997: 2). As a result, studies of the ageing body have proliferated (Furman,1997; Pearsall, 1997; Bytheway, 1998; Fairhurst, 1998; Gannon, 1999; Gardner and Johnson, 2002), including how the ageing, ill or disabled body is hidden in favour of the Western norm of the young, thin, white body (Shilling, 1993). A body is something we both have and are, and is experienced as something we prepare for public display (Nettleton and Watson, 1998: 1). Gender is just one way of preparing the biological sexed body for display to embody cultural ideals; as Blake points out, 'gender differences are not only biologically determined, culturally constructed, or politically imposed, but also ways of living in a body and thus of being in the world' (2000: 431), and Betterton notes that 'the body is the site on which feminine cultural ideals can be literally manufactured' (1987: 8).

The history of women's bodies has been 'mapped in various areas of social life and attention has been devoted to how institutions and cultural discourses shape women's embodied experiences' (Davis, 1997: 5). Women's bodies are fragmented and objectified in contemporary culture, and are 'more embodied than men ... in popular culture and popular imagination' (Morgan, 1993: 69): they are used as a casual commodity in representations in the media and popular culture (Craik, 1994; Macdonald, 1995) and are seen to be available for use in many other ways, for example, from being judged from a building site or in a Miss World contest to the attitudes to rape and assault (Brownmiller, 1986; Gregory and Lees, 1999). Women's experiences with routine aspects of maintaining their bodies have been explored, such as beauty culture, fashion, cosmetic surgery and fitness (Brownmiller, 1984; Chapkis, 1986; Wolf, 1990; Davis, 1997), because, as Smith drily comments, 'women's bodies are always imperfect. They always need fixing' (1988: 46). Women's bodies are also subject to what Chernin calls 'the tyranny of slenderness' (1983) and other studies have highlighted how women can be affected by eating disorders and body dissatisfaction (Orbach, 1988; Grogan, 1999). Wolf argues that 'dieting is the essence of contemporary femininity ... Where the feminine woman of the Feminine Mystique denied herself gratification in the world, the current successful and "mature" model of femininity submits to a life of self-denial in her body' (1990: 200) and Furman asserts that 'being overweight represents the clearest failure in the maintenance of an ideal femininity, that is, of a femininity defined by the dominant culture' (1997: 68). Bordo describes how Marilyn Monroe, once revered as the very embodiment of 'femininity', has been superseded by a more athletic, youthful body shape (1993: 141): there is now a 'universal equation of slenderness with beauty' (1993: 102). As Giddens argues, 'routine control of the body is integral to the very nature both of agency and of being accepted (trusted) by others' (1991: 157). Not only are women expected to discipline their unruly bodies to achieve slenderness, women often experience their bodies as 'out of control' through menstruation, pregnancy and the menopause (Gannon, 1999; Greer, 1999; Maushart, 1999); as Shilling points out 'women frequently have to learn to live with what can be termed "overburdened bodies" ' (1993: 32). Often, though, the burden can be other bodies: women are not only primarily responsible through pregnancy and childbirth for the 'reproduction of existing and new bodies' (1993: 22), they are also the primary carers of existing and failing bodies (see, for example, Dryden, 1999, on the gendered division of domestic labour and care). A woman's body, then, can be seen to be 'a built, that is socially and discursively constructed, body' (Mansfield and McGinn, 1993: 50), and resists the embodiment of essentialist definitions of what a woman is and should aspire to be. Women's sexuality has also been a key area for feminist studies of the body, from sexual desire to the restrictions of heterosexuality being seen as the 'norm' (Richardson, 1996, 2000) to highlighting how the body has been key in constructing 'race' and ethnicity (Davis, 1988; Hill Collins, 1990; hooks, 1990).

Body-building has been highlighted as a way in which women seek to resist the model of slenderness (Schulze, 1990; Tasker, 1992; Mansfield and McGinn, 1993; Tate, 1999) and instead create bodies which 'take up space' (Tate, 1999: 33) and challenge gendered bodily norms. 'A gym ... whilst of course not being used exclusively by muscle "freaks", can best be described ... as being situated within a discourse which makes the outlandish body possible' (Mansfield and McGinn, 1993: 51) and female bodies doubly outlandish as they strip away essentialist notions about women's bodies being smaller and weaker than men's (Morgan, 1993). However, as Bordo has argued, both the anorexic body and the muscled body exist on a continuum, both seeking to fight against 'excess flesh' (1989: 90) to produce 'docile bodies'. Other ways of 'disciplining' the female body have also been analysed as oppression (for example, Blake, 2000, on the practice of foot-binding) but also with potential to denote resistance (see El Guindi, 1999, on women's adoption of the veil, also discussed above. She argues that many women see wearing the veil as a strident feminist statement, placing the veiled female body in an entirely different, complex and more positive context from that understood by Western commentators).

Recent studies of both the body and of subcultures have included sections on body modification (for example, Cahill and Reilly, 2001) and there are now an increasing number of dedicated studies (such as DeMello and Govenar, 1996; Sweetman, 1999; DeMello, 2000; Mifflin, 2001), but body modification is still a relatively new area and is closely tied to the rise of academic interest in the body. Neither does the increased demand for tattooing mean that it 'has become an accepted aspect of Western culture; it is still seen as "other" despite its increasing popularity' (Hardin, 1999: 82), although Mifflin counters that tattoos 'defy conventional standards of feminine beauty and force the recognition of new, largely self-certified ones' (2001: 117). Mifflin examines the history of tattooing, focusing on how *women* have historically been closely associated with tattooing, despite historical and current disapproval, and mainly in association with freak shows and circuses. But she uncovers more positive examples, such as the nineteenth- and early twentieth-century women who trained as tattooists, and the Victorian middle-class love of discreet tattooing (for example, Winston Churchill's mother had a snake tattooed around her wrist and other upper-class women had their lovers' names tattooed on their toes). One of the first tattooed circus women was Irene Woodward, who, at age nineteen in the early 1880s, 'began working at Bunnell's museum and quickly became an international sensation: she was paraded before European royalty and studied by scientists. By the time she died in 1915, there were allegedly thirty eight wax figures of her in European museums' (Mifflin, 2001: 12). Like the anti-fashion women described by Wilson and Crane, the 'tattooed women leapfrogged beyond bloomers and short skirts to unheard of thigh-hugging trunks, donned not for freedom of movement, like pants [trousers], but for public display' (Mifflin, 2001: 15). Another woman who sought to challenge traditional femininity head-on was Betty Broadbent, only seventeen when she joined the circus, and

billed as 'the youngest tattooed woman in the world' [who] enjoyed a 40–year career during which she traveled with every major American circus, as well as independent shows in Australia and New Zealand … She took her wholesome looks to the 1939 World's Fair to compete in the first televised beauty contest.

She knew that as a tattooed contestant she didn't stand a chance of winning, but gladly reaped the free publicity. (Mifflin, 2001: 30).

Mifflin also examines how women who have undergone mastectomies have tattoos to both cover and celebrate their scars. One of her interviewees said that 'her decision was not ony aesthetic but also political: "This is an invisible epidemic: everybody looks 'normal' cause they're wearing prostheses"' (2001: 152). As Hardin observes, 'the reclamation of the body [through tattooing] provides the means for the woman to alter the objectification of the female and to establish a space from which to speak' (1999: 82). DeMello's (2000) accounts are very similar, including a history of tattooing in the USA, a contexualisation of the 'freak show' and a section discussing the narratives of her empirical research, but primarily arguing that multiple tattooing can liberate the objectified body. The meanings and significance of tattooed women have a particular relevance to my own research as all of the participants had at least two tattoos. However, as with historical attitudes described by both Mifflin and DeMello, my interviewees were aware of the continuing disapproval of their body modifications and how it may be perceived to erode their femininity. As Furman argues, women are expected to maintain an 'appropriate' body in order to fit into the ideals:

It would not be an exaggeration to suggest that for many contemporary American women, feminine identity is likewise importantly, perhaps centrally, signaled by the body. Appearance takes on a critical role in the life of a woman and, before that, the girl child. Consequently the acquisition and maintenance of femininity – female gender identity – requires continuous and unfailing attention to the body as an instrument of self-presentation. (1997: 44)

In conclusion, this book would fit into some of the above areas of enquiry, such as the study of tattooed women, the history of anti-fashion and ways to embody resistance. However, it seeks to fill gaps in other areas, mainly those around women and age, in subcultural theory and accounts (both academic and cultural) of age.

# *Negotiating Fluffy Femininities*

## What is Femininity?

This, the first empirical chapter, examines how the participants talked about traditional femininity and their relationships to it, and the many contradictions highlighted by their discussion. This is established by asking: how the women in this study defined femininity; whom they named as being traditionally feminine; what they used which they considered to be typically feminine; and how they felt this 'placed' them within a continuum of femininity. The central focus of this chapter is on the way the participants have constructed an 'alternative' feminine identity through their appearance, at the same time as demonstrating a great deal of commitment to a variety of disciplined and time-consuming, traditionally 'feminine' pursuits to maintain this appearance: what Craik calls 'the tension between techniques of being female and techniques of femininity' (1994: 61). The participants saw their appearance as 'different' or 'alternative', whilst nonetheless seeing themselves as feminine. They were prey to the anxieties and pleasures that 'normal' femininity is tied to, anxieties such as ageing and compromise, and pleasures through make-up, clothes and hair. They *were* feminine: they just did not maintain a traditionally feminine appearance. This is examined further in Chapter 4.

'Femininity' as a concept would be easily recognised by most people but less easily described; it holds many shifting, subjective components and expectations and there can be no one definition; it is a 'curiously intangible and fluid term' (Thesander, 1997: 8). Fixed definitions reduce femininity to an inappropriately static phenomenon for something lived by millions of women who are constantly changing and evolving. If we see femininity as discourse (that is, as a set of ideas, rules and beliefs), we 'shift away from viewing it as a normative order' (Smith, 1988: 40) and in doing so we see more clearly how femininity is constructed. The connotations of being described as a typically feminine woman encompass assumptions about, amongst other things, vulnerability, physical strength, intelligence and sexual availability. Yet feminine behaviour is a 'task' of imitation (Craik,

1994) rather than inherent skills or traits: what Bordo describes as the obsessive pursuit of the 'elusive ideal of femininity' (1989:34). Male drag artists, transvestites and transsexuals learn to explicitly render femininity (Garber, 1992) and it is arguably no less of an on-going learning process for girls and women. However, the difference is, of course, that the man in drag can 'go back' to being a man, whereas ' "femininity" is learnt behaviour which is recreated every day of a woman's life through her interaction with men and other women. 'Feminine' behaviour shows deference' (Jeffreys, 1996: 76), drag artists do not.

One method of rendering 'femininity', used more often to represent 'female' rather than to 'pass' as female (what Jeffreys calls 'gender femaling'), is the use of exaggerated 'feminine' behaviour, such as pouting, shrieking, the batting of eyelashes – acting both childish and knowing (Ekins and King, 1996). These traits, even when adopted by men, are instantly recognisable as being 'feminine', because of cultural knowledge and assumptions which are held (for example, that women are coquettish, hysterical or deceitful). They have less to do with how actual women live, act or dress than how the ideas and notions of womanhood are presented, taught and perpetuated in society – but of course, women do have to conform to certain stereotypes. In these ways women have come to embody certain cultural ideals of femininity (Sciebinger, 2000b) and, as various studies have argued, gender is something which people 'do' rather than what they are (Ainley, 1998; Dryden, 1999). These exaggerated traits serve to highlight the elements of masquerade present in 'femininity', the constructed nature of gender and the ways in which cultural products and behaviours form a 'false identity on the surface' (Wilson, 1992: 8). Masquerade illuminates the ways that 'natural' femininity is constructed via a series of acts and items to create this surface effect. In masquerade, 'instead of stripping away layers to reveal an authentic self, it plays with cultural representations of femininity ... Masquerade becomes a way of provoking and confounding the male gaze. The traditionally feminine "trivial pursuit" of fashion and self-adornment is reclaimed as a reinvention of the self' (Reynolds and Press, 1995: 289).

Masquerade, then, is a way to deconstruct and reorganise elements of gender without assuming that there is such a thing as 'true' femininity. Masquerade, as Reynolds and Press argue, 'plays' and 'provokes' and 'confounds'; it is the knowing adaptation and reconstruction of meanings, although arguably not as self-consciously as they suggest. It is important to delineate a distinction between the terms 'mask' and 'masquerade' when applied to femininity. Evans and Thornton (1991: 17) describe it as taking 'control of the mask, the disguise, that is femininity'. Both masks and masquerade are a form of disguise. The difference in the use of 'mask' and masquerade indicates different levels of control of our social roles.

## 'I Am Not a Bit Fluffy'

There were a variety of terms used by participants to describe themselves; for example, the terms 'townie' and 'freak' are discussed in Chapter 2. Three more terms were used consistently by most of the participants when referring to traditional femininities. These were 'fluffy', 'girly' and 'frothy', used to denote a particular type of femininity to which participants placed themselves in opposition. For example:

[I am] *just not fluffy rather than not traditionally feminine.* (Flong)

*I've never been girly-girly … I have never been a frothy girly.* (Claudia)

*If I was a girly, which I am not!* (Vash)

'Girly', although conflated with 'girl', actually has wider meanings than simply a young female, not least its use as a descriptive term for top-shelf soft-porn magazines. 'Girl' is not always an age-related term and can be used to refer to adult women 'to imply childishness, dependency, conformity, purity, delicacy, non-aggressiveness, and non-competitiveness' (Kramarae and Treichler, 1985: 176), and to 'remind us of our status as honorary children' (Whelehan, 2000: 37). Adult men, in contrast, are rarely referred to, especially singly, as boys but more commonly as lads.[1] 'Girly' is used by participants to demarcate shades of gender; describing a woman as 'girly' is because she is more traditionally feminine but it does not mean that she is any more feminine than they are: it just means she is further up the 'fluffy' scale. This is a distinction they draw. 'Fluffy' and 'frothy' are evocative words[2] and bring to mind images of a 1950s type of femininity: flouncy petticoats, little angora cardigans, the embodiment of a particular type of passive and conformist (yet still sexualised) femininity (Douglas, 1995; Thesander, 1997). The category 'feminine' is still seen as a narrow, restrictive one and this kind of distinction creates slightly wider categories for my interviewees to locate themselves in (or outside), effectively separating them from 'girly' girls.

In contrast, Whelehan discusses other meanings of girl. In African-American and African-Caribbean culture, 'girl' has been used in a 'positive, sisterly fashion' (2000: 37), as in the cry common on American talk shows

'You go, girl!' Following Madonna's 'Girlie Tour' in 1994, Channel Four's 'The Girlie Show' in 1995 marked a media harnessing of the term, using the double meaning to attract both sexes. Girl was also reappropriated, ostensibly as a term of empowerment for a new breed of 'girls' such as the Spice Girls (five women in their early twenties), whose rallying call of 'girl power!' claimed to celebrate all that was positive, modern, sassy and independent about being a 'girl'. But could their 'manifesto' (if it could be called that) be taken seriously? Although the Spice Girls talked about girls supporting each other and prioritising friendships with other girls over romantic relationships, their image remained one of aggressive heterosexuality. As Whelehan notes, 'mainstream girlie culture, needless to say, sets great store by the visual, and its stars are young, slim and conventionally attractive, and come under quite different scrutiny in the press from their male counterparts, especially in their relationships with men and each other' (2000: 41).

Thus whilst the Spice Girls (and other similar groups such as All Saints or Destiny's Child, now all split up) did in some ways, for Whelehan, 'mark a positive shift in the gendered arrangement of the music establishment' (2000: 41), they also remained a 'manufactured', initially tightly controlled, mainstream group of women who sang and danced but did not play instruments (a situation continued with such bands as Girls Aloud or Mystique). Also, despite having one black member, the Spice Girls remained primarily a 'white' group, with Mel B known as 'Scary Spice', marking her out as Other: threatening and unknowable. Ultimately, their cries of 'girl power' did not link to wider feminist issues and were about individualistic, atavistic self-fulfilment rather than 'the common good', thus placing them firmly within the establishment status quo they claimed to be fighting. Because of this, even their reappropriation of the term 'girl' didn't lend the term any 'bite', locating it still as the repudiated 'girly' as used by my participants. Another more recent pop group, also identifying themselves as girls, are Girls Aloud: five white women who are the collective result of the UK television version of *Pop Stars*. Girls Aloud appear to have no 'manifesto' at all, which arguably puts them in a position which we could label pre-Spice Girl in that they have no rallying cry or particular allegiance with other women. Their only message may be the pun their name (girls allowed), which then begs the question: who is giving them permission?

'Grrl' fulfils the same function in that, since feminism insisted on adult females being called 'woman' (to denote a mature, empowered individual), the term 'girl' became disempowered and its meaning and importance became devalued (Leonard, 1997: 232). Young feminist women also did not necessarily wish to identify themselves in the same terms their mothers used, so the term 'grrl' was a reclamation and revamp of 'girl', identifying it with angry, politicised, feminist young women (although arguably the term 'grrl' has now become just as exclusionary). Again, none of the women in this study identified themselves as 'grrls', although several mentioned it.

## Describing Traditional Femininity.

Sugar and spice and all things nice
That's what little girls are made of

As the nursery rhyme tells us, girls are traditionally seen as sweet and nice. The definitions and understandings of traditional femininity voiced by the participants did not stray far from this version. For example, Zeb said she would define femininity as being *'a pink, fluffy twinset and pearls'*. Frequently these rather outdated or stereotyped versions seemed to be how participants perceived the general view of traditional femininity and an effort to capture the essence of traditional femininity. Additionally, the ways they described femininity revealed many of the paradoxes and tensions negotiated by them in their everyday lives. To make clear how each woman defined and understood the category 'feminine', I asked a number of questions to find out how participants described mainstream and alternative femininity. These included their own descriptions of traditional and unconventional femininities; famous women they would place in these categories; and what products they themselves used (such as make-up) which they considered to be 'feminine'. After all, as Ussher argues, women need not 'throw the baby out with the bath water, rejecting everything deemed feminine' (1997: 442) in their quest to resist or rescript their version of femininity. There are pleasures to be had from traditionally feminine activities and most of my participants refuted any notion of not being feminine *per se*. Schulze, writing about body-building, states that 'some pose the question in terms of "how far" a female ... can go and still remain a "woman". The most pervasive tendency, however, seems to be a recuperative strategy, an attempt to pull her back from a position outside dominant limits into a more acceptable space' (1990: 59). With women body-builders this is done through the employment of 'feminine' hairstyles, bikinis, make-up, and frou-frou accessories such as hair ribbons. As Coles comments, 'on such a body a subtle hint of femininity would achieve nothing. Instead it must be high glamour, overdone and overplayed' (1999: 447).

This idea of a 'recuperative strategy' can be adapted in relation to the participants: they were anxious that their 'alternative' femininity did not render them unfeminine and so employed ways to recoup any loss of femininity they perceived. They did this by describing and talking about femininity in very traditional ways (often as if they saw femininity not as a tyrannical orthodoxy!) and by their descriptions of the feminine items that they preferred to use. Although Schulze refers specifically to how female body-builders are often seen to become 'masculinised', the participants also demonstrated fears that they would be seen as less feminine and so automatically more masculine. Several of my interviewees insisted that their femininity be recognised and acknowledged:

*I mean, I wouldn't call myself unfeminine.* (Miss Pink)

*I see myself as a feminine woman, rather than as a girly woman.* (Sparkle)

*I certainly never get up in a morning and feel like a man ever!* (Gwendolin)

Similarly, Claudia identified her make-up as something that marked her as distinct and different from 'hyper-femininity':

*Obviously with my hair and all my make-up on I'm not trying to look like a guy ... I wouldn't say I was girly girly. I would see myself as doing a lot of things that a very feminine person would not be doing like getting your hands mucky and that, they don't do that.*

Claudia's views are problematic in that her anxiety about being seen as masculine are at odds with feminist sexual politics. Resistance to sexism, a political position, becomes embodied in the 'masculine', 'defeminised' feminist body. Additionally, assuming that being unfeminine equates with masculinity is at odds with my interviewees' use of the terms 'fluffy' and 'girly', which created broader definitions of what femininity means. As Brownmiller puts it:

Femininity always demands more ... To be insufficiently feminine is viewed as a failure in core sexual identity, or as a failure to care sufficiently about oneself, for a woman found to be wanting will be appraised (and will appraise herself) as mannish or neutered or simply unattractive, as men have defined these terms (1984: 3).

For Claudia to state that she doesn't *'look like a guy'* reveals a much more rigidly demarcated line between feminine and masculine with no discernible grey area between. Even the pseudonyms chosen by the participants could not be mistaken for anything other than 'feminine' names (see table A1.2 in Appendix 1). In addition, Claudia used a recuperative strategy (also used by other participants) to convince me of her difference from '*a very feminine person*': she distanced herself by saying she would get her hands dirty whereas a 'girly' person would not. In this way she was aligning herself against (her version of) traditional femininities whilst stressing that she herself was none the less feminine. Gaines notes that a woman's appearance 'delivers gender as self-evident or natural and then recedes as "clothing", leaving the connotation "femininity". In popular discourse, there is often no distinction between a woman and her attire. She *is* what she wears' (1990: 1). Many participants seemed aware of the enmeshed relationship of femininity to a 'feminine' appearance and so were at pains to stress that their own femininity was not eroded by their less traditionally feminine appearance.

Feeling feminine (and being able to mark out clear personal boundaries and then stay within them), and being acknowledged as such, was key to many of the participants. They did this by closely watching mainstream femininities: only by knowing what the current governing codes are and sifting through what is currently fashionable could participants choose how not to follow fashion (Davis, 1992; Ussher, 1997) – but without straying too far from those governing codes. As Ussher suggests 'to examine fashion and clothes is to examine what it is to be (or to reject) "woman", in a specific cultural sphere' (1997: 60). In this way the participants can choose to ignore or utilise aspects of what is currently fashionable (and so also accessible) and because of this constant weighing up of different elements they are, in some ways, more aware of the ways femininity can be constructed and reconstructed.

The participants had clear ideas of what was currently 'acceptable' for traditional femininity and they were willing to name or describe it. Eloise's idea of mainstream femininity was:

*Supermodels I suppose ... Princess Diana. You know people who are very sort of classically dressed.*

But then, as if to ensure that I did not align her with such people, she said:

*I don't really have an opinion of her [Diana] to be honest. Or women like her. I think they are boring.*

Princess Diana held a strong hold over the public imagination for sixteen years – not least after her death in August 1997 (Campbell, 1998; Merck, 1998; Kear and Steinberg, 1999; Walter, 1999) – and was said to be the most photographed woman in the world; her treatment at the hands of the media proves that old stereotypes about what women could or should be/do are alive and well (Macdonald, 1995: 1). Opinion was divided over her but there can be no argument about her appeal: she fulfilled a variety of roles and images of modern womanhood, from devoted single parent and charity worker to wealthy, fashionable, 'jet-set' princess, and 'representations of the embodied Diana' (Kitzinger, 1999: 65) in these roles were hard to miss. Yet, as Macdonald asks, 'why [do] women, many of whom would disown these very myths of femininity if they were presented as explicit points of view, happily collude with them, and indeed find pleasure in them, when they are reproduced in the popular media?' (1995: 1). Eloise did not do this and had made a conscious effort not to even engage with the images of *'women like her'* [Diana] – indeed, Eloise said the very fact of admitting she was aware of Diana made her feel compromised. However, her answers were just as brief when questioned about famous unconventional women and her reason for this was:

*I try not to look at famous women anyway. They have nothing to do with me.*

Famous women and the representation of femininity in popular culture has a history of fascinated scrutiny (from film theory, Tasker, 1993, 1998; to cultural studies, Gammon and Marshment, 1988; sociology, Bordo, 1993; art history, Betterton, 1987; and so on) and the arguments about role models, negative messages, stereotypes, the 'beauty myth', and the perpetuation of gender roles and attitudes, have raged for decades. Famous women are hard to miss. Eloise was the only participant who claimed to have absolutely *no* interest in famous women: the others' interest in famous women took various forms (from approval to derision). Eloise explained this as a kind of superstition: that to even look at or judge famous women would in some way compromise how she herself looked, might unconsciously affect her own look. And, even in discussion with me, this extended to being unable/unwilling to even imagine or describe how a traditional or 'non-traditional woman' might look. This is a complex and unorthodox approach since, as Stacey argues, 'in a culture where the circulation of idealised and desirable images of femininity constantly surrounds us, the phenomenon of fascination between women is hardly surprising' (1988: 114) – and not just fascination in a masculinised or transvestite way, as Mulvey argues (1988), but also in a pleasurable way, for example, the costume and appearance of female stars (Gaines and Herzog, 1990). But Eloise claimed not to be able to even look (or want to look), for fear of traditional femininity somehow affecting her by a process of osmosis – and, of course, it must do so. To define herself against the 'Diana model' is espousing a particular view of femininity, but there are undoubtedly other ways in which the culture has affected Eloise, for example, her 'fairy hair', which is discussed further below.

In contrast, Gwendolin and Delilah named the same examples of the 'typically feminine':

*Pamela Anderson .... [or] for just ordinary feminine someone like Felicity Kendal I would have thought. Men ... feel they can dominate her.* (Gwendolin)

*the traditional feminine ideal is like Pamela Anderson ... Felicity Kendal. Dumb or girly but controllable, not too much of a handful, likely to ... know the rules.* (Delilah)

The ways that the participants talked about what or who represented traditional femininity to them reflects many of their own understandings of ideals of femininity as seen by a male spectator and the pervasive influence these images have. Both women embody particularly 'typical' feminine traits, Anderson (like Marilyn Monroe) literally embodying a hyper-femininity of large breasts, long blonde hair, pouting lips and so on. Delilah explained what she meant by 'the rules' which described the sort of hyper-femininity characterised by Monroe and Anderson:

*Wear this or that. Giggly girly. Daft ... doing things that make you seem smaller than you are, weaker and available. Always available ... Sex objects. That's what women's clothes are usually supposed to do ... say ... Like stiletto heels crippling her or all that stuff. Acting dumb.*

Zeb described traditional femininity as if it were an affliction. She described weakness and softness and vulnerability:

*she'd be slim, she'd be willowy, long flowing hair and wearing a Laura Ashley print dress ... She'd have that sort of washed out kind of look ... blurry round the edges ... a vulnerable thinness.*

Claudia and Vash echoed this idea of traditional femininity being defined by wearing 'nice, safe' dresses or having a particular attitude of being 'frothy'. Both said that it was the attitude added to the clothes which made a person traditionally feminine, and Sparkle made much the same point:

*A bit giggly. The flirty type ... It's more in a mannerism... just by their man-nerism come across as very feminine, very frothy.* (Claudia)

*When they don't really think for themselves, they are quite weak, giggly, wear sexy clothes, do that thing where they pout or giggle.* (Sparkle)

Delilah was the only one who defined 'femininity' as being the opposite of Zeb's 'blurry' woman. Instead she described femininity as being someone definite and strong:

*To me it is someone who is strong and sexy and good to other women, to her friends ... someone who makes the best of herself without, you know, making stupid concessions ... and positive ... but the opposite of it to mainstream ... someone like me. Or a lesbian. Or someone who does things on her own terms, she's good at what she does, you know, successful. So the women who can't be packaged and labelled properly. Someone who is going to get all the shit from those types of shitheads.*

Delilah, who said she was a feminist, defined femininity in a positive (if embattled) way, and was the only participant who did not automatically equate 'femininity' with traditional femininity. Ussher notes that 'there appears to be a contempt for femininity' from women who resist 'girly' femininity (1997: 452) and this was a sentiment echoed by the participants who said they had little or no interest in feminism. So Claudia, Miss Pink, Flong, Gwendolin and Eloise in particular displayed hostility both towards 'girly' femininity but almost equally towards feminist women. Others – such as Vash, Zeb, Sparkle, Louise and Bee, all feminists – also saw them-selves as different from traditional femininity but expressed no hostility towards traditionally feminine women. Such divisions are examined further in Chapter 5.

## The 'Tools' and How to Use Them

A person's external appearance is commonly thought to provide informa-tion about their internal self (Kaiser, 1990; Davis, 1992; Craik, 1994). Yet, although the external appearance of the participants resisted many ideas about traditional femininity, they continued to use many of the accou-trements of it, 'behind the scenes', or what Goffman refers to as 'the front region with fixed props' (1984: 245), in order to maintain their own feel-ings of femininity. Ussher describes women who are apparently tradition-ally, but knowingly, feminine, and compares them with those who entirely resist the trappings of traditional femininity (1997: 450). Both categories of femininity entail some resistance or transgression but there is a distinction between 'doing girl' and 'resisting girl'. 'Doing girl' is when a woman uses feminine masquerade (using all the 'trappings' of traditional femininity), appearing to be authentic, whilst knowing that the part she is playing consists entirely of 'front' with 'props'. But in the category 'resisting' girl: 'that which is traditionally signified by "femininity" is invariably ignored or denied (often derided) – the necessity for body discipline, the inevitability of the adoption of the mask of beauty and the adoption of coquettish feminine wiles' (Ussher, 1997: 455). Ussher points out that resisting need not involve discarding all that is involved in being 'woman': managing one's body and appearance, having children, being in relationships with men are not necessarily resisted[3] (although they might be, as some of the participants of this study illustrate). Within this type of resistance are women whose sense of themselves as 'feminine' is not traditional: they dress 'down' and avoid 'girly' clothes and adornment. Women who resist 'girl' 'take pleasure in their appearance and are fully able to engage in many of the rituals of feminine beauty. But it is never the centre of their lives and their sense of self does not come from being able to manipulate or beguile' (Ussher, 1997: 456). Some participants fitted into the former category of 'doing girl' others fitted more easily into 'resisting girl'. But, whilst Ussher acknowledges that these two categories cannot contain all women, and that women may move between and beyond the two at different points in their lives, she does not suggest that women may occupy both categories simultaneously. The women in this study 'do girl' (and have many rituals of femininity as an integral part of their lives) whilst also deriding much about traditional femininity (including some of the very things they themselves practise). This complex, and seemingly confused, relationship to femininities reflects their own perceptions of where they are located within the discourse of femininity: they 'do' girl and feel like girl but also feel like, and are seen to be, resisting girl.

I asked participants what they used or liked that they saw as particularly feminine. The reason for this was to find out if claiming to resist traditional femininity meant it was also possible, indeed desirable, to entirely jettison what my interviewee Jody described as *'feminine trappings'* and what Delano calls the 'tools', the 'lived practices of female embodiment' (2000: 5). Smith argues that trying to define femininity is like 'assembling a miscellaneous collection of instances apparently lacking coherence ... Its descriptive use relies on our background and ordinary knowledge of everyday practices, which are the source and original of these instances' (1988: 36). These 'everyday practices' are central to the participants' sense of their own femininity. The replies given illustrated another strategy of 'recuperation', although their external appearance challenged many norms of traditional femininity. They used frilly underwear, perfume, make-up and other items which denote luxury, indulgence or glamour, thus drawing themselves back into the safe arena of traditional femininity and its emphasis on feminine beauty rituals. It became clear that, whilst they resisted and derided these traits, they also watched them closely and, to varying extents, could be seen to adopt some of them. The main way was through the revelation that they used such items, as if to reassure other people that their external appearance did not negate their femininity. In a similar way some women 'flash' their femininity. 'Flashing' femininity can be adapted to this study since the participants consistently alluded to how feminine they were 'despite' their appearance. In addition, they more explicitly gave examples of how 'authentic' their femininity was. Until relatively recently, middle-class women were the last bastions of a rigid attention to fashion detail and dedication – gloves, matching shoes and handbag, hats, different outfits considered appropriate for day or evening wear (Thesander, 1997) – and did not need to 'flash' their femininity since their attire announced it for them. Still today, femininity – as a construct – relies on, and is defined by, restraint (Tseëlon, 1995), and the appearance of my interviewees was not restrained. Their hair colour was not restrained, or their body adornment, make-up or clothes in fact, everything about their appearance signalled a disdain for traditional feminine 'restraint'. Doane, on masquerade, describes 'a femininity which knows it is excessive but uses its own overload parodically' (1990: 25) and to a great extent this is how the participants appeared to be using their appearance: as parody, as excess.[4] They talked about how they loaded on the details (more and more piercings, tattoos, hair dye and hair extensions, jewellery and make-up, and many of the participants used different layers of clothes to achieve a particular effect). Although this can be construed as a slavish devotion to one's appearance, it can also be read as a disciplined and creative practice where the woman presents herself in a series of rigorously created 'looks'.

Although they appeared to be stepping beyond the boundaries of the 'traditional place' that clothes can keep women in (Gaines, 1990: 1), my interviewees exercise a great deal of care and control over how they look. There is a contradiction here between what I describe above as the unrestrained nature of these women's appearance versus the control that goes into producing it. The two aspects were always warring. Because of this, it is impossible to argue that the 'difference' of the participants' appearance unshackles them from the traditionally feminine, time-consuming adornment rituals of traditional femininity. It is not their external, finished appearance which 'places' the participants but instead it is the rituals and activities they chose to undertake to build this appearance. Indeed, as the 'appearance diary' of one participant evidences (see Chapter 4), the participants spent more time and money on their appearance than would be seen as a 'reasonable' norm for the modern working woman. But, as several participants asked, why should self-decoration and adornment signal oppression? As Eloise said, *'it can't be "dressing-up" cos I am just getting dressed'*. Gaines (1990) also asks why 'making up' and dressing up are connected to female oppression and Steele (1995) argued that clothes and fashion need not be seen to be disempowering – she points out that they can be defiant or even 'feminist'. Wilson (1985) disagrees with the notion that to resist fashion is to liberate oneself and argues that fashion, including cosmetics, provides women with an opportunity for choice and pleasure. She argues that some women may not want to give up dressing in fashionable clothes, may not feel oppressed by the use of nail polish or high heels and may see these aspects of female clothing and appearance as enjoyable and 'looking one's best'. Yet in a later work, discussing Veblen's views on women's fashion, Wilson comments that a love of fashion and its 'mania for change' could be seen to indicate a woman's 'inherent frivolity and flightiness or ... [her] subjection and oppression ... Fashion was nothing else than women's bondage made visible' (1990b: 29). Again, we can see this in terms of the restraint/lack of restraint binary. This is crucial to understanding the participants' appearance: they do not follow 'fashion' as such, and their appearance makes this very clear. In this way, then, they are able to evade (to some extent) the label of 'frivolity or flightiness' being attached to their appearance. Despite this, they continued to demonstrate recuperative strategies, 'flashing their femininity', as Tseëlon puts it, through their use of indisputably feminine items. For example, Eloise mentioned she often wore false eyelashes (*'I wear false eyelashes and some make-up as obtrusive as possible'*) and Claudia used a small, lady-like leather handbag (*'I have a little proper handbag ... If you're girly-girly it tends to be like a big shoulder bag'*).

Underwear was discussed by many participants. Sparkle said she hand-washed her silk underwear every week, and Bee had a collection of bustiers all of different colours and materials. Gemini listed several items:

*I like pretty bras. And knickers. I like my silky dressing gown. That's me dressing up ... underclothes really. Not sex shop type of peep hole bra type but something really pretty and attractive. Perfume, I'd rather have perfume than any amount of make-up really ... I love bubble bath.*

Each item has the weight of pleasure with it, and these are accepted pleasures for women just as glossy magazines and chocolate are (Winship, 1987) – and are culturally considered to be particularly feminine for women. When I asked Lara what she used that could be seen as typically feminine, her answer was also, primarily, about underwear. She was particular about the sort of underwear she preferred:

> *I like nice underwear, quite structured, pinks, reds, black, lacy, frilly underwear, ruffles and little roses and underwiring ... my boyfriend calls it chocolate box underwear, he says my underwear is a confection.*

There were many similarities in the description to how she had described being dressed as a child by her mother:

> *dresses, frilly dresses, white socks, cute-sey shoes, girly things like daft hair bobbles, frills and flouncy and ... yuk. Always over the top and pastel colours and pink and flowers ... and the thing is, as a child you have no power, you have no money and no say in it. So you are stuck.*

Lara seemed completely unaware of the similarities between the two, for example, lacy and frilly, pink and flowers. Thesander reports that in the early 1970s, with the rise of second-wave feminism, 'many women refused to wear sexy or decorative underwear, associating it with seduction and eroticism, which were the new taboos' (1997: 191). However, the 1980s saw a return to 'sexy sophisticated underwear ... a sign that many women had become sufficiently self-confident ... without fear of being labelled sex objects' (1977: 208). This change was also connected to anxieties about being seen as masculine, because of a certain kind of political resistance where women were labelled 'manly'. Although Lara's description of her underwear echoed her childhood clothing, it is also part of her recuperation of femininity through 'doing girl'; additionally, as an adult woman she now wore black, lacy underwear in a sensual or erotic way, and she had the power and the money to choose (all of which she lacked as a child), which was the main bone of contention about her appearance as a child.

Both Zeb and Delilah expressed a preference for perfume and make-up. Zeb replied:

> *make-up and perfume ... stereotypically female, aren't they? Female? Feminine?*

when asked what typically feminine things she used. Delilah replied with a detailed account of perfume names and lipstick colours (and was able to the perfume I was wearing):

*'Eternity' me, or that new one – CKBe I think. But I use 'Obsession' as ...at's quite a heavy scent ... and some Body Shop scents if I'm just in on ... n, working or whatever, 'Dewberry' mainly ... Feminine things ... well, ... , I love very very dark lipstick, dark plums, dark purples, I used to wear ... but black but I made a sideways move with lipstick ... I don't wear ..., as much make-up, as I used to.*

... participants said they wear less make-up than they used to, or ... ll, although Miss Pink told me she had worn make-up every day ... was fourteen:

*Because ginger hair's the other thing though because ginger eyelashes and eye-brows, they just disappear into your face, like to make a feature of them and bring them out you have to wear make-up.*

Wearing make-up every day for thirteen years is not a partial commitment and, although Miss Pink said she did it because she enjoyed it, she also made clear that she felt obliged to 'make a feature' of her 'inadequate' eyes. 'Such pleasures are frequently undercut as liberatory by the claim that the ideal female body is always an impossibility, an unmatchable ideal' (Finkelstein, 1997: 155) and Miss Pink illustrated this: she wore make-up to 'improve' herself but in the process had to wear it every day. Otherwise it would be apparent that really she did not match the ideal, her lashes and eyebrows were too pale. However, on the whole, the participants claim they are not trying to match the ideal and this is apparent by the clothes they wear, how they have their hair and their body modifications, thus attempting (if not always successfully achieving) a 'liberatory' approach. However, there were several instances where participants discussed how they intended to approach something in a traditionally feminine way with no conditions about it being 'liberatory', or even 'alternative'. For example, Miss Pink had recently become engaged to her boyfriend and much of her interview was about her wedding plans.

*I do want my hair to be like a million different shades of pink when I do it and I want a lilac and gold dress so it's not like way out, like I don't want to get married in black leather or anything like that... I like to be feminine as well and getting married is the time to do it.*

Miss Pink was definite about her wish to be 'feminine' and anxious that she did it successfully. Tseëlon argues, the effort to be 'authentic' implies a twofold paradox [which] suggests that originally 'one is being what one is not'. In other words: a woman is not originally authentically feminine but can become one with effort. Second, 'being authentic' implies an act of objectifying oneself, of seeing oneself through the eyes of the Other. And a being which is for-others cannot be for-itself (1995: 38).

Miss Pink did intend to get married with pink hair in a gold dress – still her own version of feminine and so 'authentic' by her own standards but negotiated via an insistence on not going too 'way out' so that she was still more traditionally 'authentic' as a bride. As Furman comments, 'the only constant [about ideals of femininity] ... would be women's imperative to look attractive for the men of their dreams' (1997: 46). Miss Pink wanted to look 'alternative' for herself but also acceptably feminine for her fiancé and guests so that her wedding day could 'authentically' be 'the happiest day of a woman's life'.

In these ways there is pleasure to be had from 'doing' feminine, however partial or ambivalent (see Table 3.1). As Silverman comments, 'oppositional gestures are never absolute' (1986: 149), and Gemini echoed this, although she embedded in a description of the very things that she thought made her rebellion partial:

*I make small rebellions. I suppose such as the tattoos and yet ... I love rustling silk and gold slippers. I don't see that as a bad thing. It's just a part of me, it's how I have always been. The romantic side.*

Gemini, and other participants, seek to balance the 'oppositional' with the 'feminine' through different aspects of their appearance and demonstrate a variety of approaches and reflections on the success of this balancing act. In Chapter 4 I examine three ways in which they discussed their femininity which was harder for them to balance with assertions of 'difference': the fairy princess, the importance of hair and the routine of shopping for (or making) clothes.

**Table 3.1.** The things listed by participants when asked what traditionally 'feminine' things they liked to use.

| Participant | Feminine Things Used |
| --- | --- |
| Louise | Underwear; perfume |
| Kiki | Nail varnish; perfume |
| Sparkle | Nail varnish; make-up; hair dye |
| Morgan | Perfume; underwear |
| Vash | Make-up; perfume; underwear; hair dye |
| Zeb | Make-up; crimpers; perfume |
| Claudia | Handbag; underwear; make-up; hair dye |
| Jody | Underwear |
| Miss Pink | Make-up; hair dye |
| Gwendolin | Make-up; hair dye; jewellry |
| Diz | Perfume; underwear |
| Flong | Perfume; underwear; make-up |
| Bee | Underwear; hair dye |
| Delilah | Perfume; lipstick; hair dye |
| Eloise | Underwear; perfume; make-up; hair dye |
| Gemini | Underwear; perfume; bubble bath |
| Lara | Underwear; perfume; hair dye |

# *How To Be a Fairy Princess*

This chapter examines the way the fairy princess figure features in constructions of femininity and how the participants talk about their hair and their clothes (buying, making and maintenance) to create their own femininities. There have been many studies of how girls learn to be 'feminine' (for example, Lees, 1993; Sharpe, 1994). The 'body training' received by boys and girls is different in all ways, from walking and talking to arguing and fighting (Shilling, 1993). There are a host of images and narratives which train a child culturally and among the most lasting of these are the stories and images perpetuated in fairy tales (Davies, 1989). Beautiful, often helpless, innocent girls are the victims of cruel treatment, often at the hands of an older woman, an interloper of some kind (a jealous witch, a bitter stepmother) (Zipes, 1986). Rivalry and discord between women function to foster divisions between women of different ages ('divide and conquer': beauty and youth opposing age and experience), thus investing the relationships between men and women as the more valuable and reliable. Despite this, 'romantic tales exert an awesome imaginative power over the female psyche' (Rowe, 1986: 218). Several participants talked about the enjoyment of playing as a figure from a fairy tale – princess, fairy, mermaid – as a child – and how they still liked this image. A random and easily recognisable example is the Barbie doll, which has been sold with 'fairy tale' outfits.[1] Barbie advertisements frequently use words such as: ' "dream", "enchantment", "fairy tale", "magic", "romance" and "nostalgia" as well as "fantasy". These are the adjectives of modern middle-class femininity ... youthful femininity, heterosexual femininity, and white femininity' (Rogers, 1999: 3 and 11). These descriptions of qualities attendant on 'true' femininity index the ways in which particular types of feminine traits are privileged (although held by a small minority of women) and how they are woven into the mythology and pleasures of the fairy tale. The participants' version of the fairy princess owed her existence primarily to romantic Victorian images of femininity such as Pre-Raphaelite paintings (Pearce, 1991) and, later, Disney versions: she is young, blonde and white, has blue eyes and is waif-like. And, despite the difference from their own appearance, they talked affectionately of this figure. Brownmiller notes the persistence of the fairy princess motif:

> Who can imagine a fairy princess with hair that is anything but long and blonde, with eyes that are anything but blue, in clothes that are anything but a filmy drape of gossamer and gauze? The fairy princess remains one of the most powerful symbols of femininity the Western world has ever devised, and falling short of her role model, women are all feminine failures to some degree. (1984: 44)

Gemini said that, although she had been a tomboy,[2] she resented the fact that the clothes she was wearing were not typically 'girly':

> *Mum always put me in shorts and T-shirts for the summer, because they were more sensible for playing outside. I loved dressing up in Mum's old clothes and playing princesses and fairies and things like that.* I really wanted to be a fairy princess, which is much more the norm [my emphasis] *so I don't think* [the clothes] *affected the way I thought of myself. I knew I was a girl.*

Here Gemini stated that she was as 'normal' as any other little girl, despite her practical playing-out clothes, and that she was able to imagine herself a fairy princess via a route that her mother could not make 'sensible': that is, via her fantasies in play. This is something several participants referred to in various different contexts: a 'normal' girl. By 'normal' they were alluding to the model of 'girl' which fulfilled some or all of the criteria of 'true' femininity. Yet could she live up to the role model? As Brownmiller (1986) points out, most women fall short of this standard and Gemini had already failed before she began, simply by being dressed in practical, sensible clothes – by saying she felt 'normal', Gemini indicated her awareness of the potential for failure.

## Faries at Play

Marsh (2000) argues that young girls are offered relatively narrow options for 'super-hero' play and many will respond to any gendered images even if they are repressive, simply because what is available is so limited – yet Marsh's study was amongst primary school children. The women in this study saw the fairy princess as a 'misunderstood' figure: a feminine figure derided for her femininity and more positive than is usually thought. This defensiveness about the fairy princess is akin to defensiveness about 'dumb blonde' jokes: why are women assumed to be weak or stupid because they are attractive? This attitude was implicit or explicit in all the participants who mentioned the fairy princess. Gwendolin stated that she thought fairy play was the 'norm' despite the high expectations that were necessarily associated with it. Gwendolin said she and her friends would get dressed up

*like fairies ... they're supposed to be feminine and floaty, and the blonde hair, the long long blonde hair ... all little girls want to be a fairy. But you don't have to be a weak fairy, do you?*

Although this is a rhetorical question, the answer is that actually yes, you do, if you wish to be seen as beautiful. Strong fairies are ugly and wicked. For example, Tinkerbell in *Peter Pan* appears to have power (in that the Lost Boys will do her bidding, which is to shoot Wendy, her rival). Ultimately, however, it is Peter who has to rescue Tinkerbell – she has no real power because she is small and delicate and pretty. Yet very few little girls live up to this ideal, for example, because they do not have the long blonde hair[3] or simply because they have parents, like Gemini's, who put practicality before 'enchantment':

*I probably looked like* [a tomboy] *because my mum cut my hair really short but I hated it. No, I wanted to have long flowing hair and really flowing skirts and stuff like that. I think I was a very feminine little child, I just wasn't given the chance to be.* (Eloise)

*Well of course I played at fairies and all that stuff, I didn't have the clothes though, just wrapped some old curtain netting stuff round me, got some kitchen foil off my mum and put it around a garden cane for a wand, I enjoyed playing that and I looked the part I think ... on the inside I was never a fairy. I knew that all the time.* (Sparkle)

The fairy princess is the antithesis to the tomboy but is also more than simply the opposite. She is the epitome of everything that constitutes 'girly' femininity: passivity, docility, conformity. Yet the participants who talked about fairy princess play as children described physicality and pleasure rather than physical repression and weakness.

All the participants who mentioned fairy play as children also evidenced and/or admitted to an adult fondness for the fairy princess (what Bee called *'the fairy issue ... it's a shameful hankering of mine'*), the 'belle of the ball', if not the persona. For example, Lara described a tattoo she has on her hip:

*the one on my hip is just a little representation of me when I had long red hair. It was pillar-box red and it is just a little woman curled up asleep, like a princess or a mermaid, with all this hair billowing around her. Longer and much bigger*

*hair than it actually was really at the time; a boyfriend did this little sketch and
I thought my hair looked so beautiful I thought I would have it tattooed on me.
So when I am old I can see how beautiful my hair was.*

And yet this tattoo, this permanent *aide-mémoire*, is not accurate; Lara has
said that it shows her with hair 'longer and much bigger' than it actually
was, hair that was 'billowing' around the figure in the picture. But this is
how she wants to remember her hair; she wants to remember herself with
'fairy princess' hair. She is creating her own myth: as an old woman she
will be able to believe that she did look like a fairy tale princess. One of the
problems with Lara (future, old Lara) looking back on an idealised, fairy
tale version of herself in tattoo form is that it underlines a desire and a willingness on her part to maintain a status quo and not to challenge the fixity
of the images of femininity. Issues of permanence and ageing are discussed
further in later chapters.

Miss Pink revealed that various people had described her in 'fairy
princess' ways:

*I've been called Barbie. This girl in a restaurant, her mother came up to me and
said 'Excuse me, my daughter thinks you're Barbie'. Hoola Barbie, she's got pink
hair. I was like 'Yeah, nice one'. And I got called Ariel in Cornwall, you know
Ariel the mermaid with red hair, this little girl said to her father 'Dad, why has
Ariel got her nose pierced?' Oh, it's quite funny.*

It is interesting to note that Miss Pink has been described as looking like
Barbie and Ariel (from Disney's *The Little Mermaid*) as both are representations of a particular 'fairy princess' type of femininity (long hair, slim,
doe eyes, young) and therefore very traditional and mainstream representations of femininity. Barbie, for example, has been identified as a negative
role model for young girls (Rogers, 1999; Urla and Swedlund, 2000) –
socialising children to the pressures and privilege of beauty via constantly
updating in tune with current fashion and beauty ideals (Thesander, 1997)
– and such representations have been linked with eating disorders in girls
and young women (Chernin, 1983; Bordo, 1989). Miss Pink did not
object; she welcomed this description of herself and was amused by these
incidents. Partly this seemed to be because they were so inappropriate considering her multiple piercings and tattoos but also because they reinforced
her belief in her own femininity.

Both Flong and Miss Pink's business cards depict 'fairy princess' images,
which they designed themselves. Flong and Miss Pink each produced a
form of iconic/ironic self-portraiture – Flong's depicts a flowing-haired

woman reminiscent of a Pre-Raphaelite romanticism (very like Rossetti's *Pandora*); Miss Pink's is more 'modern' and playful (similar to Jessica Rabbit or Disney's Ariel). Other participants likened themselves to this kind of motif: Lara's tattoo with its 'billowing' red hair, for example, and Eloise, who described her own long, red hair, when back-combed to go out, as 'wild fairy hair'. The type of appearance is 'different' from current ideals of femininity and yet the dress of Pre-Raphaelite or bohemian women (discussed further in Chapter 5) that they draw on was also 'different' in its time (Wilson, 1990a, 2000). In using the iconography of traditional femininity they create images of femininity which are not 'townie' or mainstream (and so cannot be categorised as 'girly'); neither is it practical or even desirable for the majority of women; nor is it masculinised. In this way many elements are mixed to deconstruct traditional femininity: the 'high' femininity of Victorian paintings with the exaggerated femininity of cartoons or graphic art, and the unconventional and non-traditional femininities of subcultures, such as goth or punk.

Flong also created her own adult fairy princess scenario. At a tattooists' ball, where everyone wore their normal day clothes (*'leather trousers or black clothes'*), Flong persuaded her friends to dress differently:

*full-length ball gowns and my friend ... did all this nice bouffant hair and these ringlets down the side of my face and all that. We walked into this party and everyone just ... dropped! In fact the head of our [tattooists'] union came over and he said he had to come over and say that 'You girls just looked like princesses walking down the stairs and I'd like to buy you a drink, what would all your friends like?' There was ten of us! Ten tattooed princesses.*

There are several strands to this. One is that, at a social event where everyone would look very similar, Flong found a way to look 'different' via a very traditional spectacle: embodiment of a model of hyper-femininity. Much has been written about 'spectacle', particularly in subcultural theory, for example, Hebdige (1979) and Muggleton (2000) on 'spectacular' subcultures, and Leonard (1997) on how riot grrls criticised traditional notions about female display through the spectacle of their appearance and performance. Russo states that as a child she was often warned against making a spectacle of herself: 'Making a spectacle of oneself seemed a specifically feminine danger. The danger was one of exposure ... For a woman, making a spectacle of herself had more to do with a kind of inadvertency and loss of boundaries' (1995: 213). The participants of this study aimed to make a spectacle of themselves; they had consciously made a project of staying a spectacle (despite narrowing boundaries of age and gender), and Russo acknowledges that, like Leonard's (1997) riot grrls, the shame of making a spectacle of oneself can be channelled into 'the bold affirmations of feminine performance, imposture, and masquerade' (1995: 213). Although Flong's spectacle did not challenge traditional notions about female display, she did challenge what was expected of her in the context she was in. Others at the ball also played a role, for example, the man who called them all princesses and gallantly offered to buy drinks. 'The immediate and predictable result of being beautiful is being chosen, this word having profound importance to a girl. The beautiful girl does not have to do anything to merit being chosen; she does not have to show pluck, resourcefulness and wit' (Gilbert and Gubar, 1986: 188). Flong was chosen for what she 'was' (by the man who bought the drinks). But it was done mostly in an ironic way (illustrated by Flong's dry comment about 'tattooed princesses') so that no one thought she was taking it seriously or that she was not aware of its connotations – in this case, she was using resourcefulness and wit. Flong's use of masquerade was successful because it was doubly effective: because of her own usually 'alternative' appearance and because of the particular event. As Finkelstein notes, 'styles in appearance simultaneously attract and deflect attention. When clothes are misappropriated … they fracture conventions; when they are parodied, they satirize those same conventions' (1997: 163). Flong was still 'different', still 'alternative', both parodying and fulfilling a fantasy, and managing to fracture conventions in a situation where she would have otherwise been just another tattooist in leather trousers.

The fairy princess is the 'good' fairy; she is the height of delicate, acceptable femininity. Yet, whilst the participants aligned themselves with her, they also contradicted themselves and made statements to place themselves in opposition to her – they liked how she looked but they did not like the fact that she stood for complicity and passivity. Several tentatively and defensively said they saw her as a strong or positive figure, although as many said they preferred the look and character of the evil stepmother figures. As Bryer comments, 'dark hair has connotations of mystery and evil. The long black hair of the witch contrasts with the golden tresses of the fairy princess' (2000: 11). Several participants said they preferred the evil stepmother in Snow White because she was strong, intelligent, wicked, had black hair and looked like a goth with her white face, red lips and black clothes – that is, someone who looked more like them. 'The good and bad woman reminds the young reader of her dreadful fate, should she stray from the path of perfect femininity – denunciation as wild woman or witch' (Ussher, 1997: 11). It would seem apparent that the participants might feel more attracted to the idea of themselves as wild woman but it cannot be polarised so simply. As Gemini and Eloise proved, it is possible to feel like a fairy princess on the inside even if you do not look the part – or, as Sparkle and Flong proved, it is possible to be a fairy princess on the outside but not really feel like one. Most participants were unwilling to ally themselves with either one role or the other. As Edie asked, *'Why Snow White had to be so lily-livered I don't know. She could have made friends with her stepmother and got rid of her stupid dad instead.'* Although, again, a rhetorical question, it does reveal how patriarchal versions of femininity work. In addition, it uncovers the fact that, for all their challenges to the norm, some of my participants had not worked out precisely why they had to both resist and conform – or that that is how the ideology perpetuates itself.

### 'My Hair is Everything'

Hair can provide information about societies and their wealth, structures and beliefs. How do societies deal with hair? Are men and women expected to treat their hair differently? And what does this say about gender roles? For example, Bryer quotes Greer disputing the myth that women have more abundant hair than men, which is untrue; neither do only men go bald (2000: 11); yet women are expected to have little or no body hair, like children. Steele points out that 'hairstyles are an important part of fashion and identity ... Many people ... are extremely interested in hairstyles ... yet surprisingly little research has been done on the significance of particular fashions in hair' (1997c: 337). Women's hair has always had a powerful effect and has been used in images and stories throughout history: Medusa's hair was made of snakes; Rapunzel, locked in a tower, let down her hair for a prince to climb up and rescue her (although only the prince and the witch could climb in and out at will); Lady Godiva rode naked through Coventry with only her hair to cover her; in *Little Women* Jo March sold her hair so that her mother could visit her father (Alcott, 1994). Bryer points out that long hair has embodied Western beauty and femininity for centuries: for example, 'the length and abundance of the [woman's] hair is the prime feature of Botticelli's evocation of beauty' (2000: 8). Famous (young, primarily white) women with 'signature' hairstyles have captured popular imagination and include Jean Harlow's bleached bob in the 1920s, the Veronica Lake 'dip' in the 1940s, Marilyn Monroe's platinum hair in the 1950s, Farrah Fawcett-Majors's 'flick' in the 1970s and Jennifer Anniston's 'Rachel' in the 1990s. More recently, famous women of colour, such as singer Beyonce Knowles and actor Halle Berry, have influenced popular hairstyles.

Hair has always had a place as one of the most important elements of a person's identity and hair was a key signifier for many of the participants. Most of the women I interviewed responded with a detailed 'hair history'. Hair was a crucial sub-theme to the participants' preoccupation with both traditional and unconventional femininities. The participants' hairstyles varied but in general were 'different' from mainstream styles in that they were brightly dyed, or shaved, dreaded, backcombed, or crimped. Yet, despite this difference, their concerns and the amount of time they spent on their hair were arguably stereotypically 'feminine'. Gwendolin knew at a young age that she wanted to change her hair: *'I first started making decisions about it when I was about eleven, colouring my hair'* and other participants said much the same: for example, Eloise was twelve when she wanted to dye her hair pink and Sparkle was eleven when she started by colouring her hair with felt-tip pens. Miss Pink started to dye her hair as a teenager to outwit those who teased her for having ginger hair, and several participants, including Gemini, were resentful about having short hair as children:

*My mum cut my hair really short but I hated it. No, I wanted to have long flowing ... I had this horrible tomboy haircut ... I won't have it [short] now, the shortest I had it for years was about [shoulder-length] and even then I had to grow it again.* (Eloise)

*I haven't had my hair short since I was little. My mum used to make us both have it short so we wouldn't get it in a mess. Then she'd say we weren't like proper little girls and we were there with this ... this bloody little boys' haircut ... So I guess because of that, having that inflicted on me, I grew it long as soon as I could. And my sister just went the other way!* [shaves her hair off completely]. (Lara)

Lara showed me a photograph of herself and her sister when they were aged seven and five. Two dour little girls in frilly dresses and lacy socks stared out of the photograph, both with very short, shiny hair. Yet, as with many tensions that participants were apparently unaware of, Lara complained on the one hand about her mother forcing her into wearing 'girly' clothes and yet also complained that her mother insisted on her having a very practical, short haircut.

The cutting of women's hair has been the arena of much debate and protest, not least since women's hair is so closely associated with a woman's beauty, femininity and sexuality. By the time of the Great War (1914–18) women's desire and right to cut off their hair had become a matter for public debate – and it was more than simply a matter of independence or protest (Wilson, 1990a) or practicality and cleanliness (Brownmiller, 1984). It was those things and more – it became chic and fashionable but the arguments raged on about this 'frightening challenge to the masculine–feminine polarity' (Brownmiller, 1984: 44). Although Gemini, Lara and Eloise's mothers were cutting their daughters' hair off, this remained an issue of control, in theory for the sake of manageability, but also against their will. When Lara moved away from home at the age of sixteen she was immediately at liberty to do whatever she wanted with her hair:

*I moved to [area of Sheffield] and just went mental. I just let rip. I grew my hair. I dyed my hair, I backcombed it, I left my crimpers on twenty-four hours a day … I stuck my hair up – it was like [indicates a foot above her head] … All the colours of the rainbow, one after the other and sometimes more than one at once.*

Several participants voiced anxieties about losing their hair (notably amongst them were all the women who resented having short hair as children). Gemini spoke at some length about women who shaved off their hair, and women's attitude generally to their hair:

*[I admire] women who shave their heads … For me to be completely bald would really challenge, I would be pushing myself far too far. Although I like to be rebellious I am also a bit of a scaredy cat. 'Oh your lovely long golden hair', it is one of those things that men seem to go for … you've got to be a decorative rather than an intelligent person. I don't think it's much of a surprise that most dolls have long hair … Hair is quite a big signifier in our psyche, people feel able to comment if we cut it or change the colour.*

Gemini alternated between resentment at the value put on a woman's hair and anger at herself for not feeling able to shave her hair off. Others also had specific anxieties:

*Sometimes I wake up in the night and just start worrying, what would I ever do if I got cancer, if I lost my hair and my eyebrows and just bloated up … I've seen people who are having chemotherapy and they look awful. I mean, I know they are ill and can't help it, it is the best option I suppose but I think I would rather kill myself than have to go around bald. I don't know how or why my sister does it. But I suppose that's different, that's from choice.* (Lara)

*I sometimes wake up in a cold sweat. I have this dream, this nightmare, where someone cuts my hair off against my will and my dream is just so full of this sorrow, this fear, that it wakes me up.* (Sparkle)

Bruzzi discusses the loss of hair in films and argues that scenes including the cutting of hair 'function as metaphors for loss, not acquisition or growth' (1997: 180). This is what many of the participants referred to: hair loss as trauma rather than hair loss as a signal of independence or freedom, and the fear of not having the choice whether to cut your hair or not. Bee was growing her hair at the time of the interview:

> *I still wear men's clothing but for the first time in twenty years I am starting to grow my hair. Too many girly-girls have short hair now, I want to be different to them ... My hair, I don't know what colour it really is, would probably be mostly grey I think. I was dyeing it purple and other colours, red, blue, long before it was, you know, 'in', fashionable.*

Jody, Bee, Janet and Louise had all previously had long, blonde hair and in their twenties or thirties cut it all off. All four of them had cut off their hair in response to a life change: Louise, Janet and Jody had ended relationships; and Bee had decided that she wanted to look *'more like trouble'*. The other three said they had no interest in their hair now it was short, it was easy to manage and that was the key. Short hair on women can still be seen as unfeminine or 'butch' and many feminists and lesbians have used short hair as a signal of both their politics and their sexuality – their liberation from heterosexual standards of 'beauty' (Garber, 1992). Hair is a key cultural signifier of femininity, particularly long hair, from 'big hair girl' Barbie (Sciebinger, 2000b: 16) to the carefully coifed styles of Hollywood actors, and the loss of hair can signal loss of sexual attractiveness to many women. The women in this study who demonstrated fear of hair loss believed that they would experience what Goffman calls a 'spoiled identity', that is, that their femininity rested in large part in their hair. Goffman defines stigma as 'bodily signs designed to expose something unusual or bad about the signifier' (1964: 11); for example, a permanent stigma is the missing hand of a thief; an impermanent stigma is the shaven head of a convict. The body modifications undertaken by the women in this study cannot be taken as stigma as they adopted them voluntarily; they were instead 'deviators' (from conventional norms). However, the involuntary hair loss which they feared would be linked to the stigma of losing their feminine gender identity. Kiki likened the loss of her long, dreaded hair to the loss of Samson's hair, saying it, along with her tattoos and piercings, gave her strength and confidence. Miss Pink felt that she would feel both much less confident and much less feminine if she lost her hair:

*I tell you what, if I had all my hair cut off I probably wouldn't feel half as feminine as I do now. Cos I am ... six foot and quite ... I mean, not excessively big but I am big built and things like that. And I always wear make-up, I never go anywhere without it on – just little things like that that enhance your femininity.*

Miss Pink's need to 'enhance her femininity' suggested anxieties about not being feminine enough: she evidently felt that she had to 'tread carefully' in order not to be seen as threatening – again, using the twin strategies of 'flashing' (or in this case, perhaps, 'tending' to) her femininity in order to recuperate it. The participants explicitly linked their hair practices to their sense of femininity. For example, Kiki started by saying she had dreadlocks to avoid having a feminine hairstyle and finished by saying, rather sadly, that she does not think people see her hairstyle as feminine despite the fact that it is very long:

*I've got dreads now but before I've always had mohicans and stuff like that. I've never had a sort of, feminine hair style ... it is feminine to have long hair but I don't think ... people see it as being a feminine hair style at all, although it is really long.* (Kiki)

Yet despite these concerns many of the participants continue to do things to their hair which created the possibility of hair loss or damage.

*Eighteen years isn't it, from thirteen, so eighteen years I've been bleaching my hair, why aren't I bald yet?* (Flong)

Alongside the preoccupations with hairstyles and anxieties about hair loss, several participants mentioned using electric hair crimpers. Many participants said that they had used crimpers a lot when they were younger (Vash, Zeb, Delilah, Eloise, Lara, Sparkle, Gwendolin and Miss Pink all said that they had kept their crimpers plugged in twenty-four hours a day). Several participants lamented the way crimpers had ruined their hair, an irony considering their fears about hair loss. For example, Miss Pink, when discussing the most outlandish hairstyle she had had whilst also having a full-time job, said:

*I used to crimp it about three times a day to get it to stand up, which wrecked my hair ... I haven't got time to crimp my hair three times a day any more, it doesn't fit into my working day ... I'd mess about with it more if I had time, yeah. Definitely. But I ruined it crimping it. I mean, it took years to grow it four inches at one point!*

But there were only two who still used crimpers regularly. Zeb explained that she:

> *couldn't imagine going out of the door without crimping my hair … I have even taken them to festivals and had to plug them into the car battery so I could still crimp my hair. Or if not put so much yak in my hair that it wasn't going to, you know, go flat … but I could never ever not crimp my hair. It would be very difficult.*

Zeb said she could think of no other way to manage her hair and that even if she thought of something she would not be happy to adopt it because she was so attached to her crimpers. Crimping hair is not always practical or even possible and this was something she was aware of and even fearful of – to the extent that not being able to crimp her hair made her feel less confident generally. She acknowledged that her fear is only a fear of having 'flat' hair and this was something echoed similarly by other participants who had previously backcombed, crimped and sprayed their hair until it was taller or wider than it naturally was: avoiding flat, shiny hair proved a hard habit to break. These concerns can only be a product of the ethnicity of the participants: Black women have different struggles to control their hair, such as straightening (Mercer, 1987; Banks, 2000). Delilah also still used them and mentioned them when asked if she used anything that was typically feminine. She expressed concern about the health of her hair and said that she thought she would be 'as bald as a coot' by the time she was fifty but that she would continue to crimp her hair every day regardless:

> *crimpers and hairspray, they're still mostly a feminine thing, aren't they? And I use them every day. I see men with crimped hair sometimes but it's mostly women, I mean alternative women.*

Why did the participants continue to treat their hair despite their anxieties about losing it? The answer is that in many ways they were using their hairstyles to make a statement, rather than issuing a direct challenge through what they said or how they behaved.

The investment of time, money and gender identity that the participants demonstrated in connection with their hair is indicative of their overall commitment to their appearance and their 'femininity'. This is explored further in the next (and final) section of this chapter, which discusses the 'appearance diary' of one participant.

## Commitment: Time and Money

To understand how much time and commitment this type of appearance demands, one participant, Delilah, agreed to complete an 'appearance diary' over a period of one month. Delilah's diary serves only as an example – using more diaries would produce a whole other study all on its own; for example, Miller's study of one shopping street involved seventy-six households (Miller, 1998). Delilah addressed herself to her diary with enthusiasm and produced a detailed and lengthy record of all her activities and expenditure. The most time-consuming activity was shopping.

Shopping environments inscribe masculine and feminine stereotypes and shopping can be seen to be a primarily 'feminine' activity, both both necessity and for leisure; cultural products, from Barbie dolls to romance novels (aimed at girls and women), share the same emphasis on the consumption of an ever-widening range of goods (Rogers, 1999: 132). Veblen (1994) describes the slavish devotion to buying more and more 'things' in order to signal your lifestyle: 'conspicuous consumption'. Veblen used as his model the new middle classes of the late nineteenth century but the idea is still current today in 'celebrities' (such as Jennifer Lopez and Ben Affleck, and David and Victoria Beckham) whose expenditure on possessions is frequently featured in the press. Women became equated with shopping and consumption in the nineteenth century because, as Davis notes, they became the 'expressive vehicle for announcing the status claims' of a family, in particular of the 'man of the house' (1992: 41). The nineteenth century saw the rise of the department store, which offered a great deal of choice for the shopper. However, only those with the means to do so would have been able to avail themselves of the shopping opportunities of a department store (Lancaster, 1995) since, 'well into the nineteenth century, used clothing constituted the effective market for much of the population except the very rich' (Hansen, 2000: 248).

In contrast, women in the 1960s were called on to reject fashion symbols of economic achievement as conspicuous consumption and therefore a symbolic embodiment of ideology (Rubinstein, 1995: 258). Fashion, being a way to continually redefine the female body, was reviled as 'false consciousness' (Wilson, 1985: ch. 11). In the early 1970s perhaps the most conscious style that many feminists engaged in was Oxfam-shop and jumble-sale dressing, or retro chic. It had the merit of being cheap (maintaining a distance from the dictates of consumerism); in addition, it could keep its distance from fashion's denial of contrivance by being so obviously like dressing up in costume' (Evans and Thornton, 1989: 8). Delilah's approach to second-hand clothes echoes this 'distancing' and 'costuming' framework but the participants' general attitude to their overall appearance is also the same (discussed further in the next chapter).

Second-hand clothes differ from new clothes (whether home-made or shop-bought). There remains a 'strangeness' about second-hand clothes because of their close association with the body of the person who first wore them; people are often superstitious, or say that second-hand clothes are dirty, because the clothing might 'bear the trace/s of this habitation' (Gregson and Crewe, 2003: 155 and discussed fully pp. 143–72). As Wilson notes, 'clothes without a wearer, whether on a second-hand stall, in a glass case, or merely a lover's garments strewn on the floor, can affect us unpleasantly, as if a snake had shed its skin' (1985: 2). Similarly, Hansen reports that second-hand clothes are 'known by local terms that mean "dead white men's clothes" in Ghana [and] "died in Europe" in north-western Tanzania' (2000: 245). However, Delilah's appearance diary revolved around her quest to find the 'right' clothes, particularly second-hand clothes, 'to enact both distinction and skill' (Gregson and Crewe, 2003: 86), as a key aspect of her overall appearance. As Gregson *et al.* argue, most people who habitually wear second-hand or retro clothes do not wear them from nostalgia, that is, they do not wish to re-create an accurate 1950s look but intend to make their look 'different' by mixing their styles (Gregson *et al.*, 2001: 3). Hebdige (1979) (adapting the term from Lévi-Strauss) called this mixing of styles and eras *bricolage*, meaning the creation of new patterns and styles from the kaleidoscopic bits and pieces of cultural debris (Craik, 1994: x), and second-hand clothes should be viewed as an important, but undervalued, aspect of subcultural history (McRobbie, 1989b: 24). For example, 'thrift shop dressing ... later [became] the hallmark of hippie style ... The punks took this a stage further and gave it new meanings ... [but] it did take over from the hippies their use of the profoundly unfashionable, items that cost little, the disregarded detritus of the fashion world' (Wilson, 2000: 173).

The distinctive feature about Delilah's 'appearance routine' is the amount of energy she spent on finding, buying and maintaining second-hand clothes.

*I go to the second hand market and charity shops every week, which takes perhaps two to four hours in total, plus up to ten hours mending or altering them, & probably spend on average about £20 a week on not-new clothes ... I spend quite a lot of time looking after my clothes, hand-washing, ironing, mending, etc (a lot of my clothes are second hand or very old or embroidered so likely to fall to pieces!).*

Similarly, Gregson and Crewe found that some of their respondents have strict routines of shopping for second-hand clothes (2003: 94) and the primary expenditure is time. Deliah spent up to four hours a week going to particular charity shops and second-hand markets. She never missed even if she was ill: '*I might miss the find of the century! And I can always go back to bed.*' The allure of vintage clothing lies in the means it provides to salvage some aspects of old-fashioned glamorous femininity which has otherwise been 'consigned to the waste basket' by the fashion industry and feminist interventions on the restrictive nature of women's clothes (Silverman, 1986: 150). It also enables the wearer to put an 'ironic distance' between herself and the clothing she 'collects'. 'The phrase ironic distance coincides theoretically with what others have called "masquerade", and it underscores several important features of thrift-shop dressing: ... its predilection for a tarnished and "stagey" elegance; and its desire to convert clothing into costume or "fancy dress" ' (ibid., 149). But there is also the opportunity to be creative, to repair and maintain it yourself. As Hansen notes, discussing the popularity of second-hand clothes in Zambia, 'they all want to look "outstanding", "unique", or "exclusive" ' (2000: 247). Delilah offset this 'stagey elegance' with her other (new) purchases, such as fetish clothing, teamed with her brightly coloured hair: the result was a form of masquerade – vintage feminine clothes teamed with fetish wear, a constructed, subversive image which challenged the 'naturalness' of feminine glamour.

Delilah demonstrated her time-consuming commitment to her appearance, which appeared to shape her entire life.[4] She travelled more than two hundred miles from Sheffield to London to buy boots because she could not find 'any' boots in Sheffield, Leeds or Manchester, and spent £400 on boots, a top and some body jewellery. She appeared to think nothing of this day-trip and elsewhere in her diary said that she went to London at least four times a year just for clothes shopping. She went at other times too but '*for social occasions*', marking out a distinction between 'social' and 'shopping' as if the latter were a business or work activity. This cast Delilah's shopping as some kind of task to be done, which is at odds with Miller's findings that shopping is for pleasure and, because it is done voluntarily, is a leisure activity. Were it to be done out of necessity it would come to seem more like work (Miller, 1998: 69). Delilah's shopping had become a necessity for her, something she viewed in terms of a job, but the pleasure had not diminished.

McRobbie notes that, 'although shopping is usually regarded as a private activity, it is also simultaneously a public one' (1989b: 24) but in Delilah's case this kind of public/private or work/social line was one she made a point of drawing. She travelled to London regularly partly so that no one she knew would 'see' her shopping (thus she saw her shopping trips as less 'public' although, obviously, they still took place in the public arena) and so that there was less chance of anyone else wearing exactly the same clothes. Delilah was a freelance artist and her income fluctuated; despite this she did not undertake any of the strategies of 'thrift' discussed by Miller (1998: 62). She was, however, able to work 'around' clothes-buying and the maintenance of her appearance, and said this is one of the reasons she chose it as a career. Another reason is that, working for herself, she can wear whatever she wants. She told me:

*I only stayed on* [at school] *so I could dress how I wanted for longer ... I thought, if I have a proper job I can't dress how I want, they'll want to stick me in some crap old blouse or whatever, so I did two 'A' levels ... Thought if I did them I could go to college, you know, university, and ... dress weird for longer.*

McRobbie argues that shopping 'is particularly important for girls and young women because their street activities are still curtailed in contrast to those of their male peers. This fact has been commented upon by many feminist writers but the various pleasures of shopping have not been similarly engaged with' (McRobbie, 1989b: 24), but, as Macdonald notes, 'women's ebullient visibility in the shopping mall obscures their invisibility in the boardroom' (1995: 34). The pleasures of shopping for Delilah appeared to be a key activity in her life and a routine which she was willing to base her life around; interestingly, she said that, though her social life had waned, her clothes shopping had not.

Another time-consuming pastime was her repair and alterations of the clothes she bought. Sewing and mending clothes is a traditionally feminine pastime for leisure but also for economic necessity (Burman, 1999),[5] but it is also now not such a common pastime as it once was. Several other participants also said that they had begun wearing punk or goth clothes that they had made themselves, partly because at their age they found it difficult to find or afford such items, but also partly because of the disapproval of family members. For example:

[at first] *my grandma used to help me ... she made me all my bondage gear when I was like 13–14 when I first had my hair cut off. She's always made clothes and stuff anyway. I used to come back with these wild ideas ... I've painted jeans, painted designs on jeans and all sorts, painted my boots ... I've actually seen clothes in shop windows, taken a sketch pad down and drawn it at night when the shops are closed. I do* [sic] *it when they're closed and I've gone home and then made it.* (Flong)

*I used to wear tartan dresses, buckle boots, leather jacket. I was a little punk. It was a pinafore thing I made myself, I made everything myself.* (Miss Pink)

*Going about in town on Saturdays, used to see all people – obviously a bit older than me, and happy looking – and I'd think 'Oh, they look cool, I wanna be them' and, er, gradually as you get more spending power you can do things more and more ... [my dad] was in the Navy and he used to go away for like nearly a year at a time and he'd come back and I'd have this black spiky hair and all the rest of it, I'd have made myself all these mad clothes, and he just went ape, his little girl had turned into this monster.* (Gwendolin)

As McRobbie (1989a) and Silverman (1986) have argued, the rag market and making clothes at home are stand-bys ensuring both creativity and individuality. Wilson describes fashion as 'one among many forms of aesthetic creativity which make possible the exploration of alternatives [as] more than simply a displacement of protest' (1990b: 31) and in the same way Delilah's appearance was, to her, a way of both embracing and resisting different activities linked to traditional femininity. It was pleasurable and enjoyable, and was rigorously routinised so that it had become a way of life. However, as Delilah's devotion to finding the right 'look' evidences (see Table 4.1), a number of interesting tensions are created, including the preoccupation with clothes, shopping and sewing. Several other women in this study have worn, or still wear, second-hand clothes (including Lara, Flong, Miss Pink, Vash, Zeb, Sparkle and Edie) and see it as a way to find 'different' looks whilst retaining a 'feminine' interest in clothes and shopping. Even fashion magazines now periodically praise famous women who are known for wearing vintage clothing.

This chapter has focused on three ways the participants understood and constructed their own versions of femininity: through the fairy princess figure and through discussion about their hair and about buying clothes. Chapter 5 examines how the participants categorised unconventional or 'alternative' femininities and where (and if/how) they felt they fitted into these definitions, and what signifiers of this they themselves looked for in other women or used themselves. This next chapter contrasts with the previous two, which concentrated on traditional femininities, by moving on to focus on 'alternative' and unconventional femininities.

**Table 4.1.** One participant's time/money breakdown for a typical month.

| Week | Time | Money |
|------|------|-------|
| W/c 7 Aug. | '*I spent four hours in the hairdressers having my roots done & my hair coloured, & my extensions replaced. I do this once a month.* | £60 |
| | '*I also bought some more shampoo & conditioner from the hairdressers.* | £20 |
| | '*On the first week of every month I also have a facial because I have always worn makeup and am aware I am getting older so have started looking after my skin.*' | £25 |
| | Second-hand clothes | £12 |
| W/c 14 Aug. | '*I got the train to London for the day to buy some boots. You can't find decent boots in Sheffield & I used to go to Manchester or Leeds but it's all townie or clubby stuff there now. I bought some boots, a top, and some body jewellery*'. | £25 + £400 |
| W/c 21 Aug. | '*A bit skint after going to London last week but bought some black nailvarnish & a lipstick from Cole Bros., and a bra from M&S.*' | £5 + £20 |
| | Second-hand clothes | |
| | '*Spent a whole day altering a coat I bought from the second hand market and a whole morning altering a dress*'. | £15 |
| W/c 28 Aug. | Second-hand clothes | £7.50 |
| | '*Got a fetish wear catalogue & ordered some trousers & some boots – I buy a lot of new clothes as well!*' | £250 |

W/c = Week commencing

$5$

# *Categories of Unconventional*

*I have always felt that I was different, you know. I never ever fitted into those patterns, the proper girl pattern ... it's like a paper pattern, I see it in my mind, there are particular lines you have to stay in, and you end up making just this very particular outfit ... maybe there are three choices in the packet but they're all dead similar*

Lara

The previous chapter focused on how the participants placed themselves in relation to traditional or 'fluffy' femininities. This chapter develops the participants' relation to femininity by examining how they defined and understood more unconventional femininities, and their relationships to the categories they described: tomboys; types of 'non-conformity'; famous women; and how they managed compromise. The two chapters also hold some similarities, such as the fact that, when talking about either traditional or unconventional femininities, participants continued to insist upon their own femininity. Although they refuted that they were traditionally feminine ('fluffy' or 'girly'), their narratives did make clear that they felt they were none the less attractive, 'feminine' women and that their challenge or resistance to traditional femininity did not negate this fact.

First, I provide a wider context in which to place my interviewees by giving an overview of the histories of bohemian and 'anti-fashion' clothing.

## Bohemian Dress

There is a long history of dissenting fashion for men, for example, 'the beau (early eighteenth century), Macaroni fashion (1760s to 1770s) and the dandy (early nineteenth century) and the aesthete of the late nineteenth century' (Craik, 1994: 182).[1] However, 'it was not until the English Pre-Raphaelite painters of the 1840s and 1850s that a special mode of alternative dress for women appeared' (Wilson, 1985: 184). William Morris designed a dress that did not need a corset to give it form but it was taken up only by the women in his circle, with the shape of women's clothes at that time using the corset and the crinoline and/or the bustle to create 'a raised bust, a very stiff and constricted body, a narrow, corseted waist and a bell-shaped lower half' (Thesander, 1997: 89–90). This 'mainstream' look was very different from the 'aesthetic' (or, latterly, 'bohemian') style espoused by women such as Janey Morris, Ellen Terry or Lillie Langtry, none of whom wore corsets.[2]

The bohemians of the first decades of the twentieth century followed on stylistically from the aesthetic movement of the nineteenth century, and were seen to embody artistic temperament, transgression, eccentricity and outrageous appearance; they were artistic and creative (Wilson, 2000: 3) – and mostly male, with women as muses, although occasionally as artists or writers in their own right. As with the contrast between an 'alternative' appearance and a mainstream, modern feminine appearance (of any era), their 'exotically gipsy-ish appearance [was] in striking contrast to the modernist flapper style' (1985: 185). However, the later second-wave feminist movement examined and challenged many of the assumptions of the past and, as Wilson explains, 'women as bohemians were outside the remit of this feminist re-evaluation of art history' (2000: 134). This was ironic as they had considered themselves to be breaking new boundaries of behaviour and lifestyle but 'feminism delegitimated the role of muse and cast doubt on its emotional rewards' (Wilson, 2000: 134). Wilson goes on to illustrate that even modern-day 'bohemian' heroines, such as fashion designer Vivienne Westwood and writer Camille Paglia (her examples), do not sit easily with feminism. For example, Westwood 'rejected feminism because she believed it was "anti sex" … never amenable to sisterly solidarity … she looked to other men for ideas and inspiration' (Wilson, 2000: 135). Similarly, the Pre-Raphaelite women did not forge friendships amongst themselves but remained individually linked to the man for whom they acted as muse (Marsh, 1985). Some of the participants, then, fitted broadly into this pattern: they wore clothes which resisted many of the current notions of 'femininity' and yet expressed hostility or, at least, wariness about other women (whether mainstream or not, but particularly feminist women) who might otherwise have provided sources of support. For example, Flong, Miss Pink and Claudia said that they feel they have more in common with other male tattooists and body piercers than they do with most women that they meet, thus following this tradition of identifying strongly with their male counterparts in a creative but not mainstream (and predominantly male) occupation – often at the expense of bonding with or mentoring other women. Possibly this is one of the reasons they are so adamant about their femininity. As women in a male-dominated profession they identify with their male counterparts but they do not wish to be seen as defeminised by their jobs. However, the antagonism or lack of bonding with other women points more to a rejection of femininity/womanhood and an identification more clearly with men.

## Black Clothing

The history of black clothing is varied and, although often associated with resistance and opposition, this is not its only meaning. As Wilson notes, 'the relationship of mourning and rebellion [in black clothes] is a strange one' (1985: 187). Black as a colour for mourning became especially fashionable during Queen Victoria's extended period of mourning for Prince Albert (1861–71), when the wealthy showed a general mania for all aspects of mourning (from brooches made of hair to ostentatious funerals and grave-side statues) (Taylor, 1983: ch. 9; Wilson, 1985: ch. 9). This may seem a ghoulish preoccupation to modern sensibilities but it was also fuelled by the high mortality rate, particularly for children. The rules of mourning dress were rigorous and often complicated.[3]Taylor notes, referring to the time period that people were expected to wear black, that 'basically, the more remote the relative the shorter was the mourning period, varying from two and a half years for a husband, eighteen months for a parent, twelve months for a child, six months for a brother or sister' and so on (1983: 133). Yet mourning could also provide a widow of means with an independence of sorts: a 'kindly camouflage, a way of crying quits and leaving the mating game without dishonour' (Wilson, 1985: 188). Mourning dress, then, could be used as a shield or protection but should be more accurately viewed as a gendered and classed activity, more commonly restricting a middle-class woman's choices and mobility while men were not required to mourn so completely or for so long. As Craik points out men have been considered (wrongly) to have no clothing 'fashions' other than the 'civilising imperative' of wearing plain, sober suits to signal lifestyle and social standing – or risk being seen as 'unmanly' (1994: ch. 8). This was established as a 'norm' during the consumer culture of the nineteenth century and, as Veblen (1994) notes, the more sober men's clothes became, the more women's dress became extravagant in order to advertise the income and standing of the 'man of the house' (especially newly monied industrialists who had profited from the industrial revolution). As Schreier argues, 'the well-tailored suit has been a dominant emblem of male opportunity and privilege, [while] expectations of a woman's passivity have been embedded in a psychologically restrictive and physically limiting wardrobe' (1989: 5). Some groups of men (such as gay men or men in subcultures) have flouted the rigid clothing codes for men (for instance, by having long hair or wearing brightly coloured clothes), but mostly masculinity is modelled around 'restraint rather than excess ... conveying an impression of a serious (business-like) demeanour' (Craik, 1994: 184). However, Lillie Langtry was fêted and admired for wearing a cheap black dress (in mourning for a brother) when she first made her entrance into society in 1877; 'her beauty was one thing, and if it was in the much prized Greek mould then so much the better, but [it was] her poverty and her mourning dress which contrasted sharply with the opulent, "jaded and privileged classes" and which arrested society's attention and acclaim' (Beatty, 2000: 44). Langtry wearing her mourning out of poverty, rather than an adherence to societal mores,[4] was briefly seen as subversive and interesting because black was not yet seen as a colour to be simply worn socially.

After the Great War, mourning dress became seen as something of a mockery when so many had died and so many families had been devastated (Wilson, 1985: 188) – thus the meanings of black clothes could be reinscribed. For example, Coco Chanel created black 'chic'; she designed 'the little black dress' in the 1930s although it did not become a style 'must' until the 1950s (Lehnert, 1999: 127). König (1973: 198; also Wilson, 1985) locates the roots of the beatniks and their oppositional dress in postwar Left Bank Paris where black was worn as a reaction to Dior's 'new look'[5] and to the horrors of the war just finished; wearing black 'expressed political protest, it radiated black humour, and the negative philosophy of Jean-Paul Sartre, it was also intimately related to the later ... beatniks ... and hippies'. Wilson (1985: 186) notes that the 'Chelsea' bohemian style (discussed above) lingered from the 1920s to the 1950s (embodied in film by the 'gamine' looks of Audrey Hepburn), when it 'went off in two directions as the beatniks exaggerated the pale lips, straight hair and black clothes into a uniform of revolt, while Mary Quant turned it into the latest fashion'. The black clothes of the beatniks and the black eye make-up of Mary Quant were to appear again together later in the form of goth.

The next large-scale reappropriation of black clothing was with the advent of the goth (or gothic) subculture in the early 1980s (to the present), which developed from punk[6] and the more mainstream, and short-lived, 'New Romantics' (Evans and Thornton, 1989: ch. 3). The goth look, for women, could be generalised as 'sepulchral clothes, pointy Cleopatra-style eye make-up, angular, jet-black hair, deathly-white make-up' (Reynolds and Press, 1995: 282). Although there are some difficulties with defining a person's 'look' or subcultural allegiance for fear of subscribing to a stereotype (Muggleton, 2000: 120), or because many 'subculturalists' no longer subscribe to being a member of one particular subculture and dislike being compartmentalised (ibid., 2000: 60), many participants confidently defined themselves as starting out as goths. For example,

*I always wear black now ... [From 1980 to 1981] I was a goth, wearing all black, and white make-up ... dead white face and big black eyes and very tall black hair. I used to scare people to death.* (Delilah)

*I had black spiky hair, just a bit of a goth really, that's how you start really innit, in the mid-eighties you just think you're a goth ... black hair, black clothes, black eye make-up, black lipstick.* (Gwendolin)

*Five years ago I had bright red hair ... White face, probably quite traditional gothic make-up.* (Eloise)

*I was about fourteen, fifteen, when I stopped wearing what everybody else was wearing and I got into the sort of gothic look, the make-up and the spiky hair and skirts right down to my ankles.* (Diz)

The participants were happier aligning themselves with a particular subculture than being seen as 'unfeminine', although this subcultural identity does not seem to be seen by them as being key to their femininity. Additionally, many stated that they still wore only or primarily black clothes:[7]

*Tend to stick with a lot of black, mainly for comfort, I'm comfortable in black.* (Vash)

*I just like to dress in black ... Black really cos I like it and it goes with everything and basically I've got so many tattoos it doesn't clash with any of my colours.* (Claudia)

*I suppose the one thing that has continued throughout – me dressing individually, which I would think would be from about sixteen years old onward when I had a choice to buy the clothes that I wanted – is always that they've tended to be black.* (Zeb)

*Black is the only colour I wear. It's partly a comfort thing, it's easy, it's an ease thing, everything matches everything and all that but it is – as well as a comfort thing – it is a stylish thing, it's plain, severe even.* (Sparkle)

*I wore all these really very very tatty black clothes ... Now I just wear black clothes all the time but new black clothes!* (Lara)

*When I was about fifteen, sixteen, I used to wear a lot of black ... But I wear black a lot now ... I think that's cos I'm quite big and it's to make myself look smaller.* (Miss Pink)

The historical significance of black as a colour of 'difference', of opposition and a resistance (and yet also as a colour for negative emotion and grieving), does not adequately explain this overwhelming preference for black clothes. Although the participants do not see themselves as 'in fashion' as such, they are merely echoing the wider trend for black clothes. Black now cannot be ousted from its association with style and practicality, although fashion magazines frequently trumpet an alternative colour as 'the new black', but the success of this is limited – in fact, fashion writers and editors themselves famously wear black all the time – and there are occasional 'think-pieces' on the almost universal practice of women wearing black as an everyday colour choice (see, for example, Heimel, 1991: 7–10). As Wilson argues, it is possible to 'acknowledge that dress is a powerful weapon of control and dominance, while widening our view to encompass an understanding of its simultaneously subversive qualities' (1992: 14). Black may appeal to the participants for a variety of reasons (such as practicality, its 'streamlining' qualities, as cited by Miss Pink, and simply habit) but it may also appeal in part (and even unconsciously) due to the older, mythical association with witches and vampires; 'in revolt against domesticity ... the witch is potent, sexually voracious and terrifying' (Reynolds and Press, 1995: 280), drawing on these ideas of power and independence. Or, as Hollander puts it, 'black appears as the colour suitable to delicious forbidden practice and belief' (1993: 376). It was this 'different' or 'alternative' aspect of black clothing which appealed to the participants.

Another reason commonly given was that black was 'comfortable', and yet someone wearing all-black clothes, although a relatively common sight, can still create a striking and formidable look; the wearer may feel 'comfortable'[8] but can startle others around them. As Tseëlon argues, a woman's sense of self can become closely entwined with how others see her; further, she starts to associate herself only with her external self as this is what women are so frequently equated with (1995: 38). Dressing constantly in black constructed a certain 'image' to others, an image which was 'different' and not 'fluffy': 'black is dramatic and plays to the gallery, as the costuming of revolt must always do' (Wilson, 1985: 189). Williamson, in her study of women 'vampire fans', found that traditional femininity was 'symbolised in the colour pink and ... that pink frilly dresses and little pumps were not for them' (2001: 144). In the same way, the 'fluffy' femininity described in Chapter 4 equates with 'pink femininity' and, for the participants, wearing black was another way of placing themselves in opposition to 'fluffy' – as Sparkle said, one of its appeals was that it was *'plain, severe even'*, that is, not 'fluffy', flowery or pastel. As Williamson argues, these women are not 'immobilized by the paradox of femininity'; indeed, they choose to draw attention to their 'difference' (2001: 145). Many felt they had 'toned down' their appearance as they got older,[9] so continuing to wear black 'flew the flag', so to speak, for what they saw as their continuing 'difference'; as Wilson states (with reference to the male dandy but of relevance here) 'anti-fashion is that "true chic" which used to be defined as the elegance that never draws attention to itself, the simplicity that is "understated", but which for that very reason stands out so startlingly' (1985: 183). Yet the participants' attitudes to black clothes remained, at least in part, conformist, for example, Miss Pink stating that one reason she wore black was that she believed it made her look smaller.

The history and meanings of black clothing provide a wider context in which to place the participants, their understandings of oppositional or 'alternative' dress and how they manage their appearance.

## Anti-fashion and Feminism

Although many studies of fashion and clothing have included a chapter or section about 'anti-fashion' (for example, see König, 1973; Wilson, 1985; Evans and Thornton, 1989; Davis, 1992), it remains (perhaps as its advocates prefer) peripheral to the study of mainstream fashion – although Wilson advises viewing 'oppositional dress' as 'a sub-theme to the general fashion discourse' (1985: 242), rather than as something 'other' or of less importance, and stresses that 'the analysis of youth oppositional or fad styles' often misses the 'surprising closeness, very often, to the latest mainstream fashions' (1985: 191). Similarly, as Davis argues, and as I pointed out in Chapter 3, one can only avoid being fashionable by knowing what is fashionable: 'Anti-fashion is as much a creature of fashion as fashion itself ... This would seem to be obvious in that whatever form anti-fashion takes it must via some symbolic device of opposition, rejection, studied neglect, parody, satirization, etc., address itself to the ascendant or "in" fashion of the time' (1992: 161).

Studies of anti-fashion[10] (often used interchangeably with terms such as oppositional or counter-cultural dress, which are themselves associated with subcultural activity and theory) are often 'over-determined' (Davis,

1992: 161) and they are discussed here because of their associations and links with the lifestyle and appearance of the participants. However, it should not be assumed that the term 'anti-fashion' was significant to any of the women in this study, and one of the principal errors of those who write about it is the assumption that they are speaking authoritatively for, or about, those who 'do it'. Only Gemini chose it from a list of (a minimum) eleven possible self-appellations,[11] no one mentioned it in their interviews, and, in fact, on some lists it resolutely remained the one word that everyone ignored. Resistance to a term that seems politicised is not surprising considering the participants' attitude to another politicised term, feminism. Both terms can be viewed as confrontational in an intellectual way and, I would argue, it is this dimension of these terms which is rejected (probably unconsciously) by the participants.

In attempting to expose gender stereotypes feminists have argued for more functional clothing to be adopted, to draw attention to the constructedness of 'femininity' (the most famous example being Simone de Beauvoir's *Second Sex*) and how it has restricted and oppressed women. Historically, women have made various stands against the restrictions of feminine dress, from the introduction of the 'Bloomer costume' (believed, wrongly, to have been designed by Amelia Jenks Bloomer), 'a trousered costume (for comfort and health)' (Foote, 1989: 144), to the 'reform dress' of the 1880s onwards, which advocated the creation of a safer, more comfortable form of dress to replace the current 'crippling effect' of women's dress, with tight-lacing and the sheer weight of underclothes (Thesander, 1997: 99). Both failed to find success or acceptance; indeed there was an outcry, with an hysterical, mostly vitriolic response in the press.[12] Such a response may seem outdated for something which now appears so modest, but consider the relatively recent outrages about men growing their hair long or the vicious caricatures of second-wave feminists in dungarees: anything which is seen to be 'blurring the visual lines between the sexes' (Foote, 1989: 144) is still seen as a threat to the 'natural' order of things (for example, in the West, men still wear trousers most of the time but not skirts, as David Beckham found to his cost when he stepped out in a sarong). Increased independence for women in the early twentieth century made lesbian or feminist cross-dressing more possible for those with the means to do so.[13]

Later, second-wave feminists continued to challenge orthodoxies in feminine appearance. Rich, for instance, puts 'high heels and "feminine" dress codes in fashion' in the same category as purdah, the veil, rape and footbinding (1996: 132) – polemic designed to arrest attention. Although, as Macdonald points out, 'early feminist reactions to fashion were overtly hostile', various feminist scholars expressed a suspicion that 'feminist attitudes to fashion were both hypocritical (replacing one "feminine" uniform with another "anti-feminine" one) and puritanical' (1995: 211). It was this early fervour and 'backlash' against fashion that informs many caricatures of feminism to this day (for example, that feminists are all sour, sexless and either 'butch' or dowdy). Only two participants, Jody and Zeb, said that they dressed as they did partly to 'signal their politics' (both identified as feminists), but, as Griffin found, 'few studies on political attitudes have recognised feminism as a political issue' (1989: 179); so it may be this line of thinking which influenced the responses to this category. Yet, as Griffin points out in her study of feminist consciousness and identification 'feminism is not a unitary category which encapsulates a consistent set of ideas within a readily identifiable boundary' (1989: 174). Despite this, there was a general unwillingness amongst the participants to align themselves with feminism, which they did see as being a 'unitary category' and some implied that they equated it with being anti-men and masculinised. Again, this assumption illustrated their attitude to the rigid boundaries of gender: in Chapter 3 we saw how they equated masculinity with being not traditionally feminine. Wearing bloomers or other ways of expressing feminism or emancipation in dress (and therefore in lifestyle) in whatever era received much the same hostile or inflexible response. In this case, I would argue that the participants distanced themselves from feminism because they mostly sought to distance themselves from anything (including other women) which would undo or threaten their 'recuperative' strategies (discussed in Chapter 3), and they felt that an allegiance with feminism would somehow unsettle the carefully constructed balance of both traditional and alternative femininities that they had created for themselves.

## Defining 'Alternatives'

Having established which traditionally 'feminine' items the participants used and how this usage was accompanied by other 'recuperative' strategies designed to underline their femininity, they were also asked how they defined less conventional forms of femininity and how they placed themselves in these categories. Their replies included:

*I'm unconventional, nonconformist I mean.* (Vash)

*I am in it and outside of it. I am the mole in the camp. I see myself as still being on the fringes.* (Lara)

As with Blackman's study of teenage 'new wave girls', whose appearance made them a 'highly visible group' (1998: 208), the participants' visibility held particular meaning and value for them – but how did they view other 'visible' women and what made them fit the category? I asked the participants to articulate their own definitions of femininity in order to establish a continuum of 'femininity'; I then asked them to categorise unconventionality and asked them where they fitted in between these two extremes. They all felt able to do this but responses varied from feeling able to construct and 'place' themselves on some kind of continuum to saying they felt they did not exist on any kind of scale of femininity since all femininity was somehow tainted by its association with traditional femininity. Zeb's definition of an unconventional woman fitted in with the idea of being 'highly visible':

*She could be thin or fat or whatever ... or have an observable disability, physical disability, but that wouldn't make a difference. I think she would be wearing clothes that would say 'Oh, I'm here' rather than just fading into the background. So it would be like, oh I dunno, big boots and definite colours and walk more confidently and sort of signal her presence in ... through her clothes and how she walked and how she held herself instead of sort of looking like she was apologising for just being there, instead of just fading into the background.*

Zeb said that if she were to fit herself on a continuum between her 'weak, blurry' traditional femininity and her unmissable, unconventional femininity she was at the unmissable end of the scale. Delilah, however, became briefly quite upset and angry:

*I realised it sort of when we were talking about what is the ideal type of woman and I realised how angry I am ... It makes me so sorry for women and the things they do ... People need to stand up for themselves, to step out of it and do whatever makes them happy. So long as they're not hurting anyone they – I mean women actually – should really go for it and do whatever the fuck they want.*

When asked if she thought she challenged traditional femininities, Delilah replied:

*I am not un-feminine. But you mean like I don't wear blouses and little pencil skirts? So yes I do. I have pink and yellow hair! And lots of metal in my skin and ink under my skin. So it's not the norm, is it, and sometimes it upsets people ... And less pretty by their standards. Less manageable generally.*

Delilah was equating her own unconventional appearance with a reduction in her general attractiveness. She said she thought people would find her 'less pretty by their standards' and then qualified that by saying they would think this because she was less 'manageable'. Her implicit message was that to be traditionally attractive you have to be malleable and not independent. In terms of her behaviour, however, we might ask whether Delilah *was* less manageable. It is more feasible that this was an assumption made about her because of her appearance. This attitude was one I encountered repeatedly from the participants: that despite their 'alternative' appearance and their vilification of traditional femininities they continued to be aware of exactly how they were 'offending' people – and they did not always appear comfortable to be doing so. This paradox illustrates 'the problem of female subjectivity and women's agency, a problem that women encounter in childhood and must confront for the rest of their lives. This problem ... raises the question of whether women can truly define who they are and how they present themselves to the world given the expectation that they meet definitions established by others' (Furman, 1997: 52).

Many participants demonstrated that they were well aware of the difficulties in defining who they are through the presentation of themselves and the responses received when they do not adhere to the definitions of others (an example of this was discussed in the previous chapter when several participants challenged the definitions of the 'fairy princess' as being weak or passive). Claudia was aware that other people placed her in a category of unconventional woman, which threatened her sense of herself as 'feminine' and also challenged how she defined herself; she said she was constantly being called a goth when she was not. She expressed disappointment that others judged her so quickly:

> I see people look ... me up and down, you can almost sense that they go 'God, what's that!' but they don't come and say it to your face. To be honest I would rather they did cos at least it's like, well, 'Ask!', you know. Don't just judge me by looking up and down.

More than any other participant, Claudia expressed sentiments which made clear that she wanted people to see that 'underneath it all' she was feminine. McRobbie (1994b) argues that popular culture and subcultures can offer girls new possibilities in exploring subjectivities and identities (for instance, ragga music gives black and white girls a chance to 'talk back' to the sexism of the lyrics through dance. Although this exploration is an important and positive development, it is possible to develop it further to include the sometimes confusing end-point faced by Claudia and other participants. Their anxiety was about being 'masculinised' (and therefore, seen as unattractive) because of their appearance, although at first it had seemed a way of resisting and breaking away from negative connotations which frequently follow a woman's appearance (whatever that appearance is). Their subjectivities as 'alternative' women who are none the less feminine are constantly threatened by the perceptions of people around them and of whom they are aware. For example:

> *At work I said 'Oh, I'm branching out into colours' and made a big joke of it and said 'but of course, it's special for work' ... but later in the day somebody said to me 'Oh, I like your jacket, it's this year's colour' [it was dark purple] ... I was actually a bit horrified by that so obviously I do have an issue about wanting to be different but I don't think it's until somebody says something like that that I realise that ... it was like 'Oh no, somebody might think I made an effort to fit in with this year's fashions.' I was just, like, absolutely appalled.* (Zeb)

As Berger and Luckmann have argued: 'identity is ... a key element of subjective reality and, like all subjective reality, stands in a dialectical relationship with society' (1979: 180). For example, El Guindi, writing about women who choose to wear the veil, explains that the Western feminist argument that veiling is not liberatory because it perpetuates inequality renders the 'protest quality in veiling' lost in that context (1999: 163). In the same way, the participants faced a paradox in that their 'alternative' appearance represented many things and one of them, to greater or lesser extents, was protest or resistance against traditional femininities. The 'protest quality' of their appearance, however, was consistently eroded by their own 'recuperative' strategies employed to respond to (and refute) the (often perceived) assumptions of others.

When asked to categorise women she found unconventional, Claudia replied:

> *Women body-builders probably do fit that cos why shouldn't they do it? That's why I do what I do, cos I like it and I don't think 'Well I shouldn't do that' or 'Well I should.' I think 'I am a person and I fancy doing that' so I do it. Like, most girls I know can drive a car and stuff but when it comes to fixing it I'm like 'Well I can't do it.'*

Even when arguing that women should be able to do whatever they want to do, Claudia was also saying 'but I am still very feminine because I can't fix a car', using an established stereotype of femininity. Her attempt to align herself with female body-builders was also interesting. As a subculture, much has been written about female body-builders (for example,

Schulze, 1990; Tasker, 1992: 141–6; Mansfield and McGinn, 1993; Coles, 1999) and yet the body modifications they undertake are not permanent like the extensive tattoos that Claudia has. It is possible to see why Claudia would place women body-builders in a category of unconventional women and why she might also identify with them. As Coles argues, women body-builders challenge a number of traditional ideas about femininity, particularly during a performance at a competition, when they demonstrate 'that femininity, heterosexuality and even the female body are constructs' (1999: 445). It is this disruption that Claudia and other participants would identify with as, despite efforts to remain 'feminine' through make-up and accessories, they are seen to be unfeminine and therefore 'manly'. This, as we have seen, was Claudia's fear (that she would be viewed as 'manly' because of her tattoos) and yet her own appearance has more long-term significance, as women body-builders could reduce their bulk if they chose.

Kiki addressed this divide between temporary and permanent resistance and was cautious about categorising the unconventional, saying that what is unconventional now will not be in a few years; thus what or who is unconventional is a shifting category:

*There's a big fashion for piercing, so many people have piercings and you know in two years time they won't have those piercings. I think a lot of women are doing it, not to not conform, but just to be fashionable. Women aren't so willing, not young women, to play roles any more, they wear jeans all the time, they don't necessarily wear make-up, whereas women would have once worn it all the time, every day. The putting the face on thing.*

As Davis also warned, 'the very same apparel ensemble that "said" one thing last year will "say" another, quite different, today' (1992: 6). Kiki concluded that it is difficult to expose or define the truly unconventional woman – some women look unconventional but are, in fact, 'merely' fashionable; others just wear jeans and no make-up but through their refusal to 'play roles' (that is, live up to traditional ideologies of femininity) are, in fact, resisting in a more long-term way. Jody also pointed out that what is unconventional or nonconformist at one time may, at another time, be seen as a fashionable compromise. She related an incident when she was wearing combat trousers and boots as a sign of rebellion – but so was everyone else because it was fashionable: *'It was like "Oh look, it's yet another GI Jane"!'* In this way there is no fixed or 'confirmatory front' (Goffman, 1984) with which to accurately read someone's intentions.

Footwear was identified by every single participant as a site for resistance due to the discomfort and limiting qualities of traditionally 'feminine' shoes with heels. For instance, most of the participants stated that they would not be willing (or able) to wear shoes instead of boots, no matter what the occasion, as they had not owned any since childhood. Morgan's answer was a common one:

*I have never in my life had a pair of court shoes or sandals or anything along those lines.*

Kiki was vehemently opposed to the idea of wearing high-heeled shoes and felt that they not only restricted her but offered a threat to her personal safety:

*I've never worn high heels cos I just don't feel safe, and they do, as soon as you put a pair of high heels on they change the whole way you carry your body, when you put high heels on you can't look strong, because of the way they throw your whole body out of balance and stuff, and you can't look strong and assertive.*

This was a sentiment echoed by Jody, who described her own unconventionality in a more combative way:

*If I'm around, like just youths knocking around, I would feel vulnerable dressed in a skirt and heels, whereas dressed as I do I can move into a more aggressive looking posture and look like I'm trouble or look like I mean business and I'm not to be messed with ... and you can walk quietly as opposed to clacking.*

By adopting an aggressive posture, moving more quietly and not being recognisable as female, Jody had found a way to feel safe and confident – things she saw as unconventional for most women. Jody asserted that some styles of dressing mark women out as *'victim fodder'* and a way to fight against this is to look like a boy from behind – she did not 'totter' nor 'clack' in high heels. 'If fashion is one of the many costumes of the masquerade of femininity, then those costumes can be worn on the street as semiotic battle-dress' (Evans and Thornton, 1989: 14). Throughout her interview, Jody equated feminine dress with particular expected behaviours and she was clearly consciously determined to resist both traditional feminine behaviour and appearance. She saw them as 'defeatism' and used the word 'trappings' in a loaded way: women were trapped but were also trying to trap men with their 'flirty shit behaviour'. To Jody (who described herself as having been the feminine 'good girl' during her marriage) this type of behaviour lacked dignity and she recognised the masquerade of femininity; she knew that it was about presenting something to the world that may not be what you really are or what you feel yourself to be (Tseëlon, 1995: 37). Jody felt she had chosen not to do this any more, that she had exercised agency. Yet choosing to do so can also bring problems: for example:

> *I'm not doing what a lot of people think women should do to make themselves attractive. You know, I am possibly going out of my way to be the opposite of that, I am very aware of that ... I think people just get really upset by it cos I'm not sort of following the norm.* (Morgan)

> *I've had abuse in the past for looking too, well not looking feminine enough: 'Why do you do that to yourself?', 'Why do you wear your make-up like that?', 'What have you got in your nose?' and 'Why have you done that?' It's just expectations and some women fall out of them.* (Vash)

Although women may signal agency through their choice not to wear clothes which make them feel weak or restricted, others may police them. As Grogan notes, 'there can be no doubt that Western culture ... promotes unrealistic body ideals to women, and that non-conformity to these ideals leads to social disapproval' (1999: 56). But this can also work in the participants' favour, as Morgan illustrated:

> *Looking like I do, if I walked into a pub that I'd never been in before and sat down on my own I might get hassled but I'd be less likely to get the sort of hassle that you might, for instance, I'm not likely to get chatted up by some townie sort of thing.*

When asked which famous women they would fit into categories of unconventional, Siouxsie Sioux was named by eight participants.[14] Sioux's image was, and remains, attractive (albeit not traditionally), articulate and intelligent – 'her look fused the dominatrix, the vampire and the Halloween witch into a singular form of style terrorism' (Reynolds and Press, 1995: 282) but Sioux was much more than the sum of her parts: she was one of the most prominent and successful punk women but also broke other boundaries in the music industry by writing her own songs and producing her music. The participants complained of a lack of positive female role models when they were children or teenagers and claimed that women like Siouxsie Sioux filled this gap, for example:

> *Siouxsie Sioux. My first role model! My first pin-up! I was so in love with her. She was so tough and weird-looking and very beautiful.* (Lara)

Yet the majority of the participants were children in the same period (the late 1960s and 1970s), which saw the rise of second-wave feminism and a plethora of positive, politicised potential role models, who were not, however, easily accessible via the 'normal' routes of television or the magazines that teenage girls would read. The media '[does not] merely provide a mirror or a template of what "woman" is, it provides us with a complex array of contradictory representations, which produces multiple meanings and therefore affords myriad sites for identification' (Ussher, 1997: 13). In the same way, the representations that are offered are arguably limited, no matter how myriad they may be. Identification was key for the participants in choosing women who fitted into categories of unconventionality. As Wolf has noted, there are difficulties in finding female heroines for women since, due to a lack of female 'role models in the world, women seek them on the screen and the glossy page' (1990: 42). This creates a tension since heroes and heroines are, by their nature, meant to be strong, individual, interesting – none of which are theoretically possible in the ' "ideal" imagery' of popular culture where women are 'flattened' into being merely beautiful (Wolf, 1990: 42). To counter this, the participants had identified with generic 'types' of women in the real world: Claudia, a woman with tattoos covering the majority of her body, said she identifies with *'anybody that goes against what you would expect as being traditionally feminine'*. Similarly, Flong (a tattooist) said she identifies with female tattooists and Sparkle, a vegan and animal rights activist, said animal rights activists. Eloise, with long bright red hair, said Danielle Dax, a punk singer famous for her long bright red hair. Six women cited friends or family members as their role models. In general, the women all chose role models or heroines who either shared characteristics with them or who were already emotionally close to them; what the women would call 'like-minded' (a crucial requirement, which they used frequently in different contexts) even if they did not look particularly 'alternative':

> [My friend] *can pass in the normal world but she's like-minded. A lot of my friends are like that these days, can pass as normal.* (Morgan)

Along these same lines a similar answer was echoed in five interviews: in general, any women who are 'different' and any women who 'break the rules' were cited as being role models or heroines. Again, these are groups which the participants see themselves as belonging to and were women who the participants saw as having the necessary 'heroine' qualities of being individual and interesting.

## To Compromise or Not To Compromise

Ideas about the 'self' and identity have received much attention, with a plethora of debates and positions developing to encompass 'the most mundane of things and ... the most extraordinary' (Jenkins, 1994: 3). Davis offers a concise definition of the term: 'the concept of social identity points to the configuration of attributes and attitudes persons seek to and actually do communicate about themselves (obviously, the two are not always the same)' (1992: 16). Whilst succinct, this definition fails to even hint at the 'very scope and diversity of contemporary debates about identity' (Du Gay *et al.*, 2000: 2). Women's identities and their relationships to fashion have also been the focus of theory; for example, Craik (1994), Tseëlon (1995) and Barnard (1996) use the term 'ambivalence' in relation to how women use clothes and seem to ask whether clothes use women or women use clothes. By that I mean, can women exercise agency in the wearing of their clothes or will they necessarily be subsumed by gendered power structures such as 'fashion'? The participants felt that they had placed themselves, however partially, outside the tethering power of 'fashion' through their 'alternative' identities, so their own sense of ambivalence would be more likely to be connected to how to avoid compromising this position. Guy and Banim (2000) provide a helpful starting-point for understanding in that they identify three discourses related to the clothing maintained by the fifteen women in their study: 'the woman I want to be', 'the woman I fear I could be' and 'the woman I am most of the time'. The first category is about creating successful, positive images and making a good impression, the second about difficulties and mistakes made in clothing choices and the third about 'satisfactory images without too much effort ... the woman I am in my ordinary way of being with my clothes' (2000: 316–21). For the participants of this study it is sometimes more useful to conflate the first and third categories into 'the woman I wish to remain'. The reason for this is that most of the participants' narratives illustrate the fact that they are rarely willing to compromise their 'alternative' appearance, no matter what the occasion, because they already feel they have become 'the woman I want to be'. However, at the same time (rather than at a different occasion or in a different context), they are 'the woman I am most of the time'. Several participants (including Zeb, Miss Pink and Eloise) stated that at any time they were 'just getting dressed', as they had looked like (or similar to) this for so long, rather than 'dressing up', which implied making a special effort.

Banim and Guy's later work (2001) identifies three categories of clothes which the women rarely or no longer wore: 'discontinued', 'transitional', and 'continuing'. 'Discontinued' refers to clothes no longer worn; 'transitional' refers to those clothes which are no longer worn but 'their viability to their owners' self-image is being considered but has not been fully resolved' (2001: 206); and 'continuing' refers to clothes which still have a connection with a woman's self-image. Clothes that women kept but did not wear represented 'the stories [which] help women establish a personal history across their changing images' (Guy and Banim, 2000: 207) and therefore can be used to maintain and indicate subjectivity and agency. I use this analysis below in relation to Lara.

Several participants expressed the sentiment that their appearance (hard-won through years of maintenance) reflected their 'real' self and that they continually faced instances in which they felt they had to compromise how they looked – thereby threatening their sense of 'true' self or 'the woman I wish to remain' – so that 'appearance and manner ... contradict each other' (Goffman, 1984: 35). These compromises, or contradictions, were directly connected to their age (which is examined further in Chapter 6) as well as to the circumstances and context, which are examined here. An area which caused the need for most compromise was work and fitted into the discourse of 'the woman I fear I could be'. Participants indicated that there is a continuum of resistance where compromises can be made which are, on the one hand, total – and, on the other hand, very slight (something Melia also found in her 1995 study of resistance and sexuality). For instance, Vash wore a plaster over her eyebrow piercing when she went to work. And yet, whilst this was apparently hiding the piercing to demonstrate adherence to company policies, she was also drawing attention to her piercing. A plaster stuck across an eyebrow is not an everyday sight and, even if it were, is very noticeable. 'Identity is not "just there", it must always be established' (Jenkins, 1994: 4), and here Vash was resisting rules about no piercings at work whilst appearing to defer to them, creating her own unofficial 'compromise' through establishing her identity as a pierced woman.

Jody said she had no option except to compromise as she worked as a nurse in an elderly people's home and had to wear a dress and tights, and although she would prefer to wear trousers as part of her uniform she was unable to do so. As Wilson argues, 'any investigation of counter-cultural dress forces us to recognise that individuals and groups use dress in subtle ways to create meaning, to locate themselves in society in a number of ways ... also, interestingly, [it may] often involve a critique of and an alternative to current norms of beauty' (1992: 261).

Work constituted an area where many participants felt they neither located themselves accurately nor maintained their accustomed critique of 'fluffy' femininities. As Giddens notes, self-identity is about 'continuities' and is 'something that has to be routinely created and sustained in the reflexive activities of the individual' (1991: 52). Gemini demonstrated tension about her appearance and how she perceived its effect on other people, although she also told me that she felt she had never fitted in to mainstream society:

> I had it [her tattoo] *put on my arm so I would be able to show it off and startle people. It is quite startling for an old woman like me to have a tattoo especially a big one – it's a swan – a big swan – but also I wanted to be able to cover it up if I felt it was an inappropriate moment for it to be shown ... I've got to be the only tattooed magistrate on the bench.*

Gemini was happy to startle people by being an 'old woman' with a tattoo but was less comfortable about being an old woman with a large tattoo who sat on the bench as a magistrate (which, in itself, is often seen as representative of an occupation for the middle-aged or elderly middle classes). Melia argues that ' "transgressions" ... altered according to context. There were some situations where it was not deemed appropriate to use appearance as resistance, and others where the complexities of bodily signifiers could be used to deconstruct and reconstruct normative femininity' (1995: 553). Although Gemini sought to challenge ideas about what was appropriate for a woman of her age and position, she admitted that there were some contexts where it was simply impossible. This is one precise example of my participants' awareness of the 'rules' and just how far they can choose to push them: to go too far would be to become social outcasts and therefore unable to make any real challenge (or, arguably, political difference). As Banim and Guy argue, women 'used clothes to integrate various aspects of their identities and bodies in order to create the identities they felt were appropriate to the perceived demands of any given situation' (2001: 203). Zeb, too, found that she was not able to dress at work as she normally would, but she did not have any problems about compromising, as she saw this as part of doing her job effectively:

> I *wear purple and have even been known to wear dark blue* [that is, instead of black] ... *I'll not wear all my earrings or possibly not wear my nose stud ... If I was going out to see clients I would just try to look a bit smarter. And that would basically be because ... in interviewing work you want to get information from somebody so you don't want to make yourself strange to that person in any way at all. I would see that as maybe being a barrier to building a good rapport.*

Lara made the most complex compromises for work. She pointed out that she had to work to live and so had found her own ways of managing the necessity to 'tone down' her appearance:

> *I tie my hair back in a bun and I can wear one nose stud and two rings in each ear, and they never see my tongue piercing anyway so I leave that in ... and I wear glasses as well – but I wear blue contact lenses out of work. So my tatts are covered and I put eyebrow rings and nose rings and ear rings back in as soon as I finish work.*

The difference between her 'work' and 'real' wardrobes implied that she lived her life in disguise – which, when asked if she did, she said:

> *I do, I do. They would never understand about my piercings. And I have about five work outfits which I mix around and I even keep them separate to my real clothes, I keep my work clothes in zipped up bags on the back of the bedroom door and I keep all my real clothes, I mean my home clothes, in the wardrobe.*

Lara's work clothes were not even allowed in the wardrobe with her 'real' clothes and it seemed clear that Lara's 'work clothes' assisted her to feel less vulnerable since she felt so much less 'herself' at work. Giddens states that 'routinised control of the body is crucial to the sustaining of the individual's protective cocoon in situations of day-to-day interaction' (1991: 56). However, viewed in the light of Banim and Guy's findings, it is possible to identify Lara's approach to her work persona as one of shame and/or secrecy. Clothes which women no longer wore (which represented their 'discontinued' identities) were stored out of sight at the back of a wardrobe or in a box under a bed. 'If worn clothes are connected to the public presentation of self, maybe kept – or hidden – clothes represent a secret self' (Banim and Guy, 2001: 217). Lara's refusal to mix her 'work' clothes with her 'real' clothes illustrated the split between the two identities and wardrobes she managed daily, keeping her work and home personas separate through a system of how to wear her hair and which clothes to wear, even incorporating separate accessories such as spectacles, bag and jewellery. However, Lara differed from Banim and Guy's description of women who 'integrated' their clothes and bodies to assemble 'appropriate' selves. Lara did not integrate what she saw as her 'true' (her home) identity. She attempted to have no overlaps and even took her 'work' clothes from a separate collection rather than wear anything which she wore at home.

Delilah, as with Lara, clearly set out incidents which signalled her commitment to her unwillingness to compromise. For example, a shopping trip to a flea market when she was fourteen:

*set me on a certain path forever ... funny, when I look back on it like this ... properly ... I can see how many choices I made that were, that relied on how I could dress and how I could do my hair.*

For example, she decided to do two A levels in sixth form rather than leave school at sixteen:

*I thought, if I have a proper job I can't dress how I want, they'll want to stick me in some crap old blouse or whatever.*

Other participants found or created jobs where they could continue to be 'the woman I wish to remain' and where they felt they did not have to sacrifice their appearance.[15] Those who had such jobs had no need to compromise how they looked in order to earn money and recognised how lucky they were. A common phrase used in many of the interviews was 'getting away with' things. Here Claudia explains that she had to 'create' a job to get away with her piercings:

*I know I couldn't get away with it and get work outside – probably that's a lot of reason why I do it: because I can. I think if I hadn't had the opportunity to do it I probably wouldn't have had even half as much [tattooing and piercing] cos I wouldn't have dared to do it and still try and fit in. But I can so I do!*

This is a way of reconceptualising identity and 'self' and is discursively produced: what Giddens (1991) would describe as being 'knowledgeable actors', that is, people in charge of themselves, consciously producing and presenting themselves in certain ways. Morgan related how she and her friends had started out as goths, but, as time went on, she had developed her own sense of style:

*Most of my friends just carried on wearing black and the women wore a lot of black gothy make-up and I didn't ... kind of pushing me in the 'alternative' in inverted commas, direction but only a little bit, and then I just sort of developed my own sense of style and whatever I wanted to wear, and my own sense of ... myself.*

Several of the participants had spent a number of years changing their appearances to find their 'true selves' and felt they had to maintain a certain level of 'alternative'-ness to remain true to themselves, presenting a 'confirming consistency between appearance and manner ... [a] coherence of front' (Goffman, 1984: 35), which many contexts threatened. Finding contexts in which they did not have to tone down their appearance allowed them to dress as they chose without feeling threatened or compromised. For example, Morgan said:

*I would feel totally sort of lost really. You mean like, whatever situation and someone said you must wear these clothes and they weren't normally the sort of thing I would wear? Ooh dear, no, I wouldn't ... I've never really done that. I think I'd lose all my confidence. I'd feel very very strange. I wouldn't feel like myself at all. I'd feel like I was acting, which I would be.*

Some participants said there was no occasion for which they would compromise their appearance; others said they were willing to make compromises according to context but only to a certain extent, such as while they were willing to wear a dress it must be black and must be from their existing wardrobe (or 'customised' with their own accessories). 'Having items of clothing that could be depended upon to "perform" well was an important dimension of creating "the woman I want to be". The most useful, and often favourite items were those that women were confident would look good on them and are generally easily managed' (Guy and Banim, 2000: 318). For example:

*It might be something that a townie would wear but I would wear it differently with the other clothes I've got. I wouldn't say I won't go into Top Shop or anything like that. If I see something I like I'll buy it and fit it in with stuff I've got.* (Vash)

Or, whilst they were willing to look 'tidy' or smarter, they would not be willing to wear less jewellery or hide their body modifications or tie their hair up. For example:

*The only thing that I do is if we go for a meal with* [her partner's] *parents I will sometimes wear something with long sleeves to tone it down. I can cope with it, a lot of people can't. It's the only thing I can do. I can't take all this* [piercings] *out of my face, I can't take this tattoo off my hand.* (Claudia)

The most common reason to effect some level of compromise was out of respect for those close to them but they would not necessarily conform to what was expected of them. For example,

[At a wedding] *I was just wearing black trousers and a black jacket and it wasn't my normal scruffy type of thing, it was actually quite smart but ... my hair was crimped ... I insisted on wearing dark glasses the whole time ... it's really interesting actually, in the wedding photos ... the only other person that kept their sunglasses on, a bloke ... and there we both were, sort of on the fringes of this wedding party, and there we were both dressed in black wearing dark glasses.* (Zeb)

In these ways they manage the tensions that their appearance could cause in social situations and become 'someone who is projecting aspects of herself through clothing that suits/enhances her ... however, the primary frame of reference was how the women felt about themselves and not the explicit validation of others' (Guy and Banim, 2000: 318).

In conclusion, the participants fitted into broad traditions of 'unconventional' women, particularly that of the bohemian muses of the 1800s and early 1900s. Their wearing of black placed them within discourses both of modern 'stylish' fashion and of oppositional dress. Although some appeared wary of other women (mainly 'fluffy' or feminist women, with whom they felt no affinity), they named 'like-minded' women (that is, any woman who resisted traditional femininities) as those they would categorise as unconventional but also as those they admired. 'Femininity (and women) are positioned outside language (and power). For the woman to embrace the "authentic femininity" is to affirm her own disempowerment' (Tseëlon, 1995: 39). Thus, although they did embrace some aspects of traditional ('fluffy') femininity, they also refused to 'affirm their disempowerment' fully by aligning themselves firmly in unconventional (that is, what Tseëlon defines as inauthentically feminine) categories of 'the woman I wish to remain'.

The next chapter examines the participants' relationships to their bodies through their body modifications and body image.

# 'More Like Torture than Love'?

The previous chapter examined how the participants described and understood unconventional femininities and this chapter builds on this by focusing on some of the ways they employed to embody their 'difference', that is, their 'alternative' femininities, through their appearance and body modifications.[1]

The human body, once a neglected area of sociological studies, is now the subject of an ever-growing area of scholarship; although, as Morgan notes, 'the sociology of the body is a relatively late arrival on the scene' (1993: 69). Similarly, Davis, on the upsurge of interest in the body, commented that 'social scientists are retrieving a neglected topic and making it the focus rather than the implicit backdrop of their analyses' (1997: 3), and yet the body has been examined in feminist work for a number of years[2] and, as Shilling points out, 'the interest in the body is not new. In times of war, for example, governments have traditionally displayed concern about the physical health and fitness of the nation' (1993: 1). It may be that feminist scholarship felt the need to prioritise the study of the body because women's bodies have been, and remain, much more visible and objectified in daily life. "The 'life" of the body is played out through the technical arrangement of clothes, adornment and gesture' (Craik, 1994: 1).

## Bodies/Image

Being 'policed' by other people (as opposed to policing oneself, which is discussed in the next chapter) was a subject several participants discussed angrily. Potential threats were of concern to the participants since their appearance marked them out as more visible and, despite feeling defiant, they attempted to take action to circumvent any negative attention. For example, Kiki said:

*I love my build, I love being tall, always loved being tall. I don't mind being big either ... I'd never want to be tiny. I've got friends who are tiny little females and I would hate to be like that because I think I'd feel so vulnerable. And when I do walk along the street I am tall, and I do walk big, if you know what I mean.*

Through this 'presence' many of the participants said that they felt they were given slightly more space by strangers on the street:

*I walk straight and I take up room.* (Bee)

*I see people looking at me in the street and some of them are smiling and that makes me smile and some of them aren't smiling and that makes me smile even more.* (Morgan)

They reported that people backed off from them slightly – perhaps from fear or disgust at their appearance – but none of the participants found this disturbing and, in some ways, revelled in this extra few inches of personal 'space' around their bodies. Williamson also found that the women in her study told her that wearing black and looking as they did 'kept people at a distance', which they welcomed (2001: 147). In the same way, Delilah said that in her teens:

*I was wearing all black, and white make-up ... dead white face and big black eyes and very very tall black hair. I used to scare people to death ... My appearance, see, it gave me strength almost ... it was like armour and I felt invincible.*

Several of my interviewees felt that their appearance lent them what Gwendolin called a *'protective layer'.* The comparison is with the way they talked about a more traditional feminine appearance as involving clothes and behaviours which weakened the woman wearing them, and the fact that, although they realised that they would be looked at as much as, or more than, the traditional woman, they felt they could use this in more positive ways. A theme which recurred through the interviews was that of making oneself an 'exhibit', although not an exhibit in a way which would be considered to be sexually arousing to men, for example the long blonde hair and large breasts of the archetypal 'page 3 girl'. Rather, the nature of the exhibitionism was to treat themselves and their appearance as an ongoing 'identity project' (Giddens, 1991), which the participants found empowering. Claudia explained:

*It's caused a lot of people to speak to me who perhaps wouldn't have had a reason to ... something that gives you a starting point ... it does provoke a lot*

*... a much different reaction. Like you say, people see all the tattoos and think, 'Oh, there's something to look at.' They will look.*

Here Claudia demonstrates several interesting contradictions connected to the idea of provocation. Although many of the participants believed themselves to look less vulnerable and were therefore given more space, they also attracted negative attention. This attention, both negative (people looked at them with disgust) and positive (people asked friendly questions about their body modifications), would appear to work in terms of conventional understandings about femininity (for example, the attention given to the page 3 girl). But there is a difference between having breast implants so that people will look and having tattoos so that people will look: the reasons behind the two are different in that the participants wished to undermine understandings about the availability of the female body, whereas cosmetic surgery is done to adhere to those conventions.

Giddens notes that body adornment and dress are 'means of self-display, but also relate directly to concealment/revelation in respect of personal biographies' (1991: 63). Revealing or concealing can entail choice, resistance and agency: for example, Vash's method of 'hiding' her eyebrow piercing with a large plaster (in Chapter 5), or 'the wearer's ability to control that visibility' (Cahill and Riley, 2001: 151). It means that the woman has control over the display she presents. Silverman argues that we should challenge 'the automatic equation of spectacular display with female subjectivity, and ... the assumption that exhibitionism always implies woman's subjugation to a controlling male gaze' (1986: 139). Eloise said that at a young age she decided to give people something to look at, which demonstrates agency and an unwillingness to be subjugated:

*when I was sort of 12 and 13 ... I thought well if people are going to look at me, they might as well look at me for something good. But I was always looking right back.*

Morgan also said that people will look and acknowledges that she should perhaps expect people to stare at her but she also said that she stared back:

*I'm not defensive at all but if I catch someone staring at me, as they often do, you know, you've got to expect that, I will sort of stare back. Not in a challenging way particularly cos it's not fair, I can't expect people not to look at me, it would be silly. I won't look away, I won't hide myself. If someone's looking at me, especially in a disapproving way, I let them know that I know they're looking. If they smile, fine, I smile back.*

Staring back is not a traditionally feminine response and, while it may not be meant as 'defensive', neither is it submissive. Women's eyes are often downcast and to challenge through eye contact is not a common feminine retort. Kiki reiterated the importance of eye contact whilst telling me about one of the ways she had created bodily space for herself in a potentially limiting situation:

> *looking people in the eye, it's so important. Or if you've got all these piercings and stuff ... I had this driving instructor and I used to wear these massive big metal bangles, and this driving instructor would put his knee over, like next to, the gear stick so I had to keep touching his leg, you had to, and he'd sort of press his leg into you, so one time I was changing gear and I just, I deliberately got my bangles and just smashed them into his kneecap, he was like 'Arggh' and I looked him right in the eye and was like 'Ooh, sorry'. I nearly broke his knee.*

Here Kiki used both feminine adornment (her bangles) and (ostensibly) feminine wide-eyed 'innocence' as a physical warning to her driving instructor. The difference between the visibility of the participants and the visibility of women's bodies more generally is through the fact of their resistance to mainstream feminine appearance. Women are visible because their bodies are seen to be more of a commodity and more 'judge-able' than men's bodies. But these women's bodies do not conform, they resist; they do not adhere to the norm, the boundaries are different. As Vash said, some women 'fall out' of what is expected and then people react differently, most frequently with more caution or with violence. Vash told me about one of the times she had been threatened:

> *I've had abuse in the past for looking too, well not looking feminine enough: 'Why do you do that to yourself?', 'Why do you wear your make-up like that?', 'What have you got in your nose?' and 'Why have you done that?' It's just expectations and some women fall out of them ... [so] I actually thumped him. No, because it was, it's the men who tend to feel intimidated by it, then they come across as quite aggressive. This was somewhere in town, not alternative-type men.*

Both Kiki and Vash had responded with violence, confident enough of their physical strength to do so. However, Kiki related an incident when she had walked through the centre of Nottingham on a Saturday night illustrating how men's bodies predominate in public places and how men may feel that this is their 'right':

> *It was scary for me cos there was loads of them, pissed out of their heads, and they were real lads, Nottingham town centre is a nightmare on a Saturday night,*

*you just don't go through it … One guy even asked me out of a pub to have a fight with him. And it's because they don't see you, they didn't see me as being a woman, I'm quite tall and big-built, if I was really petite they might not have done it.*

She identified that she had crossed two boundaries: first, she was walking alone through the town centre on a Saturday night and 'you just don't go through it', it is the domain of men who want to fight; and secondly, her build (the space she occupied) and her appearance (*'a freak'*) made them see her as less than a woman, transforming her into both prey and a potential threat. Women are linked to 'small' and 'weak' whereas men are linked to 'large' and 'powerful'; 'muscularity and masculinity can be, and often are, conflated' (Mansfield and McGinn, 1993: 49). Thus a woman who is 'large' and 'powerful' threatens the normative order of gendered space. Gaines identifies the threat as one to the distinct gendered categories of masculine/feminine; therefore anyone who does not fit easily into one of these two narrow choices 'unsettles' cultural ideals and norms:

> The lesson in transgression we have from the transvestite as well as the female body builder is that gender ambivalence is traumatically unsettling to the culture. These counter practices of the body violate deeply felt premises. The sexual difference system around which societies are organised, after all, is guaranteed on a day-to-day basis by gendered dress, adornment, and body style. (1990: 26)

It was in this way that Kiki's size and appearance were perceived as a threat. Most of the participants were aware of these attitudes to the female body; as Tate argues, women's bodies are expected to 'take up as little space as possible' (1999: 36). Kiki was one of the participants who had thought the most about the space she occupied (no doubt because of experiences like those above):

*I'm quite big and stuff and I'll be walking along and I'll have blokes with beer guts call me fat … and it's really true. A man will look in the mirror and over-compensate and a woman will look in the mirror and under-compensate and, I said before, if a woman feels bad she'll straight away target her body to make herself feel even worse about herself whereas I don't think men do that.*

Miss Pink, Kiki, Bee and Delilah all said they were 'big-built'; for example, Miss Pink said one of the reasons she wore black was that it made her look smaller. Furman's study of older women echoed this in that many of them said they would rather be 'tiny' or they felt too 'big' or 'broad' (1997: 51). However, the overall tone of the interviews was primarily positive towards body shape and image which contrasts with other findings in Furman's study about women's relationships to their bodies: '[perhaps] women's preoccupations with weight tells us something, not only about changing cultural aesthetics and expectations about the look of the female body, but also about the appropriate use of space culturally assigned to women. Women move in space in ways that are different from – far more constrained than – men' (1997: 71).

Several participants did define themselves as being 'big' although they strenuously avoided describing themselves as 'overweight'. Only three did: Gemini, Zeb and Louise. Gemini said she thought much of this was to do with ageing and compared how she had looked in her teens and until her early twenties:

> *Lots of people had short clothes but mine were a good two or three inches shorter … I used to have a white lace trouser suit and I didn't wear anything under it at all … When I had children I put on loads of weight and spent time trying to seem invisible. I didn't want to have people look at me as a woman, and tried not to draw attention to myself. I became very frumpy and lost confidence in who I was as a person.*

At the time of the interview, however, she claimed to feel much more confident about herself:

> *I feel tons more confident in myself as a person despite the fact that when I see myself with no clothes on I don't consider myself a very attractive sight but that's to do with the ageing process and being overweight.*

However, she also said:

> *I don't know if that's culturally or if I've been browbeaten into the fact [that she is overweight] but I think I look disgusting with no clothes on. There's a very short time when people look all right with no clothes on. The time when I was very exhibitionist was the right time, I had a right and firm and crisp young body that was all right to look at. And yes I would, I think, given enough money I would quite willingly have reconstructive surgery if I felt that there would be little or no scarring.*

Gemini listed to me the many operations she would like to have on her body and face:

> *I would have my breasts lifted and reduced. I would have my tummy reduced, tucked, lipo-sucked, and reduced to as small and flat as possible. And I'd have*

*under my arms lipo-sucked and tucked cos I don't want my tattoo to sag. And the tops of my thighs, the insides. And basically if I lost a lot of weight which I would subsequently try to do, then anything that was unsightly I would have that done. But I am not into facial reconstruction*

Gemini qualified her statement about confidence by saying she was over-weight. She told me that her two pregnancies had 'ravaged' her body and that she still felt a certain amount of resentment over it. Macdonald argues that there is a great investment in 'appearance as a key identity marker' and that the body works to distinguish between, amongst other things, 'mothers from sexual beings' (1995: 192). Gemini was aware of this dis-tinction and felt it had taken her a long time to overcome it. Arguably, the idea of herself as an attractive, sexual being was still not one she was com-fortable with. The discussion about being overweight and conventionally unattractive contrasts with the discussion about tattoos, which are about resisting such conventions of attractiveness. The participants who consid-ered themselves 'big' had an ambivalent relationship to their size: on the one hand, they saw themselves as being less attractive; on the other hand, they saw themselves as being less vulnerable because of their size. Again, these two attitudes contradict each other.

Louise had a different approach to her weight. Her tattoos told a story, were part of a rite of passage which began when she became clinically depressed and had to begin a lifetime of reliance on antidepressants. One of the side-effects was that she put on a lot of weight:

*What it is for me now is that it's actually whether anyone else sees them [the tattoos] or not it's irrelevant, yeah? For me, it's a physical reminder of a rite of passage. From having being a certain, you know, thing, person, [slim, blonde] having gone through that traumatic and life-threatening experience, to having survived it, being a survivor of it.*

Louise, then, saw her increased body weight almost as a prize she had accrued in her fight against depression. Similarly, Zeb, in particular, dis-played unusual acceptance about being overweight. 'Being overweight rep-resents the clearest failure in the maintenance of an ideal femininity' (Furman, 1997: 68) and yet Zeb (who was not maintaining an 'ideal' fem-ininity in that she saw herself as 'alternative' and not 'fluffy') refuted this assertion. In her teens and early twenties she had been very underweight and promiscuous, and she linked the two together; that she had not valued herself, did not eat properly, had sex with many men (various studies have highlighted how eating disorders or dieting can be linked to low self-esteem, for example, Chernin, 1983; Wolf, 1990; Giddens, 1991; Grogan,

1999). However, she had been presenting an apparently attractive and sexual persona. At the time of the interview she was significantly over-weight and claimed to prefer her body like this (*'I feel like one of those very round fertility goddesses'*).

> *I like my body now and although I am very overweight and other people wouldn't, I feel wouldn't like it, I like it. I think it makes me look more of a woman and more womanly and it's sort of less apologetic ... now I like myself and I can treat myself better and I like me ... I just feel more comfortable about being me now.*

Grogan found that 'looking at body satisfaction throughout the lifespan, studies have found that women of all ages are less satisfied than men' (1999: 164). However, Zeb's problem, as she approached forty, was other people's reactions to her weight gain; they were not satisfied with it:

> *They act like I should be concerned about my weight, as if it's something I'm missing and they have to explain it to me.*

Zeb identified her main problem in being overweight as the prejudice she faced from both people she knew (mostly colleagues) and strangers:

> *I'm an overweight housewife. But I don't think people think I look like an over-weight housewife. I think they think I look overweight but not like a housewife.*

So, although Zeb fulfilled a traditionally feminine role as a housewife, she felt that it was somehow eroded or ignored because her weight and her alternative appearance became the primary issues that people focused on.

Lara expressed more dissatisfaction with the way her job limited her freedom to have more tattoos than she did about her body image itself. She said she connected to her body in *'minor ways'*, such as going to the gym occasionally, but that it was her body modifications which made her appre-ciate her body's limits and possibilities. This was perhaps the key issue in how these women approach their body image: activities such as going to the gym focus only on improving the body, in that people go there to get fit or to achieve a muscled or 'toned' body (the 'Holy Grail' of modern gym attendance), or for health benefits, and this necessarily requires an assess-ment of what is perceived to be wrong and how to correct it with ongoing, never-ending work. Thus going to a gym is not an end in itself; people have to keep on attending. Bordo sees perpetual gym attendance as 'extremes' (1993: 94) and does not see the pleasure or confidence gained such as that identified by Tate (1999). But the participants were so aware of their own 'difference' that they were also able to be reflective about the pros and cons of other 'unconventional' choices for women. For example, Kiki was able to recognise, and articulate, the contradictory pressures on women, using the example of body-building:

> *it's like body-building is a really positive thing and a really negative thing cos it still concentrates on image for women, it's still about a woman controlling her body and it's really good in the way it's not accepted ... by men ... it's a way of fighting back but then some of them are really unhealthy, and they're still obsessed by diet and weight.*

In contrast to this, tattoos and piercings are a finite process: choice, design and application – and, unlike the gym, they are a process with a definite, apparent end-point. The only point of connection is that a gym can be described as 'being situated within a discourse which makes the "outlandish" body possible' (Bordo, 1993: 51). As Grogan found, most women exercise to attain a slender, 'toned' body shape rather than to attain good health (1999: 57). This sentiment is echoed in the interviews of Kiki, Delilah, Gwendolin, Miss Pink, Edie, Sparkle and Vash, who all said they did not want to be muscly but would like to be 'toned' (that is, streamlined, pared down). This was then tempered by their assertion that they were happy to be 'big' or 'big-boned' and they were glad to take up the space they did. The majority of the women in this study spent as much, or more, time and effort on their appearance as the most 'traditionally' feminine woman. The 'difference' in the appearance they had crafted seemed to displace the focus of their preoccupations from anxiety about how 'wrong' their appearance was (for example, whether they were overweight) to pride that it was never 'right' in the first place (they had multiple tattoos and piercings).

## 'This is Me!'

The popularity of tattooing and piercing has increased dramatically over the last ten to fifteen years, have as has academic interest and writing on the subject. For example, Sweetman (1999), DeMello (2000), Cahill and Mifflin (2001), and Reilly (2001) have all examined various aspects of body modification, including the gendered aspects of tattooing and piercing, the history of the practice and its significance to those who do it. Mostly attention has focused on Western attitudes to, and fashions in, body modification. For example, DeMello's work is a history and examination of the tattoo 'community' in the USA and the changing meanings of tattoos.[3] Craik attempts to (briefly) rectify such omissions by pointing out that Polynesian cultures used tattooing as a technique of fashion, with designs going in and out of fashion along with social changes. Craik also points out that 'the most elaborate tattooing skills were developed by the Japanese' and a museum in Japan features tattooed skins, proving that 'the tattooed skin was regarded as a form of "clothing" and not merely as surface decoration' (1994: 24–5). My interviewees echoed this attitude to their body modifications in that they saw them as an intrinsic part of their identity as an 'alternative' woman rather than as something merely for fun or decoration.

Piercings can be private or public; for example, pierced nipples are shown only to the person closest to a woman whereas facial piercings are public piercings and are on show. However, piercings are, for the most part, only semi-permanent; rings or bars can be taken out and the piercing will partly or wholly heal. The same is not true for tattoos, which are permanent, and we can see that there are two broad (although distinct) purposes for tattoos. One is the type which is done for display; it is there to tell a story to whoever sees it; it draws attention to the tattooed female body, especially as, as Sweetman notes, 'the stereotypical image of the tattooee [is] young, male and working class … [although this is] increasingly outdated' (1999: 55). Body modifications move the participants away – rather than towards – the Western ideal of a slim, young and unmarked body (1999: 57); Sweetman's definition of unmarked, in this context, is in relation to 'body projects' such as dieting and keeping fit (which move the body closer to the ideal). However, bodies can also be seen to be marked by age, and the conjunction of age with body modifications was one which caused much reflection amongst the participants.

The other purpose of the tattoo is when it is done for private reasons, to tell a story or mark a passage which is private to the owner and those she chooses to reveal it to. Whether public or private, a tattooed female body is still, to a certain extent, a resisting body because, as DeMello and Govenar note, 'tattooed women overstep the physical boundaries of their bodies by permanently modifying them, and they overstep the boundaries of femininity by embodying a formerly masculine sign' (1996: 77). However, although this remains true, tattoos can be more than this: they may be an 'overstepping' of gender boundaries, but for the participants of this study many tattoos were far more personal than that. For example, several participants had tattoos or piercings to challenge and commemorate a particularly difficult time in their lives. Kiki believed that her own tattoos and piercings were a way of 'fighting back' against the fear and anger of her childhood, what Sweetman calls 'reasserting control *over* her body' (1999: 68):

> *we had a really bizarre childhood ... it was violent because I always fought back and shouted and I suppose that went with my appearance, my attitudes ... I used my body to fight back through piercings, tattoos, all that. I did it in a very outward way ... I do get a lot of confidence from ... my tattoos.*

Louise began to have tattoos in her thirties and not for display (*'they're not about décor'*). All of her tattoos are linked, all are private and each one tells a story. 'Women tend to be tattooed for personal pleasure, rather than [like men] public display' (Cahill and Riley, 2001: 152), but both Kiki's and Louise's reasons go beyond personal pleasure and are more meaningful; Louise explained that they act more like a 'map' in case her health again fails: she has navigated this course before and she has recovered.[4]

No matter how subversive or personally significant body modifications are, 'fashion' often intervenes, normalising what was previously a 'boundary', and the participants were aware of this encroachment, for example:

> *I've had my tongue done twice, one's been in about five years and then the Spice Girls caused this great scene where Joe Bloggs in the street had their tongue pierced so I thought 'Right, I'll have mine done again.' It's like your eyebrow though, everybody'd got their eyebrow pierced. It's all become trendy and yet we've been doing this for twenty or thirty years in the alternative scene. So we need to keep having more.* (Flong)

The 'we' who need to keep having more are 'alternative' people wanting to keep ahead of – and distinct from – mainstream people. 'The transgressor, getting under the skin of mainstream society, claims not only to expose the falsity of the society that is shocked, but also claims access to some kind of intensity of experience from which the mainstream society is cut off' (Wilson, 1994: 111). The reason that 'alternative' people need to keep having more, bigger, better body modifications is so that they can retain their rights over the 'intensity of experience', to ensure that mainstream society cannot say it understands, or even condones, it.[5] Even if this involved pain or discomfort – as some of the more uncommon piercings do – the participants showed willing to 'keep ahead of the Jones's'. This creates a significant tension between the position they occupy in regard to 'femininity': there is a 'pulling back' (recuperation) with the traditionally feminine items and activities they use; but there is also a 'pushing forward' (to maintain the 'difference' and intensity of experience) of having more body modifications. Morgan described one piercing to me:

*After my tongue it was that bit of my ear there, the tragus, that was the last one I had done ... I like that one as well. Quite unusual.*

The reason she had this piercing was that it was unusual. In the same way, Delilah wore very large rings in her nose and had a total of thirteen ear piercings and multiple facial and body piercings, including:

*two in my nose, big hoops I have, one in each side ... they are very big, aren't they? I wanted them to really show up and everyone has sweet little hoops in their noses now so I thought 'fuck that' and got these great big ones.*

Again, she felt she had to go further than just 'everyone'. 'The transgressive impulse is ultimately elitist in so far as once a transgression becomes a widespread habit it has lost its magical aura of initiation and privileged experience' (Wilson, 1994: 111), so the only way to reclaim this experience is to go further. As tattooing and piercing become more popular, it ceases to matter whether one's tattoo predates the current trend since in theory anyone could say they had had their tattoo for years. Thus the 'alternative' person has to have more tattoos to make it clear that theirs are the authentic item. 'In most cultures, styles of dress and body adornment attempt to produce a different body, that is, to reshape it into an aesthetic ideal, whether through scarification, nose- and neck-rings, hair dyeing or fashionable garments ... [and] bring theories of identity formation directly into contact with the regulation of the body' (Finkelstein, 1997: 160). This 'regulation' of the body was vital to the participants' sense of themselves as 'alternative' women; that is, the body modifications acted as signals that these were women who were not 'fluffy', with other acts reinforcing this effect, such as (as Finkelstein mentioned) hair-dyeing. But, instead of creating an aesthetic ideal, they were creating a female body which was perceived as marked and therefore less 'feminine', and so they moved consistently further away from the ideal. Although the use of 'feminine' items such as those discussed in Chapter 3 worked in a limited way to recuperate this distance (even if apparent only to the participants themselves), most of these items became 'hidden' by the body modifications. As we have seen, Claudia, in particular, stressed that people did not seem to 'see' her make-up and her handbag, concentrating instead on her multiple body modifications. Despite this, the sentiment amongst my interviewees was overwhelmingly one of choosing to make these changes (and so demonstrating agency) and enjoying the body modifications. Primarily, however, most participants said (explicitly or implicitly) that they felt in command of their bodies and saw other female, unmarked bodies ('fluffy' women) as being less in control of themselves. For example, Delilah commented on the regulation of her own body image, likening it to a blank canvas on which she could render changes or modifications:

*It was a production, if you like ... I was my own masterpiece! Or missus-piece!*

This quotation revealed her own feelings of being 'in charge' of her appearance and, by extension, of herself. And yet arguably most women feel the same about their appearance and strive to 'make the most of' themselves with cosmetics, clothes and exercise. As Shilling argues, 'treating the body as a project does not necessarily entail a full-time preoccupation with its wholesale transformation, although it has the potentiality to do so. However, it does involve individuals' being conscious of and actively concerned about the management, maintenance and appearance of their bodies' (1993: 5). Several participants said they no longer had enough time to maintain their appearance as they once had, but several said they still spent a considerable amount of time on it. Delilah was one of those who evidently saw her own 'body project' as a continuing full-time occupation around which others things, such as work, must fit (rather than vice-versa, which was discussed in Chapter 4) – which is certainly not feasible for most people. Despite having less time to maintain their appearance, not a single participant expressed any dissatisfaction or regret about their tattoos or piercings. In fact, a more common feeling was that they were sorry that body modification had become so 'common', and they would like more tattoos and piercings, bigger tattoos and 'cover-ups' to improve and extend existing tattoos. For example, Flong said:

*I've got six tattoos now, I've got others planned ... The majority of what I've got on are native American designs and I've just had a cat put at the base of my back but it's our shop logo so it's a purple cat with great big ears, it's like really over the top.*

Eloise, on the other hand, did not plan her piercings:

*My nose I first had done years and years ago ... my ears, loads there ... the lip I had done, that was basically done on a whim. It was, I was bored and it was 'So right, what can I do?', saw this girl – a freak girl, not a townie – with her lip pierced and thought she looked fantastic so there I was. I had it done.*

Lara felt she would like to plan more. She already had five tattoos and six piercings, not including her ears. She told me that she would have more tattoos and piercings if she could:

> *if it wasn't for work I would have some in more obvious places. I would actually like one on the back of my neck. That would be good, just grand, if you had one there you could never ever pretend that you had been anything other than a freak. Really. It's the same as having one on your hand. I would like a bracelet on my wrist as well, like barbed wire or something.*

In Chapter 5 I discussed Lara's two separate and distinct wardrobes, which represent her 'work' and 'true'/home personas. Her inability to have a more visible tattoo because of her work was something that she strongly resented. This resentment spilt over into disapproval of women who can, or who do, have larger, more visible tattoos which were 'pretty':

> *you see these women with tons of tattoos and they're all flowers and fairies and they say 'Well, yes, mm, I have tattoos but look how pretty they are, look how dainty and nice.' Save us from the pretty tattoo brigade ... it should offend at least half the people who see it, it should not be fragrant!*

Louise agreed that 'pretty' tattoos were not appropriate:

> *I think one of the dangers, we often go into a tattooist's and we see the stuff on the boards and we just pick 'em, because they look pretty. But tattoos shouldn't be pretty.*

One of Kiki's tattoos was of '*four men hunting three antelope*', which had significance for her (about respecting the environment) rather than because it was pretty. Similarly, she had a tattoo on her hand:

> *my tattooist, I had to argue with him for an hour to do it, cos he doesn't tattoo people's hands, most good ones don't ... I had to really think about that and how I was and I thought it's not one you can just cover up if you go to an interview and stuff, but it's such an important part of who I am I don't mind having it on my hand cos I am showing who I am all the time, sort of thing.*[6]

Sweetman found that many women opt for tattoos which are clearly 'gender-neutral' or 'feminine' rather than a design which could be seen to have masculine connotations like Kiki's or Louise's. For this reason, he argues, it is difficult to describe women's tattoos as 'resistan[ce] *per se* ... although they may be seen as empowering, a form of self-inscription that involves asserting control over the body, such marking is often sought or enjoyed not as a means of subverting hegemonic notions of femininity, but in order to detract from or disguise perceived deficiencies in relation to the hegemonic ideal' (1999: 68). Miss Pink is an example of a participant who appeared to be adopting this idea and she had taken various steps to disguise 'faults' about her appearance, including dyeing her hair (to disguise her natural ginger colour), wearing black (as she felt it was a 'slimming' colour) and having body modifications (which also worked to draw attention away from such 'faults'). She described herself as:

> *just under six foot. I've got long pinky-red long hair, pierced nose, pierced ears, um, pierced tongue. I've got tattoos. One on my wrist, one on my back. They're flowers, they're all flowery and feminine. So flowers on my wrist, flowers on my ankle, a celtic-y thing on my toe. I've got a little ... oh, it's a weird design thing on my back and flowers going right across my shoulders. That's pretty ... it's all quite dainty.*

Miss Pink did not feel that she was 'dainty' (she mentioned her height and build at various points in her interview) and seemed to be using her flowery, delicate tattoos as a tool to instil a sense of herself as feminine 'enough'. As DeMello notes, a first tattoo is often 'something little and feminine' (2000: 1) and yet Miss Pink's tattoos had remained dainty and 'feminine'. Again, this is a 'recuperative strategy' in regard to body modifications; as DeMello argues, anything but an obviously 'female' tattoo would put her femininity (or her heterosexuality) at risk (1996: 76–7). Yet this also contrasts with other participants who were hostile to the idea of 'pretty' tattoos, seeing them as indicative of a 'fluffy' femininity that they felt was not appropriate to their own sense of difference.

Claudia expressed disappointment at people's reactions to her tattoos (Claudia had two full-sleeve and two full-leg tattoos plus tattoos on her hands, back, breasts and feet, so she had the most of any of the participants):

> *I think a lot of it is a lot of people are confused because of the tattoos and piercings and because I'm a female and I do all the make-up and things ... when they can see them, a lot of the time they are covered anyway. Just cos it's too cold to get them out. I have had said to me 'How could you do that to yourself?' as if it wouldn't matter if I was a male.*

But, while Claudia was evidently aware of, and annoyed about, the double standards between attitudes to men's and women's tattoos, she also betrayed her own concerns. She said her tattoos were covered most of the time. Cahill and Riley argue that this 'visibility/invisibility offers multiple levels of resistance' (2001: 168), and yet Claudia covering her tattoos appeared to have less to do with being able to manage the levels of her resistance than being able to control how feminine she looked: she was insistent on herself as a 'feminine female' but her problem was people thinking she is less feminine just because of her tattoos.

'Clothing marks an unclear boundary ambiguously, and unclear boundaries disturb us. Symbolic systems and rituals have been created in many different cultures in order to strengthen and reinforce boundaries, since these safeguard purity. It is at the margins between one thing and the other that pollution may leak out. Many social rituals are attempts at containment and separation' (Wilson, 1985:2–3). Claudia said that her life was steeped in the culture of piercing and tattooing and so was within boundaries which contained and separated her from mainstream society. She recognised that this had set her apart and it was when she was outside these boundaries (that is, on the margins between one thing and another) that she faced the most hostility about her body modifications. Although Wilson's argument would place Claudia's body modifications as the 'pollution' (because she overstepped boundaries), she saw the prejudices that she faced as the 'pollution'. Paradoxically, she called it a 'problem' that she was around the culture of tattooing and piercing all the time, at work and at home, meaning that she did not have to hide her tattoos; they were a constant part of her life. There was no reason (or perhaps opportunity) for her to stop having body modifications even if she wanted to:

> *See, I'm a bit isolated from it cos I get in my car ... I do my job so I'm around piercing all the time, erm, and I worked in a tattoo studio for two years so I was around that all the time and then I can go home ... I think almost I'm perhaps more acceptable cos it's 'Well, she's a piercer for a living, it doesn't really matter' ... so, yeah, I do feel a bit as if I've stepped out of that really, it's actually quite scary the thought that, you know, perhaps one day I won't be able to do this and then what will I do?*

As Claudia pointed out, there is also perhaps *more* acceptance of this way of life because *'she's a piercer ... it doesn't really matter'*, as if her appearance were also part of her chosen career but also as if she lived separately from 'us'; she existed in the piercing world and she did not bother us, so it was less important or threatening. Wilson argues that transgression actually confirms the boundaries of the 'ghetto' even whilst those 'inside' seek to cross boundaries. She points out that to live like Claudia and other participants 'defines a difference, and a separation' (1994: 110) and for Claudia this had become a problem. She felt that her body modifications and the attendant (and necessarily separate) way of life was locking her into a 'ghetto' situation, which eroded various other aspects of her sense of self, primarily that of her femininity.

I asked Claudia whether her own appearance made her more aware of unfairly judging other people by their appearance. Claudia explained:

> I've recently joined a gym and a lot of people there are really into body-building and they're like 'Wow' [about her appearance]. They're doing what we've done in a different way; [body-building is] only body modification and anything you do with that is the same. It's just to give yourself more confidence, change yourself, or make you feel like you've done something that, you know, one day you can look back on and go 'Well, at least I did that bit, I wanted to and I did it.'

The gym that she attended is one of the few places where she felt comfortable; she was not the only person there who was somewhat different from the norm, and she could align herself with a whole different group of people and thus extend the space that she occupied. Although her 'difference' was not that she had highly developed muscles, she could see enough similarities to feel part of the group. It was apparent that this acceptance was mutual and the body-builders she met in the gym felt that her body modifications were as positive as their own.

Giddens (1991) argues that managing the body is the route by which modern individuals seek a lifestyle which they perceive as different or better than their own. Bodies are a means of expressing one's individuality and aspirations rather than just a signifier of where we 'fit in' on the social scale. On body-building, Schulze comments that 'since female body builders are often described as "freaks" ... "grotesque" ... it would appear that they offend bourgeois taste as well as patriarchal ideology ... This is a body that "takes up space" ' (1990: 76). If one were to remove the term 'body-builder' from this quotation, the argument could be more broadly applied to women who resist through their appearance and dress (especially as the term 'freak' was used in a positive way by many of the participants to describe themselves). Body-builders (both male and female but particularly women) invite attention – awe, ridicule, disbelief, admiration – and their bodies physically take up more space because of the bulk of their physique. In a similar way, the participants of this study attract attention – again, from admiration to insults – and take up space physically because of aspects of their appearance. Both sets of women have an 'emphasis on the spectacular, on the sheer presence of the body' (Schulze, 1990: 69) and both interrogate the idea that cultural ideals of 'femininity' are 'naturally' embodied in a female body. As Blake argues, about foot-binding

> *the embodied self is also a 'social body' in that it is an organic object of discourse. It mirrors, reflects, projects, and represents the language-based categories that society takes to be the 'natural' order of things ... But foot-binding dramatically altered and in some ways subverted this 'natural' order of things in a way that revealed the wilful and artificial aspects of the feminized body* (2000: 442).

In the same way both body modifications (and body building) subvert this 'natural' order.

Delilah was more pragmatic than Claudia about other people's attitudes to her tattoos and piercings:

> *I suppose different people think different things are feminine. I think that my tattoos and piercings are very feminine. They make me feel very ... womanly and feminine. To me they are. I know other people think they're ugly or butch or something.*

Wilson argues that there has always been a 'widespread human desire to transcend the body's limitations' (1985: 3). My interviewees had all, to varying degrees, experienced body and/or facial piercing, tattooing, the colouring, crimping and back-combing of hair, and wearing clothes which were, for example, always black or wearing 'unladylike', not dainty, footwear, such as army or motor-bike boots. In these ways they have created 'post-modern bodies',[7] which Braidiotti defines as 'artificially reconstructed' (1996: 13) and which can be a way of connecting with, controlling and experiencing one's body, which women are taught to deny. Goffman emphasises how the body enables us to intervene in daily life to negotiate how we present ourselves, and Delilah did this by stating that other people may not think her attractive but, none the less, she remained confident about her own femininity and attractiveness on her own terms. Similarly, Cahill and Riley note that when the 'pierced' woman is offered up as a sex object she 'counters this by reclaiming her "weirdness" and her "difference" ', thus renegotiating the image of herself (2001: 163) and intervening in someone else's definition. In doing this the women engage and connect with their bodies, aware of themselves in aesthetic, empowered and positive ways, something girls and women are traditionally taught not to be. Rather, women are taught to keep a distance from their bodies, to diet them away, not to touch themselves or be self-aware.[8] Gaines argues that recent feminist work has shown that 'women still have an alienated relationship to the production of their own bodies' (1990: 9), but the participants of this study repeatedly assert that their multiple piercings and tattoos, their constant hair-dyeing and their wearing of 'bizarre' or outlandish clothes make them more aware of their bodies, more in tune with themselves.

A common feeling was that their piercings tied them to a renewed sense of self-worth about their own sensuality and sexualities, and their bodies. For example, Lara celebrated her piercings:

*To me, it connects me to my body ... like it pins me down to my body in a way I didn't before. It's not the only way I connect to it – you know, I wash and use a loofah, and I have sex with my boyfriend, and I paint my toenails, and so on, sometimes I even go to the gym, but it's definitely one of the best ways to experience your body. And I suppose it may seem like piercing is more like torture than love – like having to muck about with my piercings every day – but it's not, I really think that my body responds positively to it.*

Lara's assertion was that through her piercings she had established a new, better relationship with her own body. She felt closer to it than when she was doing more perhaps mundane maintenance tasks such as washing or exercising. She enjoyed having to 'muck about' with her piercings every day (Lara took most of her piercings out for work and put them in again afterwards, saying her piercings regularly reacted badly, causing pain, bleeding and infections). She felt that her body, as if it were a separate entity, also responded well to this extra attention, even if it sometimes resulted in pain. 'Mindful of its experience in the "real world", the body becomes a "self". Here is where an intentional mutilation of a woman's body induced the (re)embodiment of her self by the application of a rigorous discipline designed to inflict and to overcome protracted physical pain ... "Femininity" came from the muted management of body and space' (Blake, 2000: 258). Although Blake is here discussing foot-binding, Lara can be seen to be employing this same sort of management of her body through the constant removal and replacement of her piercings, even though it is obviously not good for them: she is constantly 're-embodying' herself as her work persona and then as her home ('true') persona through this painful and disciplined practice. Foot-binding was often seen as a sensual practice, despite the pain and mutilation, and in a similar (although lesser) way Lara, and others, also keenly felt the sensual aspects of body-piercing:

*One of the things I love about piercing is that the pain with the pleasure makes me feel more alive ... makes me feel tenderness toward [my body] and pride in it … As well, I think piercings just simply feel good! I love my nipple piercing; it's made my nipple very sensitive and sensual – and, like, sore. My tongue piercing less so, but I love tugging and pulling it with my teeth.*

'Self-adornment links the biological body to aesthetics. The relationship of fashion to eroticism is both obvious and complex, but has perhaps been over-emphasized in our sex-conscious culture at the expense of other and equally interesting relationships' (Wilson, 1990b: 33). In Lara's case she enjoyed the relationship her body modification lent her to her body; she liked the 'pain with the pleasure'. She had changed the biological given of her body – perhaps not internally or permanently or even very obviously (unlike foot-binding) – but she had changed parts of the body and her reactions to them. Additionally, even those modifications stay which are only semi-permanent; for example:

*I mean, yeah, you could take a piercing out but I've had these years so I wouldn't … I think it gets to a point where you wouldn't take them out. (Kiki)*

Morgan also said that it made her more aware of her body:

*I never ever regretted having them [her piercings]. I would take them out if I did. I love them. The first one was my nose … I liked having this decoration on my face, and I like the actual piercing process – particularly now that it's done with needles rather than guns. It's … not a sexual thing, particularly, but it does something, makes you aware of your body … it's strange.*

Like Lara she enjoyed the physical act of being pierced despite the physical side-effects such as swelling or bleeding, for example:

*I heard it, I heard the needle going through, it made a very strange sound, but none of them actually hurt, well, they do but the needles are so sharp and it's over so quickly. They're sore afterwards obviously but … a bit sore to sleep on to start with. I couldn't sleep on that side for months.*

It made Morgan more aware of her body and, although she could not explain why or how, it was clear that she engaged with her body in a more sensual way.

*I do like to see pierced nipples, I think they look really pretty … I wanted asymmetry. I didn't want them both doing. One plain and one adorned. And after that my tongue. I play with it all the time, this is the original bar. You have it done and your tongue swells, put a long bar in to allow for the swelling then when the swelling's gone down you're supposed to keep going back and they give you a smaller bar each time till it's tight, you know, it fits tightly to your tongue but this is the original one with loads of room so I can play with it and poke it out and stuff.*

Other aspects of the participants' resistance was partial or ambiguous, and created tensions they had to manage, such as their reliance on traditionally feminine items or their insistence on being seen as very feminine women. Craik argues that 'the act of beautification draws attention away from the individual as a person and thus detracts from individuality' (1994: 22); yet the participants generally insisted on their own individuality and felt that their body modifications expressed individuality or 'difference'. In fact, body modifications were a way of 'recouping' their 'difference' from the typically feminine activities that they undertook. Their body modifications were one area in which their commitment was total: it was visible, often painful and expensive, and mostly permanent.

Central to this discussion in this chapter has been the fact that the participants occupied space; they had created extra space for themselves through their appearance and enjoyed the results of this, such as people giving them slightly more room in passing on the street. There was also an element of either apology, or having learnt not to apologise, for the space they occupied. Several participants mentioned being tall or 'well-built' women and were (often painfully) aware of the cultural ideal of a woman's body as petite and extremely slim. However, these were bodies which did not conform to traditional ideas about female bodies because of the ways which they were dressed or adorned or modified. Wilson describes such a body as one which "flirts with [the] dangers of the boundary' (1985: 132) and here the participants flirted with the boundaries of 'femininity'; they cultivated an appearance which did not comply with traditional femininities whilst insisting upon their own femininity. Another result was that their bodies had become 'exhibits', things which other people looked at. Although women's bodies are typically more visible than men's, these bodies were not visible for the same reasons: they had multiple tattoos or piercings, or they had pink hair, or they were wearing fetish clothing with big boots. Their bodies had become 'the site of struggle over the power to define beauty' (Tate, 1999: 47). They were looking back at people.

The next chapter turns to how the participants discussed their anxieties and ideas about ageing, in relation to their approaches to femininity and their 'alternative' bodies.

# *Defying the Crone?*

In the previous chapters I examined how the participants talked about traditional and unconventional femininities, and what these categories meant to them. In this final empirical chapter, I focus on the anxieties and concerns of the participants about ageing. Much has been written about the prejudices and stereotypes faced by ageing women, particularly by feminist scholars (for example, Bordo, 1993; Friedan, 1993; Pearsall, 1997; Sontag, 1997; Gannon, 1999; Greer, 1999). Lyons and Griffin discuss the construction of women's ageing with reference to linguistic and visual representations of menopausal women. They found that primarily negative words were used in connection with the menopause, such as the body would 'suffer' and certain parts become 'deficient' necessitating 'management'. 'Terms such as "deprive", "degenerate", "decline", "withdrawn", and "deteriorate" are frequently used' (Lyons and Griffin, 2000: 470–1). Similarly, Gannon notes that 'in cultures where aging is despised and feared, and women are valued for fertility and beauty, the aging woman is often the target of pity and ridicule – portrayed as lonely, sick, frail, and unhappy' (2000: 476). The participants were evidently aware of these stereotypes and sought to discuss ageing in more positive ways. However, tensions arose in the accounts, particularly in regard to their awareness of themselves as 'alternative' women and how they could (or could not) combine their 'difference' with being middle-aged or elderly.[1]

## Age Catches Up with You

The participants sought to make it clear that they intended to defy cultural expectations and age 'differently', and indicated that they thought that older women are expected to begin to 'dress down', perhaps even take less trouble and care with their appearance, or to dress more carefully and restrainedly. Jody commented that

> *as you're older it may be more acceptable to let yourself go, whereas if you're a certain age you may be expected to care about your appearance.*

This is an example of Jody subscribing to the stereotype of a particular type of old age which is in conflict with the general attitude of the participants: although they claim not to care about conventional norms about femininity, they clearly put a great deal of effort into self-presentation. Melia notes that 'there [is] a recognition that dress codes [are] not static, and indeed [are] often age-specific' (1995: 551). But the question is, 'letting herself go' from whose standard? Jody defined herself as 'different' and non-conformist; she was not 'girly'; 'letting yourself go' implies that there was a rigorous set of rules (in this case traditional 'femininity') which one was adhering to in the first place. The answer appears to be that Jody did recognise that her current appearance, although not 'fluffy', was still 'age-specific' and that she intended to continue to be 'different' by 'letting herself go' (which can also mean to have a good time) and wearing whatever she chose.

Kiki echoed what Jody had said about the pressures on women at different times in their lives:

> *When you're young you can be different from normal femininity, and when you're old you can be, but in that middle bit there's a lot of pressure to conform, grow up, be normal as well. Being part of a youth culture you can get away with it to a certain extent. But from thirty onwards there's that pressure. But old women ... they go mental, they stop doing it, they're like invisible people and not seen as sexual, and I think some of them would find that really liberating, and they start to be and dress a bit more like they want to ... and some old women are great, really eccentric, do their own thing.*

Often the image of old age is one of loss: 'children leave home; then follow the losses of fertility, work, husband, health and finally death. Yet many of these so-called losses can be a source of new-found freedom and energy' (Leonard and Burns, 2000: 487). Kiki (and others) identified old age as potentially liberating and the middle of life (between youth and old age) as more restrictive, more subject to rules and expectations. Friedan states:

> The lives of older people can be characterized socially by a theme of loss – of social positions (roles), of expectations (norms), and of reference groups ... However, one consequence of the decrease in social expectation may be the increase in personal freedom. Enhancing the competence of older individuals [no longer] involves adequate role performance [but] adequate coping plus doing what the individual himself [sic] wishes to do. (1993: 547)

Similarly, Kiki described a scenario where elderly women are released from the pressures of being sexualised into a new freedom where no longer being perceived as a sexual being (even if, in fact, you are) is a release. One can dress how one wants without such a strong requirement to conform; thus being 'unruly' when you are elderly has the potential to be less difficult, because one is subject to fewer social expectations.

Both Zeb and Kiki discussed social expectations, what was 'appropriate' for ageing women to wear and how they thought they would fit in:

*I think they* [people in general] *make assumptions about what women should wear but also about what women of a certain age should wear as well and I don't fall into that kind of category ... I dress inappropriately for ... you know, for being a woman, for being my age, for situations that I'm in.* (Zeb)

*I can see myself having more tattoos. I think I'll still have my piercings, I want to be a mad old woman with dreadlocks down to my ankles. I'll always have the dreads ... I want to be one of those mad old women in town that everyone knows. I want to have loads of cats.* (Kiki)

Yet in discussing non-conformity one particular stereotype of age was used:

*Those old ladies who wear slippers and have thirty cats.* (Diz)

*Women who've got like twenty cats and they live on their own and people think they're crackers, and they may well be, but they're not harming anyone.* (Gwendolin)

Several participants referred to this stereotype, using words such as 'crackers', 'eccentric' and 'mad'. As Russo notes, such women are by their nature isolated: 'hysterics and madwomen generally have ended up in the attic or in the asylum, their gestures of pain and defiance having served only to put them out of circulation' (1995: 67). Other, equally negative, stereotypes include 'the ludicrous "bawd", or the "shameless old lady" ' (Fischer, 1997: 167). This 'mad cat-woman' stereotype relies on a non-sexual as well as a non-conforming old age where human company has been superseded by that of pets and one's appearance has become almost grotesquely eccentric. The attitude to such women is one where the disgust about the woman is often displaced on to her many cats. The participants' references to the stereotype did contain an element of fear; the implications were that such 'mad' women had gone too far: they had not attempted to recuperate their femininity, they had not policed themselves by watching others, they had not 'toned down' their appearance and, in fact, they didn't care. They exhibit what Russo calls a 'loss of boundaries' (1995: 53).

Elderly 'mad' women had used none of the strategies that the participants had developed to safeguard their femininity and their own boundaries. This type of older woman is seen as being somehow out of control, 'out of the loop' of the beauty myth. Tseëlon argues that 'the ageing woman serves as the *memento mori* to that which the beauty system is trying to defend against' (1995: 93) and this particular stereotype functions culturally as a warning. Ford and Sinclair comment that 'the danger of such stereotyping ... is that the elderly, perceiving that society has little regard for them, thus come to have little regard for themselves ... Both men and women suffer from these stereotypes, but they are particularly detrimental to women because they add to their already disadvantaged position in terms of status, power and rewards' (1987: 1–2).

Bee was a performance artist and had noticed her own ageing primarily in connection to her work:

*I'm entering a new stage in my life. My age is catching up to me. I feel some pressure from my environment to adapt to 'middle age' conformations. Not from my friends, who are in the same boat as me but ... from general society ... I'm considerably heavier than I was ten years ago. I'm trying to analyse my feelings about all this and come up with some kind of resolution but it's quite hard.*

Despite a certain amount of bravado and genuine anger in Bee's words, there was also a vulnerability and dread about what might happen. Bee, like many of the women I interviewed, felt that age was 'catching up to her', making age seem like something she had done her best to outrun and had, in the end, proved unable to. The extent that appearance for women interconnected with self-worth, sexuality, sexual identity and other social constructs is evidenced by comments made by participants about their own experiences of being more attractive, more confident, generally happier when they were younger. It may be that other factors such as being healthier, having fewer responsibilities or having more money then also contributed to this feeling, but the overwhelming message is that life was better as a young woman. Delilah felt that her appearance when younger reflected most accurately how she wished to be seen:

*Well, I'm comparing myself to how I used to look and I used to love how I looked. You know, I really felt it was me and I wasn't putting on an act or anything ... [now I am] still me, I suppose ... but a different version, an older model, watered-down.*

Goffman notes that 'a performer tends to conceal or underplay those activities, facts, and motives which are incompatible with an idealised version of himself [*sic*] and his products' (1964: 56) and in the same way Delilah and other participants were playing down this current version of themselves in favour of the more idealised, 'truer' versions when they were younger.

Gemini, the oldest participant, mentioned her favourite poem, in which the voice speaking is that of a woman warning how badly she will behave when she is older:

> *Jenny Joseph's poem. When I am an old woman I will wear purple …. I am with Jenny Joseph. I've already got the purple suit! But I don't have any problem with women dressing with what society would think inappropriate for their age providing they're doing it for the right reasons. Pleasure for themselves. Yeah, pleasure. I don't think there should be any rules at all.*

Gemini, who was in her late forties at the time of the interview, said she felt herself to be getting closer very quickly to being an old woman. And, although participants had broken particular rules around appropriate 'femininity' at their current age, they were obviously more painfully aware of the difficulties in breaking rules as they grew older.

## Policing Yourself … and Others

This fear of being 'inappropriate' may appear not to apply to the interviewees since they had all maintained an 'alternative' appearance. However, there were two main strategies used to 'measure' how far they were drifting towards too inappropriate. The first strategy was for a participant to watch carefully what other women were doing and gauge from that how inappropriate she herself had become, thus using other women as a mirror in which to reflect how far to go, or how much, to recuperate her appropriate femininity. As Sontag argues, 'Women look in the mirror more frequently than men. It is, virtually, their duty to look at themselves' (1997: 22). But at some point women stop seeing an attractive woman and see instead an ageing woman.[2] In order to more accurately judge how far they can safely go, the participants stepped back from their own reflection and watched other women. I call this 'policing' other women (and themselves) because the boundaries they were setting were stringent and the connotations negative. The second strategy (discussed in the next section) was a response to the first and involved 'toning down' their appearance (most said this was involuntary). Both these strategies arose because of the participants' anxieties about ageing; if, as discussed above, women find that their choices become narrower as they age, then this is doubly so for 'alternative' women and begins to reveal the im/possibilities of being alternative. For example, having bright pink hair does not hold broad social meaning and so has little ambiguity; therefore, as one ages bright pink hair becomes (even) more outrageous than when one was young. Similarly, body modifications work against the idea of women becoming less visible as they age; in fact, an elderly woman who has multiple piercings and tattoos would be far more visible than a young woman with the same – and much more likely to be subject to derision and rejection.

The fear, then, is one of being not only outrageous or 'different' but also monstrous, grotesque. Such words collude with the sense of women (and particularly ageing women) as being grotesque:

> Naming represents a particularly vivid way of recalling the persistence of those constrained codings of the body in Western culture which are associated with the grotesque: the Medusa, the Crone, the Bearded Woman, the Fat Lady, the Tattooed Woman, the Unruly Woman, the Hottentot Venus, the Starving Woman, the Hysteric, the Vampire, the Female Impersonator, the Siamese Twin, the Dwarf. (Russo, 1995: 14)

Russo's categories chime closely with many of the tensions and concerns voiced by the participants: the Crone (Gemini), the Fat Lady (Zeb, Miss Pink, Louise), the Tattooed Woman, the Unruly Woman, the Vampire. All hold particular cultural resonance; they are words with power (like slag and slut) but they are not positive words. For example, Russo's list (discussing the grotesque) includes the Bearded Woman. Chapkis describes being a 'moustached' woman as a source of shame and of being an outcast from a hostile society in which men shave and women are simply expected to be hairless (although, of course, most women are not naturally hairless). 'The moustached woman – like all women who fail to conform – is not only Other she is Error; flawed ... in her ability to appear as a normal female' (Chapkis, 1986: 5). Kiki mentioned her 'hag hairs' and said that she did try to accept it but others around her 'policed' this aspect of her appearance:

> *I'm really aware I've got quite a dark moustache ... I've got hairs on my chin but I call them my hag hairs! I quite like them. I've got this friend who tries to pull them out but I won't let her ... I've made a conscious decision that I have got a moustache but that's natural and I'm leaving it like that. And the hairs on my chin, I'm not going to pull them out. And this little girl, yesterday, she said 'You've nearly got whiskers, you have'. I said 'Yeah'.*

Kiki was not allowed to remain unaware of this 'flaw' (in the same way, discussed in Chapter 6, Zeb said that other people constantly pointed out to her that she was overweight). While it may be possible to accept 'hag hairs', Kiki commented that she always shaved her legs and under her arms and found the sight of women with hairy legs *too much* – thus demonstrating a strategy to recuperate her femininity, that is, to keep herself appropriate enough (not too grotesque) by policing others.

Russo's categories of grotesque hold other, more detailed, requirements:

*We may begin a long list which would add to these curiosities and freaks those conditions and attributes which link these types with contemporary social and sexual deviances, and more seemingly ordinary female trouble with processes and body parts: illness, aging, reproduction, non-reproduction, secretions, lumps, bloating, wigs, scars, make-up, and prostheses* (Russo, 1995: 14).

Again, we can see how easily the participants could fit into the category of grotesque, not least because many of them described themselves (in a positive way) as freaks or ex-freaks, and many related tales of how they had been treated as 'curiosities' because of their appearance. One example is their body modifications: tattooing and piercing are permanent, visible scars they have chosen – but the marks of age are not chosen and cannot be avoided. As Sontag argues, 'in a man's face lines are taken to ... show he has "lived"... Even scars are often not felt to be unattractive; they too can add "character" to a man's face. But lines of aging, any scar, even a small birthmark on a woman's face, are always regarded as unfortunate blemishes' (1997: 23). Similarly, Russo (1995) mentions wigs (which could include the hair dye, hair extensions and dreads of the participants) and make-up (used in excess when many were younger and still used daily by several, for example, Claudia, Miss Pink and Delilah).

Bee described a common reaction when she visited the town where she grew up (in Canada), where other women policed her because of her appearance:

*Since my twenties I've had short hair. Because of my size and hair and clothing I'm often confused for a man. I mean, at a cursory glance. Some people, particularly older women, women my own age and older, insist on calling me 'sir'! Even after they realise I am female. I suppose it's meant to express their disapproval, or coerce me into 'proper' behaviour ... How I react depends on how I feel.*

Bee's reactions ranged from '*stony silence*' to '*being rude to them right back*' to '*going home and crying*'. She said that as she got older the latter reaction had become the most common.

*Sometimes I go home and look in the mirror and say to myself 'You should really change how you look.' Because of my age and size. But other days I think, 'Well fuck them, I shall grow old disgracefully.'*

Tensions were evident between a need to continue being 'out there' and an opposing need to avoid censure and feel vulnerable – several participants used the phrase 'mutton dressed as lamb', utilising the phrase as a kind of controlling barrier, the ultimate measure of having 'gone too far'. Any discussion of the terms and ideas applied to ageing revolve around being less valued and less attractive (mutton being tougher and less palatable than lamb). 'The connection between youth, attractiveness and chronological age is conveyed in the phrases "growing old gracefully" [which none of these participants mentioned in connection to themselves] and "mutton dressed as lamb" ' (Fairhurst, 1998: 260). Asked to give an example of 'mutton' (having just used the phrase in connection with herself), Gemini responded violently with her opinion of the late Barbara Cartland:

*She's held so closely to this frilled up icing sugar sweet complacent femininity, fluttering round men, she's held to it for so long, that her only eccentricity is to hang onto the youth that she seems to think is the only thing worthwhile for a woman in society. I don't think she's growing old disgracefully, I think she's just lost the plot. I think she is very sad, she isn't rebelling in a healthy way ... She makes my skin crawl to be perfectly honest, there is something unhinged about a[n old] woman who says she has the body of a nineteen-year-old.*

Unpacking this quote reveals several issues: one is that Gemini, a woman in her late forties, resented Cartland apparently colluding with the general cultural norm of equating beauty with youth. The *'frilled up icing sugar sweet complacent femininity'* that Cartland embodied (or attempted to embody) was grotesque in that it demonstrated Cartland's refusal to acknowledge that she was ageing, something which Gemini herself was struggling to do with courage, and negated the possible power that a wealthy, successful old woman could have by persisting in enacting the worst sort of 'fluffy' femininity. Gemini's apparent anger at Cartland's refusal to grow old gracefully (saying, she was not growing old disgracefully either) contradicted her own stated desire to be an *'old woman in society's face'*. Yet this attitude also illustrated one of the most puzzling contradictions exhibited by the participants: their own resistance did not negate their disapproval of the resistance of other women if those women were still conforming to a 'fluffy' approach now seen to be inappropriate because of their age. Non-conformity *per se* was not enough; the impetus had to be an 'alternative' one.

Vash discussed how she might choose an outfit to wear for a night out whilst being careful to avoid appearing, like Cartland, as 'mutton dressed as lamb':

*I might see someone and I think 'Hh yeah, that looks brill' and then I suppose there's this little voice at the back of my head saying 'You're getting on a bit, you can't do that any more.' I do get a bit worried that I'll end up looking like mutton dressed as lamb so I do try to keep it as ... sort of, appearing not as ridiculous as possible. Ridiculous to yourself.*

Vash explained this reticence by saying that women of a certain age cannot 'get away' with as much – even if they are the same body shape or size as someone ten years younger:

*There are some things that would look brilliant on someone in their mid-twenties but put it on someone in their mid- or late-thirties and it would feel uncomfortable, I mean in myself. As much as I would like to do certain things, I don't any more.*

Vash was clearly aware of other women ageing and watched them to see how they looked: did she think they 'got away' with it? Or were they grotesque? Did they horrify her and put her on her guard against making such an error herself? In this way she was policing herself by using other women as a mirror:

*I think too that made me think of what I was saying before, about mutton dressed as lamb. When you were in there* [a particular nightclub] *... some of those women needed a hammer and chisel to get their make-up off and I thought 'Oh no, I don't want to get like that.'*

Here Vash echoes Gemini's feelings about Barbara Cartland. Ussher argues that beauty ideals and the 'magical' transformation that make-up can work are presented in women's magazines as an 'exciting adventure' – an adventure that is an option at fourteen but becomes a constraint, a necessity, by forty:

The art of artifice is still alive, yet the aim to be achieved is reversed ... the older woman wants to look younger, her hours of cosmetic ritual attempting to accomplish the impossible, the achievement of immortal youth ... these visions of beauty [images of models] partly work through perpetuating fear – the fear of getting old, and therefore being unattractive (as beauty equals youth), but also the fear of 'getting it wrong'. (1997: 58)

Thus, although Vash appeared to lack sympathy or empathy for some women, it was her fear of her own potential mistakes which was the issue; she was afraid of 'getting it wrong'. She was seeing her own vulnerability reflected back at her from other women.

Similarly, Gwendolin voiced disapproval of how some women look. In particular, again, it is women who wear a great deal of make-up:

> *Lots of heavy tarty make-up and fake fur coats and loads and loads of gold and I look at people like that now and think 'Oh, you look like an old slapper.'*

'Slapper' – like slag – is an insulting term used only in regard to women who are (whether true or not) promiscuous – yet promiscuity is rarely the real issue when using these words. Instead, such words are used as forms of social control, to indicate disapproval or hostility.[3] When I asked Gwendolin if she thought her appearance had changed and would change more as she got older, she was certain that it would:

> *I think it more applies to people who change their appearance suddenly because they're frightened of getting old and they haven't got the personality to go with the clothes and ... like I get taken for younger but I think that's more to do with attitude than looks, I might look a bit younger than what I am but that's prob-ably the hair, the clothes, but ... if I was old in mind I would look a little bit stupid cos I'm still quite young in mind, I'm still a bit silly, it helps cos you can actually get away with acting younger – not that you do it on purpose cos I don't see myself as old yet. I thought I would be old when I was this age when I was sort of sixteen but now I'm actually here I think I don't feel no different, just as silly.*

Again, the phrase 'getting away with it' was used and Gwendolin even implied she 'acted' younger than she actually was. She then hurriedly amended that statement and said she didn't 'act' younger on purpose. The implication of her remarks was then that other people assumed she was younger than she was because of her appearance, and her outlook on life, neither of which were deliberately contrived. In her study of the regulars of a beauty salon, Furman also found that some of the women claimed that old age was not a problem as they felt their 'true' age (how old they actu-ally *were*) did not show (often through 'genes and ... cold cream'), and that it was common for women to feel younger than their chronological years whether they looked their age or not (1997: 105). Skelton and Valentine (1997) note the ambiguity around the terms youth and youth culture. They point out that some people who are legally adults resist this definition and 'perform their identity in a way which is read as younger than they actually are; whereas others may actually perform their identity so that they can "pass" as being older than the actual age of their physical body' (Skelton and Valentine, 1997: 5). Obviously, wishing to 'pass' as older or younger than one's actual age is not peculiar to youth. Gwendolin was presenting herself as someone younger than she actually was and she was apparently happy to allow this misconception: this illustrated her own anxieties about ageing and her desire to 'pass' as younger than she was (and possibly, by extension, her desire to be younger).

There is a tangible sense of participants' awareness of growing old dis/gracefully through their use of such terms as 'going too far', 'getting away with it' and, most tellingly, 'mutton dressed as lamb'. However, the terms were not comfortably used and were more likely to be used in negative ways about themselves or in reference to other women. A lack of positive terms does prevail when discussing ageing femininities. For women who have spent perhaps at least half of their lives rebelling against traditional 'girly' femininity, growing older presented some problems and there was not a single participant who had not begun to address these problems in some way. Delilah's hair, at the time of her interview, was pink with yellow hair extensions. Yet she had decided to forego purple and blue hair extensions in addition to yellow because she had recently celebrated her thirty-sixth birthday and felt that three different colours of hair extensions was too much. She said it was part of *'toning down'* and that she felt herself careering towards forty: *'the big 4–0'.* However, 'toning down' is not a straightforward matter for the participants, as the next section illustrates.

## 'Toning Down' Your Appearance

A common assertion amongst the interviewees was that, although they may have 'toned down' their appearance, they were still the same ('alternative', 'different') person they had ever been. As Pearsall comments, 'women do not willingly accept old age; there is surprise, incredulity and indignation. They reject the image others provide, at first, only to capitulate eventually. And yet a question asserts itself: Can I become a different being while I still remain myself?' (1997: 3). This question is echoed in other studies (for example, Furman, 1997; Bytheway and Johnson, 1998), where the ageing participants say they may look older but they remain the same inside. In this context, 'toning down' functions as a metaphor for general ageing. The participants consistently refused to say 'I am ageing' and instead replaced this with the term 'toning down'. Although they appeared to embrace the ageing process as one they would experience positively, the ways in which they spoke about 'toning down' revealed a tangible resentment about it. Delilah's very first answer, referring to her appearance, included this sentence: '*I think it's a lot tamer now than it used to be.*' Delilah went on to describe her appearance by telling me how much she had dyed her hair, again referring to being older and what condition her hair might be in in the future:

*I suppose it's too late for it [her hair]. I'll be like bald as a coot by the time I'm fifty ... I've had it this colour for... well, for ever really. I'm really happy with it, it feels absolutely right for me. Up till Christmas I had purple and blue and yellow extensions in it as well but I thought, well tone it down a bit cos I was thirty-six in December and it was part of me accepting that. I was a bit depressed about it cos it's more than halfway to forty so I thought I'd have my hair done and while I was there I decided to just have more yellow in it and no purple or blue ... but I went and had my lip pierced as well so so much for toning down.*

Delilah claimed that she was accepting her own ageing by having fewer hair extensions – then she had an extra facial piercing instead. Clearly, Delilah was not accepting her ageing. Delilah attempted to downplay her concerns about approaching forty but her final question to me in this paragraph dispelled her breezy tone:

*The big 4–0, that's what they say innit and here I am just careering towards it, that's what I was thinking when I got it done [the extra piercing]. I don't feel thirty-six, I feel about fourteen. I've decided I'm going to ignore numbers. Age numbers. For myself, I mean. I'm going to do something I'm not supposed to do, like I'm going to wait till I'm sixty and then learn to skydive and ... How old are you?*

Again, Delilah referred to what was, or was not, appropriate for an older women: they are 'not supposed' to go skydiving which, was why she said she should do it. Jody also asked me about my own reactions to being thirty to contextualise her own anxieties, to place them as acceptable on a general canvas of 'alternative' femininities.

Several participants expressed anxieties similar to Delilah's, as if they had little or no control over the 'toning down' process; as if it were a regrettable, inevitable aspect of getting older. For example, Flong told me about a conversation she had had with a friend about her hair:

*She said to me, 'You can't have bleached blonde hair for the rest of your life because when you start getting into your late thirties it'll look tarty', I went 'Yes, we'll see' ... and as I've got older I think I have tamed it down and I am just normal now ... It just happened. I don't thing it's gradual at all, it just happens ... But I don't know why that is. I think that all your life you're still going to be that alternative person ... but I think you do tend to tone down as you get older.*

'It just happened' is a phrase used when people have done something they wanted to do but also do not want to take responsibility for. They have abregated control and taken a step away from the act. Another reading of 'it just happened' is that the participants were aware of the process but did not want to admit 'defeat' (that is, that they could not comfortably reconcile an 'alternative' femininity with an ageing femininity) and so claimed to have no control over it. As Pearsall argued above, most women resist the image of 'ageing' woman which is foisted on to them but they do capitulate eventually.

'Toning down' had its own meanings and significance for every individual and, whilst rinsing or tinting one's hair (rather than dyeing it) may seem necessary to certain kinds of women (more 'traditional' women who want to 'grow old gracefully'), my interviewees had spent years perfecting the art of being dis-graceful – and one of the key ways they had done this was by having brightly coloured and outlandish hairstyles. For example, Kiki stated:

*When I was younger and I was a punk ... I had, oh, coloured hair, bright pink, blue.*

Fairhurst argues: 'colour of a woman's hair is potentially problematic ... Dyeing hair is inappropriate [for her participants] but tinting or rinsing (excluding blue rinsing) is acceptable. It is interesting that dyed hair carries the connotation of harshness much more than rinsing or tinting' (Fairhurst, 1998: 264). This quotation relates to Fairhurst's own work, which was with women and their experiences of the menopause, and it contrasts sharply with the attitudes of my interviewees. None of the participants saw tinting or rinsing as a by-product of ageing as this would have seemed as alien to them as having multi-coloured hair would to Fairhurst's participants. Vash talked about her hair colour in a way that had two layers of meaning: one was, 'it's not as wild as it was' but the other message was 'I'm still wild for my age':

*I suppose that's why I stayed with the black – and put purple in it. Cos although it's a lot tamer than it used to be it's still got that certain something ... Making an effort. I'm still here!*

Vash's comments were interesting. Like Delilah and Flong, she used the word 'tamer' in relation to her appearance (the opposite of tame being wild, independent, unbroken) but qualified the statement by making it clear she had not stopped maintaining her appearance. [4] As Tseëlon argues, women are caught in this double-bind:

> The ageing woman portrays an unashamed undisguised ugliness that society has placed on the category of woman. And she is beyond the control of the beauty system. Yet even here she is caught up in a paradox. She is threatening if she has given up the fight for beauty and failed to defeat the inevitable. But she is equally threatening if she tries to do just that: defy the inevitable. (1995: 94)

Vash said she was still making an effort (so had not 'let herself go') and was *still here*. This phrase revealed her awareness (and fear) of the increased invisibility of old women and she clearly linked spending time on her appearance with trying to outrun age (although, as Bee found above, this is ultimately impossible).

Claudia used the phrases 'toning down' and 'getting away with'. She said she had a number of issues about ageing which she had already considered at some length:

> *It changes as you get older. Obviously what I can get away with at my age ... you can get away with less at my age. I have to be a little bit careful so it's not silly. I can probably get away with more at a [tattoo] convention when everybody does what they want there and they don't worry what they look like ... I don't wear the old leather frock for shopping in Tesco. So I suppose I am careful in that respect but other than that I'm sort of like ... sometimes I would do things cos I know it would cause offence. Just cos you do get a little bit tired of toning it down. Sometimes it's just like 'Well sod it, I will wear this dress and go for a meal there and be damned with it!' It's mostly trying to respect who you're with.*

In common with other participants, Claudia saw some situations as more sympathetic than others and, mostly, she responded accordingly by 'toning down' her appearance. She said she did not want to cause offence but she also said that sometimes she felt that it was unfair for other people to judge her by her appearance so she occasionally deliberately chose not to 'tone down'. This revealed not oly Claudia's hostility to the 'toning down' process but also her ambivalence about her own acceptance of it.

Gwendolin also discussed 'toning down', saying she did not know why her appearance had become less extreme but that it may have been due to her having *more* confidence about herself as she grew older. Earlier in the interview she had spoken of her appearance as a protective layer around herself, something she found helped her cope with being bullied at school, and she felt that she no longer needed to 'hide' behind such an extreme appearance:

> *I wear less make-up now than I used to and my clothes aren't as extreme as they were for like going out in the day. I used to get really dressed up before I'd set foot outside the door and now I just clomp about in boots and leggings ... I think that comes with more self-confidence as well as you get older cos ... I don't know what it is really but it's something that seems to happen as you get older, I don't know whether you actually care less but something happens so I ... gradually, gradually wore less and less make-up and become more normal-type make-up whereas before I would go about looking like Alice Cooper.*

She described this change as 'something that seems to happen', again as if she had no real control over it. Similarly, Eloise said that her day-to-day appearance was less extreme:

> *I think in my day-to-day appearance I have* [toned down] *because it's too much like hard work* [she has ME] *but not when I go out. Then I am toned up!*

Eloise was one of only three participants who said they had complete control over the 'toning down' process. Kiki was the only participant who said that she would now consciously 'tone down' without feeling she was compromising her usual appearance, using the example of a job interview:

> *When I was younger I was adamant that I'd never do all that, but I think I'm calming down a bit, but when I was younger I was a really really big rebel, but, er, nowadays I think I'd smarten myself up to a certain extent.*

Zeb was able to pinpoint why her appearance had become less extreme:

> *I would ... dye my hair every five minutes ... I don't dye my hair any more ... I think it was gradual. It didn't feel like there was just one day when I decided to stop doing it, erm, I think it sort of tailed off over the years so it I was sort of hard-core for a while and had like a mohican and loads of extensions and things and then it was like 'Oh well, can't be bothered to keep up that amount of effort'... And I suppose it was when I started doing other things really and stopped being unemployed, I just didn't physically have the time to spend on my appearance so it became less important. You know, that wasn't of primary importance any more, I had other things to do so it wasn't my only interest.*

Thus, whilst she still considered herself to look 'different' she also recognised that she was not as 'different' as she used to be. In many ways, the participants' insistence on telling me how different they used to be seemed to be as much to convince themselves, and me, that they were still alternative women. As Brownmiller argues,

> In a culture where the chief criteria of feminine success are ephemeral youth and beauty, a woman's sense of failure is likely to begin at the moment she is perceived by others as no longer young and desirable. Society offers a woman few objective reasons to feel successful as she grows older. More insidious, society offers her few ways to *look* successful as she enters her middle years. (1984: 129)

But Zeb, Kiki and Eloise felt (or admitted) that they had complete control over the 'toning down' process – choosing when they wished to look more successful than 'alternative' – and in this they differ from Flong and other participants.

In contrast, several participants said that they had never felt more confident about themselves than they did now that they were in their thirties or older – and yet at the same time they lamented the loss of their youth. For example, Gemini stated:

> *I am more in tune with who I am I think at this particular time in my life. I guess this stage could have come on me when I was thirty rather than forty eight. I suppose it would be nice to look back and think I had spent my time being confident and more in control but no point looking back ... It would have been nice.*

This somewhat wistful and nostalgic tone was heard in many of the interviews. Gemini seemed unaware of the tension between wanting to change her body and feeling disgusted by it[5] and feeling 'in tune' with who she now was. The fact that many of the participants insisted on how they had been more alternative when they were younger and yet continued to 'tone down' their appearance revealed a lack of self-confidence, rather than the increasing self-confidence they professed to feel.

## You're as Young as You Feel

Having told me that they were anxious about age catching up with them, most of the participants also said they were happier now about themselves than they had been when they were younger. For example, Eloise said that she was now more 'obtrusive' than ever:

> *for three years while I was ill when I first got ME, I stopped going out and dressing up altogether and then over the last year I've just, rather than tone it*

*down I've got worse – or better, whatever – well my hair's not as bright now, but that's because of all the hassle that comes with it as well, but I wear false eye-lashes and some make-up as obtrusive as possible ... [I asked if she welcomes the attention it brings] Yes, yes I do because the older you get, I always imagined that when I got to thirty-one that, you know, I'd be past it and nah, if anything I am better now than when I was younger. Much.*

Vash said she too was more content at the time of the interview than she had been for at least ten years:

*I think I've got worse as I've got older. Or better. I think as you get older you become more, sort of, you know what you want, you know how you feel, so it does make you a bit more ... in a different way. You're not as rebellious in some respects but you think 'All right, I'll compromise in this way but I'm old enough to know what I'm doing, this is me'. You do become more sure of yourself ... I feel much better now, I look better, I feel more confident ... than when I was twenty-seven.*

Vash was saying that, although she was willing to make some compromises, they did not compromise her sense of self; she is more sure of herself and so will not compromise so much that she is not comfortable. As Pearsall asks, 'Now that we see our faces slowly assuming the visage of the older woman, our ... rejection of beauty standards is put to its most exacting test. Can we resist being undermined by the lack of self-worth we feel when arriving, finally, at the most stigmatized stage in a woman's life cycle: old age?' (1997: 1). It is tempting to suppose that these assertions of feeling 'better' and of increased confidence as they aged were an attempt to convince themselves as much as anyone else. However, it is equally possible that, in order to remain 'alternative', they felt they had to retain some semblance of youth to legitimate this 'difference', even if only in outlook. For example, Vash likened herself to some of her contemporaries:

*Yes, I do actually [thinks she is resisting expectations of how a woman should look]. Certainly with my age. I mean, you know, I walk round and see people I went to school with – I bet you do too at your age – and they are old. Old. And there are people on the degree I'm doing, they're not much older than me but they do seem very old in their ways. You can really tell the people whose attitude to life is different cos there are a few of us, say my age, and we're mixing with the eighteen-year-olds cos we've got the same outlook. Clinging on to youth, determined.*

Here Vash appeared to be justifying herself with the old adage 'You are as young as you feel' (also used by Gwendolin when she said it is not about age but, rather, about a person's attitude). 'The only thing you can do if you are trapped in a reflection is to subvert the image' (Reynolds and Press, 1995: 289) and Vash was subverting the image of herself as a single mother in her late thirties: she had returned to education, and felt more confident and attractive.

> *Obviously, there's going to be one day you look in the mirror and 'Oh my god!' and get the Zimmer frame out and think 'Maybe I shouldn't do this any more.' They say that it's getting, that it's an older society now and people's attitudes to age are changing. Years ago when you were hitting forty you were probably seen as past it whereas now it's nothing. I just think ... you also see differences in generations, differences in attitudes to age. Like my mother's attitude is oh, I shouldn't be doing this now, I shouldn't be going clubbing, I should be staying at home and sitting with my son, nice family life and everything.*

Here Vash unpicked both a generational and a cultural shift in attitudes to age and gender. Vash's mother expected her to be much more domesticated and this was because she was a product of her age and believed in more 'traditional' values about a woman's role in the home and family. Vash, on the other hand, believed she was quite domestic enough and would like more freedom – and believed that this attitude had become much more acceptable.

Louise had radically changed her appearance and lifestyle whilst in her thirties and therefore was experiencing her forties with acceptance. This attitude is one echoed in Leonard and Burns's study: 'Overall the picture was not one of decline after mid-life but one of improvement with age. Those in their fifties or sixties identified less illness, fewer adversities and more personal growth than those in their forties' (2000: 488). Louise did not specifically refer to ageing although she did say she was happier now than she had been up to the age of thirty. Similarly, Claudia had been very traditional in both her appearance and lifestyle until she was in her early thirties:

> *It's evolved over the last four and a half to five years, I would say. Before ... conventional is the only way to describe it. I used to work in an office so it was normal, sort of, blouses, skirts, short hair, etc.*

She felt that the changes she had made to herself (for example, she had approximately one hundred and eighty hours' worth of tattoos[6]) had improved her life in various ways, including giving her a new career direction and the confidence to be the centre of attention because of her appearance. She felt that this was specifically because she had more self-confidence as she aged:

*I think that's why I'm like this now* [because she is in her late thirties] *and I couldn't have done this ten, fifteen years ago. I don't think I would have dared do anything that drew this much attention to me. I was even less confident then and as I've got older ... yeah, perhaps it's the getting older that's given me the confidence to do it as opposed to doing it to give me the confidence to be happy with it.*

Claudia did not have her multiple tattoos and piercings to mark, defy or celebrate her ageing. She did it despite her ageing and with the full intention of changing herself and her life: 'before it was too late' was unspoken but implicit in Claudia's interview.

## Marking the Occasion

Most of the participants chose to mark events, particularly birthdays, with body modifications. Partly, they did this to defy the expectations of ageing but also to acknowledge their anxieties. So, although they may have been ageing, they were doing it in their own ways; they were doing things that, for them, had significance and which were often visible to other people. For example, Jody commemorated the first few years of her thirties, which, she said, had presented concerns for her:

*When I was thirty I felt very bad about thirty, it sounded harsh, twenty-something is OK. I was twenty-eight for a couple of years, because I liked it! I didn't want to be a responsible adult, I don't know, I just felt old, it just felt ... it was a thought-out decision rather than anything hasty and then when I was coming up to thirty I thought 'Oh, this is a nice way of marking that passage.' So I had my nose pierced then and got the tattoo. Thirty-one I changed my name ... and thirty-two, I got my clit pierced, and I skipped last year, I didn't do anything.*

Of the four things she did to mark birthdays, two are piercings and are not necessarily permanent. But two are permanent – a legal name change and a tattoo – and represent a permanent reminder: of her 'difference' and her age. Similarly, Morgan had another tattoo to mark her thirtieth birthday:

*My last one was a tribal-y thing round there, my mum paid for it for my thirtieth birthday, I wanted a new one, I wanted it quite big. It's very pretty ... A great present, a permanent present from my mum.*

This has an air of ritual about it: a mother marking the thirtieth year of her daughter with a permanent body modification (Morgan even described the design as 'tribal-y'). The participants seemed to be acknowledging that they felt a need to create their own ceremonies around their ageing (as Gemini demonstrates, below). DeMello notes that women find that undergoing some kind of life crisis is a key motivator for having a tattoo as a way to regain control: 'The body is both the site for the inscription of power and the primary site of resistance to that power' (DeMello, 2000: 173). Although ageing may not appear to be a 'life crisis' since it is an inevitable result of life, the response of having body modifications is not an insignificant one. It is a form of control over one's body and signifies a level of decision and independence.

In Chapter 4, I discussed Lara's tattoo, a 'fairy princess' representation of herself with 'billowing' hair. Lara said she would be able to look at her tattoo in later life and remember how she looked as a young woman. However, tattoos of this nature would also illuminate the degeneration of the body – the tattoo's 'permanence' is only as permanent as the body which wears it and the very look of the tattoo will change as the body changes. Chapkis states:

> The body beautiful is woman's responsibility and authority. She will be valued and rewarded on the basis of how close she comes to embodying the ideal. Whatever the current borders of beauty, they will always be well-defined and exceedingly narrow, and it will be woman's task to conform to them – for as long as humanly possible. While beauty is a 'timeless' quality, the beautiful woman is tightly fettered to time. (1986: 14)

In the same way body modifications are 'tightly fettered to time' but also – in addition to the distance created simply by age – create a greater and greater distance between the wearer and the 'ideal'.

Gemini's first tattoo was done at the age of forty-four:

> *I always wanted to draw attention to myself and to be looked at and I've always wanted to rebel. The first one* [tattoo] *was just for me so I would have the opportunity to show it off, so it would be in society's face, so they would know I was back, it was me again. And I don't think really there will be an opportunity for society to put me in my place again or the place it thinks I should be in but it's not going to happen, it might be a bit late but it's not going to happen again. The second one happened almost because I'd got into the swing of thinking what am I going to do next. After I'd had my piercing, I had my navel pierced.*

Gemini said 'it was me again' implying that her real 'self', the rebellious, attention-seeking self had been submerged for most of the years of her adulthood. This feeling, and the acts which symbolised it, followed several life-changing events, of which the most significant were the death of her mother and her hysterectomy, both (mostly) signals of ageing. DeMello found that the women in her study 'explain[ed] their tattoos in terms of healing, empowerment, or control' (2000: 172). Gemini also talked to me about the rituals she had created for herself after she had had her hysterectomy.[7] She said her hysterectomy was like a death to her and she wanted to mark the occasion in a way that was both traditional and bizarre. It was in this same way that she saw her decision to have two large tattoos and a navel piercing whilst in her mid-forties. It was grieving and it was defiance.

The act of having body modifications despite ageing creates tensions with recuperating 'femininity', since tattoos, although now much more acceptable for women, are still 'inappropriate' for old women (primarily because they have been unacceptable for 'nice' women until relatively recently[8]). It also creates tensions with policing oneself and 'toning down' one's appearance since policing oneself would involve holding a tight rein on any act which could be construed as too inappropriate, and 'toning down' is the response to being too inappropriate for one's age. However, literally marking time on the body is a defiant response to ageing as 'bodily deterioration is enacted on the female body' (Fischer, 1997: 165). As DeMello argues, perhaps the participants were 'working to erase the oppressive marks of a patriarchal society and to replace them with marks of their own choosing' (2000: 173). In addition, it may be a way to recuperate their 'alternative' femininity and to remain 'different' in the face of anxieties about old age and its perceived invisibility and grotesquerie.

In conclusion, this chapter has focused on the contradictions exhibited by the participants when discussing positive aspects of ageing and how they felt they would deal with old age; their feelings were ambivalent and ranged from marking their ageing with some kind of body modification to hoping people took them to be younger than they actually were. Those participants who were experiencing particular anxiety about their impending middle age also appeared to be experiencing a double blow: they had been seen as radical, different, daring in their appearance – whilst also still feeling feminine and attractive. As middle-aged or old women, they were fearful they would be seen only as ridiculous or powerless.

The next chapter, 'Reflections and Conclusions', discusses the issues and paradoxes raised in the empirical chapters, and considers possible future work.

# Reflections and Conclusions

> The pathologies of female protest function, paradoxically, as if in collusion with the cultural conditions that produce them, reproducing rather than transforming precisely that which is being protested.
>
> Susan R. Bordo,
> 'The Body and the Reproduction of Femininity'.

The empirical chapters (Chapters 3 to 7) began with a discussion about how the participants experienced and described femininity and ended with their thoughts about becoming elderly women; themes such as body modification and unconventionality held the two together. Overall, this book has been about the trajectory of the lives of women who appeared to resist many (but not all) of the more traditional physical aspects of womanhood (for example, clothing and body modification) and has explained how appearance can be used to signal continuing resistance to certain concepts about femininity. Femininity, in turn, links to wider discourses about the body, finding or creating jobs (such as working as tattooists or body-piercers) which allow this resistance to continue, and anxieties about ageing. A key point which emerged throughout was that resisting certain elements of traditional femininity did not mean that participants saw themselves as unfeminine. On the contrary, they insisted on their own femininity and enjoyed many of the pleasurable aspects of being feminine whilst strongly disputing the idea that they were in any way 'girly'.

## Tensions and Paradoxes

In this book I used empirical data to explore the personal meanings of dress and appearance and how they were expressed through the narratives of a group of women who were ostensibly resisting traditional femininities. Furman comments that such a study, although concentrating on a small group, can be (quoting Blake) 'to see the world in a grain of sand' (1997: 6). This resistance was rife with discrepancies and tensions; for example, there were both angry defiance and careful negotiation. Some of the participants were clearly aware of the contradictions in their narratives; others seemed less aware. Either way, the contradictions were rationalised in a variety of ways using several key strategies (see below). Overall, the main tensions for the women were: Did being alternative erode femininity? And did being feminine negate being alternative?

One way that the participants demonstrated their anxiety about whether their alternative appearance had a negative impact on their overall femininity was their assertion that being perceived as unfeminine, or 'differently' feminine, equated with masculinity. By 'differently' feminine I mean the distinction between traditional femininity (walking a fine line between the restraints of what is 'ladylike', what is inappropriate, what is un/fashionable) and the participants' own versions of 'alternative' femininities; they are no less bound by particular cultural expectations but manage to challenge the boundaries, if not actually move them, by their use of what Doane calls a 'parodical overload' (1990: 25) of body modifications, hair colouring and outlandish clothes. For example, in Chapter 3, in reference to their own 'different' femininities, Gwendolin said she never felt like a man and Claudia said she was not trying to look like a man, as if their 'difference' automatically imbued them with masculine traits. This perception therefore presented no grey area or broad category – no ambiguity – within which the interviewees could comfortably place themselves (unlike the category 'girly', discussed further below). Rather than constructing a 'sliding scale' of different sorts of femininities, I found instead that often the participants were more likely to see masculinity and femininity purely as two separate poles which offered no opportunity for anything other than the narrowest of definitions. Conversely, at other times they described femininity as an arena where negotiation and variety were possible but within the context of my own request that they devise a continuum of femininities and place themselves on it. Further, many offered a sophisticated analysis of the construction of femininities and of gender roles generally. It was through these kinds of contradictions that the richest material was derived and, although many participants exhibited such contradictions, there was no indication that they were confused or unhappy by the often marginalised position they felt themselves to occupy. Reinharz describes how a woman she interviewed displayed many contradictory feelings about herself but notes that none the less 'she is engaged passionately in the contradictions of her identity rather than being debilitated by them' (1992: 13), and this was the overriding feeling that I found: that the contradictions they displayed were a vital part of the 'alternative' femininity they had constructed. Indeed, the many contradictions that the participants managed were not straightforward but involved elements of negotiation, adaptation, acceptance, resistance, attempting to create a new discourse of femininity: an alternative to a traditionally feminine appearance but not to femininity itself. Even when the participants appeared to be embracing some aspect of traditional femininity, their narratives could often be unpacked to reveal their own concerns and perceptions.

A primary example is that the participants disclosed that as children – and often, still, as adults – they had admired a 'fairy princess' type figure, dressing up and playing it as children and still occasionally hankering after the look as adults. The Western version of the 'fairy princess' (familiar through popular animations and images, from Disney to pantomime to art) is a key signifier of what the participants defined as 'girly' femininity through her appearance, her vulnerability and her reliance on others. She is certainly not a figure known for her resourcefulness or her unconventionality. Yet several participants argued that they felt the reputation of this figure should be questioned; through their own experiences they explained that a girl or woman could feel that she is a fairy princess but not look the part, or she could fulfil the 'visual requirements' but not feel she was fulfilling the role on the inside. From this argument they extrapolated that such a figure need not automatically be seen as weak or compliant just because of her appearance. This development reveals their own perceptions of the complexities of femininity: caught between the old-fashioned/traditional image of woman as home-maker and nurturer, and the modern image of woman as a sexualised 'Superwoman' who is still expected to fulfil a range of roles. The analogy of the fairy princess as modern woman caught between the two opposing images of womanhood illustrates how femininity can occupy a dual (and confusing) position. However, it also reveals yet another contradiction: the fairy princess is surely one of the most feminine icons of femininity and yet several participants defended her reputation in much the same way as they would have hotly defended their own right to 'femininity'. The entire 'fairy princess' argument was the mirror image of their own experience in that the fairy princess is judged on her appearance and not on how strong or intelligent she may be, and illuminates how they saw reactions to their own appearance. They felt they were not given an opportunity to demonstrate that there was more to them than simply 'alternative' women who looked 'weird'; they also wanted to be accepted as feminine and attractive women despite the fact that they had consciously chosen not to fulfil the popular cultural requirements of feminine attractiveness.

A further, linked (but contrasting) contradiction, which became apparent when the participants discussed ageing, was their disapproval of elderly women who resisted dressing 'appropriately' for their age. Their disapproval did not extend to unconventional women but only women whose appearance clearly marked them as traditionally feminine women (a prime example was Barbara Cartland) and so different from themselves. This disapproval directly contradicted their defence of the 'fairy princess' figure (an often intensely personal understanding of a generic image) because they were subscribing to a 'mutton dressed as lamb' mentality rather than striving to see beyond the appearance of the woman. As Wolf argues,

> the [beauty] myth does not only isolate women generationally, but because it makes women hostile to one another on the basis of appearance, it isolates them from all the women they do not know and like personally ... Something that makes all male social change possible [is] how to identify with other women in a way that is not personal. (1990: 56)

The types of women whom the participants did identify with also proved to be intensely personal, to the point that they named women who were, in fact, just like themselves: not just 'alternative' women but, for example, the tattooists said they most admired women tattooists.

The narratives of self-fashioning challenged ideas about what is natural or contrived, comfortable or difficult. Every single participant cited comfort as one of the main reasons they continued to dress as they did. For example, Claudia said, *'I just like to dress in black. For work it's sort of leggings and shirts cos that's comfortable more than anything else.'* Yet the participants also described to me episodes of pain and discomfort related directly to their body modifications or other aspects of their appearance. In particular, Morgan, Lara, Delilah, Louise, Jody and Flong all talked at length about the pain, soreness, bleeding, infections, swellings and lasting discomfort they had experienced as a result of a piercing or tattoo. Did the pain legitimate the continuation of their identities as 'alternative' women, which perhaps could be seen to be losing their authenticity because of their age? A parallel example is that body-building for women sets 'unconventional ... standards of attainment' (Tasker, 1992:142) and, in the same vein, maintaining an unconventional femininity sets an unconventional standard of appearance – therefore, like any standard, it needs to be kept up. Arguably the need to perpetually maintain, and add to, existing body modifications would indicate their continuing commitment, even in the face of other acts, such as 'toning down' aspects of their appearance. Gaines asks, 'What if self-decoration gives women a sense of potency to act in the world?' (1990: 6), making the discomfort they often experience worth the overall comfort and agency it lends them through their continued identities as 'alternative' women. The very nature of an 'alternative' appearance is that it is very obviously and deliberately neither entirely comfortable nor 'natural', but there has been ample debate over what is natural about anyone's appearance. Steele (1995) points out that blue jeans are no more 'natural' than high heels and it is only the gendered nature of clothing which lends a symbolic power and that fashion need not be seen to be disempowering or sexist – she points out that it can be defiant or even 'feminist'. However, there is a clear rebuttal of anything natural in the appearance of the majority of the participants: for example, pink hair, black lipstick and full sleeves of tattoos cannot be mistaken for 'natural' by any stretch of the imagination. But, instead of distancing themselves from traditional femininity, I would argue that this unveiling of the contrived and fragile nature of 'difference' instead links them more closely to the constructedness of gender. As Craik argues, there will always be an 'ideal' against which women will seek to match themselves, and these ideals will be no more 'natural' or uncontrived in appearance than the participants: 'Models currently epitomise the ideal female persona in Western culture ... Modelling epitomises techniques of wearing the body by constructing the ideal technical body. Through those techniques, the body is produced according to criteria of beauty, gender, fashion, and movements' (1993: 90–91). Thus, although the participants did not choose to construct the 'ideal' (that is, traditionally gendered) feminine body, they did employ changing and often challenging techniques to construct their own versions of femininities.

## Strategies

Although Ussher describes 'girl' as a term which can be used to typify and label 'the archetypal fantasy of perfect femininity' (1997: 445) the participants used 'girly' as a negative category. The use of the term 'girly' was an important strategy as it enabled the participants to locate themselves differently and more flexibly within the wider discourses of 'femininity'. I called this a 'recuperative strategy', adapting Schulze's phrase for the ways that female body-builders attempt to retain (and claw back) their femininity through their use of accessories such as hair ribbons and jewellery, even if their overall body strength and bulk has rendered them 'unfeminine' (and, therefore, seen to be masculinised) (1990: 59). The participants talked about traditional femininity negatively (it was oppressive, restrictive, not creative or original) in order to harness their own descriptions of femininity as the more positive, definitive versions (unconventionality, freedom, wildness, creativity). Wilson argues that 'value systems are inevitably embodied in our dress' (1992: 14) and the participants' value systems (being 'alternative' and 'different' and 'individual') were necessarily opposed to those of 'girly' dress (which they saw as being mainstream, mass-produced and restrictive). In this way they were able to frame their own appearance and femininities (and value systems) as desirable and understandable, rather than as 'Other' and threatening.

Another recuperative strategy was 'flashing their femininity', which I adapted from Tseëlon's description of how successful professional women use their appearance (from high heels to lipstick) to signal that they have not become 'unfeminine', and are therefore not a threat to their male colleagues (1995: 37). Similarly, because of their anxieties that their 'alternative' appearance would erode their femininity, the participants would 'recuperate' it through the use of items they considered traditionally feminine, such as perfume or frilly underwear. They did this in order to claim their allegiance to femininity in general but in particular to their own femininity. Of course, this was not the *only* motivation in using items traditionally associated with femininity. A feeling of pleasure and self-pampering, not to mention personal hygiene, were also reasons.[1] However, the way that participants spoke about these items strongly indicated that they felt that much of their 'lost' femininity was recuperated through the use of perfume, make-up, luxurious underwear, perfume, bubble bath and hair products. In the same way, sometimes the key to recuperation could be easily achieved by something about themselves. For example, Morgan explained that:

> *a lot of people thought I was a lad, at first glance, or from behind, bus drivers who weren't properly looking would say "Sixty-five, son ... oh, sorry, love.' I didn't mind at all. A lot of the time it was only at first glance ... But once they look for more than two seconds there's no doubt, I've got a girl's face so it doesn't bother me.*

Morgan did not mind this mistake because she believed herself to 'look like a girl' on closer examination – if this had not been the case, she would have had to find other ways to 'flash' her femininity.

Claiming that they had no control over 'toning down' their appearance enabled the participants to avoid facing two potentially uncomfortable results. Did 'toning down' mean that they were less committed to being alternative or 'different'? As discussed above, their continuing commitment could be safely interrogated because of their willingness to endure pain and discomfort when having extra body modifications in order to maintain their 'alternative' appearance. The term 'maintaining' an appearance is paradoxical in itself in this context as usually the term would refer to taming something (for example, to maintain a house or garden would mean the 'upkeep' of care, repair and general tidying up) whereas with my interviewees 'maintaining' referred to how they continued to negotiate a certain level of wildness. However, the phrase 'toning down' also facilitated a distancing from the ageing process; if 'toning down' just happened, it meant that the women did not need to reflect (and in fact were prevented from reflecting) on their ageing and its implications for how it would ultimately have an impact on their appearance. In many ways, 'toning down' was linked to strategies of recuperation in that the participants used it to ensure that they did not become too grotesque and too removed from 'acceptable' levels of difference. They policed themselves and other women by watching out for, and measuring, mistakes. What was too much? How far could they go? Two things were at stake and were in direct opposition to each other: their alternative appearance and their femininity. 'Toning down' was a strategy to bridge the distance between the two.

The participants drew on various influences and eras to evade a 'girly' appearance through the adoption (and possibly alteration) of second-hand or vintage clothes teamed with brightly dyed hair, multiple body modifications and new clothes such as fetish clothing, motor-bike or army boots, or custom-made goth clothes. 'We can ... see that subcultural use of fashion is a rhetorical usage of formalized styles, a sort of slang or argot of the "standard English" of fashion' (Brake, 1985: 13). The availability of such outfits was not as straightforward as shopping on the high street, thus necessitating a degree of commitment, knowledge, time and energy simply to find these kinds of items. It could be seen as a further legitimisation of their continuing resistance to traditional femininity, a strategy to prove they had not 'sold out' even though they claimed they had noticeably 'toned down'.

## How To Do 'Girly'

The participants demonstrated that they were tied to many of the same traditional anxieties and preoccupations as the 'fluffy' women they derided, such as their weight (too much?) or height (too tall?). Their definitions of femininity were often outdated and stereotypical. For example, Zeb defined femininity as twin set and pearls, and both Lara and Sparkle suggested that femininity consisted in wearing an apron and making bread! In contrast, many participants at the same time defended their own right to 'femininity' by pointing out, as Gwendolin did, that *everyone's got their own ideas of what's feminine or what's not feminine* and Delilah said that *different people think different things are feminine*. An important tension was that the women did not feel as if they were resisting femininity itself.

It would be easy to assume they would argue that they were 'different' and not comfortable with any traditional categories at all. But they offered reflections and meanings which made clear that they did wish to be seen as 'alternative', as different, but they also wished to be seen as feminine, as women, as womanly and were anxious that this should be understood. They were not only one thing or the other. By this I mean that it would be incorrect to see their continued resistance as a challenge to being feminine *per se*. Rather, it was a challenge to culturally bound ideas of traditional femininity. Flong said that she was *'just not fluffy rather than not traditionally feminine'* and the participants were happy defining themselves as women who were feminine. In this way, then, they existed on a continuum of gendered roles: there was a tension between the tomboy/'alternative' aspects of themselves and their being feminine but not 'girly'. They felt able to move between the poles of this continuum without jepoardising their own sense of what was feminine enough and what was too 'girly', or was too 'alternative' or not sufficiently 'alternative'.

The narratives reveal a great deal of commitment to time-consuming and often convoluted or expensive 'beauty' rituals, recalling earlier eras when it was more feasible for (certain) women to spend much more time on their appearance. Wilson notes that 'women have been so wholly identified with mainstream fashion that it is hard for them even to have oppositional styles. Sartorial excess and deviance readily equates with rebellion for men. It *can* signify revolt for young women – but even the bizarre can be fashionable' (1990b: 32). Many participants railed against how the 'bizarre' was often subsumed into a current fashion, thus disenfranchising them from something they considered their own because of its 'difference'. But glamour is not fashionable, and neither is spending such a long time on your appearance. For this reason I would argue that 'alternative' dress can be seen as a rebellious form of glamour in a society where very few opportunities to really 'dress up' exist any more (for the majority). Although the subject did not arise in my interviews, I would be interested to find out where the participants fit themselves in relation to past eras of fashion and beauty. Do they see themselves as glamorous?[2] Is there an inherent 'glamour' in being so committed to, and investing so heavily in, your appearance?

The ways that many of the participants defined traditional femininity were in outdated caricatures which were more appropriate for the 1950s, an altogether more glamorous period (for those who could afford to wear the New Look), thus placing themselves in relation to this type of femininity rather than a more modern version. Second-wave feminism of the 1960s and 1970s was notable for its hostility to 'beauty culture' and glamour

(Gaines, 1990: 3). Wilson highlights the difficulties that feminism has grappled with since second-wave feminism: 'the thesis is that fashion is oppressive, the antithesis that we find it pleasurable ... the alternatives posed are between moralism and hedonism; either doing your own thing is okay, or else it convicts you of false consciousness' (1985: 232). This may explain the hostility of many of the participants to feminism; they were aware of the old stereotype that feminists take the conservative view, have short hair, do not wear make-up or dress up and disapprove of those who do. However, as Wilson also argues, 'it is mistaken to set up something called "alternative fashion" as a morally superior idea' (1985: 241). The participants really did not set themselves up as 'superior' to mainstream fashion because they kept a close eye on it, and when asked to compare themselves with femininity most of them instead chose to compare themselves with a different era of femininity (including, through their pseudonyms, mythical names such as Delilah and Morgana). The women's commitment to this type of 'different' glamour could also function to reiterate their own feelings of femininity, a way to 'flash' their femininity through the products and time-consuming rituals they had adopted.

An example of one participant who demonstrated a number of interesting contradictions was Miss Pink. (She only just fitted into the study because of her often very traditional attitudes to femininity and gender roles, while still fulfilling the needs of the sample because of her appearance .[3]) Miss Pink described herself as very feminine (although she felt herself to be both too tall and too big, and was worried that her size made her less feminine). She was soon to be married and said that the wedding ceremony was a chance for her to dress in a very feminine, very pretty way. She was a tattoo artist and described her own tattoos as *'flowery and feminine ... pretty* [and] *dainty'* (pretty tattoos were derided elsewhere by Lara and Louise). On the face of it, these things taken individually do not seem to place Miss Pink in any more of a contradictory position than any of the other participants. However, several things did set her apart. For example, she was the only participant who chose role models who were conventional (famous married women who seemed to combine a very traditional but still happy marriage with a successful career, which particularly interested her). She was pleased to have been likened to very traditional images of femininity ('Barbie' and Disney's 'Little Mermaid'). She said she had to be *'very careful'* about what she wore and how she wore her hair because of her size, saying also that she could easily look 'unfeminine', would not even feel feminine if she did not have long hair (many participants demonstrated that hair practices and having long hair were key to their sense of femininity)[4] and could never go a day without wearing make-up (and, in fact, had worn make-up every day for the last thirteen years since she was four-teen years old). But other participants expressed similar feelings (for example, Kiki said she would not cut her long hair and Zeb said she would not leave the house without having crimped her hair and put on eye-liner). As Giddens argues, 'to be a man or a woman depends on a chronic moni-toring of the body and bodily gestures. There is in fact no single bodily trait which separates all men from all women' (1991: 63). The difference between Miss Pink and the other participants is that Miss Pink was the most anxious to be seen as feminine in as many traditional ways as pos-sible, which set her at a pole of the continuum of femininity constructed by all my interviewees. At the opposite pole would be Bee, Jody and Louise, who all had very short hair, never wore make-up and described themselves as not subscribing to most of the feminine 'trappings'. Other participants would move between the two poles but existed primarily somewhere in the middle.

In these ways Miss Pink, and other participants to varying degrees, con-founded expectations: their resistance did not necessarily take the form of being 'butch' or boyish (although it could be sometimes, always, or not at all) but most importantly their 'alternative' personae did not unshackle them from the protracted anxieties traditionally linked to women. The women did not wish to 'un-woman' themselves (no matter which part of the continuum they existed on) in order to resist traditional femininities but would rather transcend and transform what was available, seeking to feminise ideas about the meanings of 'alternative' and resistance. Subcultural theory and fashion theory are both noticeably silent on the subject of 'alternative' adult women and several participants told me that they were aware that they were a group who had not previously been 'studied'.

## Resisting 'Girly'

The participants signalled their resistance to traditional femininity in various ways. But knowing what to resist and what to accept or adapt from the ever-changing worlds of fashion and popular culture is only pos-sible because participants kept a close eye on mainstream developments (such as clothes, images and modern icons and representations of femi-ninity) and so were able to react accordingly and stay up to date (both on what was 'in' and what they were consciously keeping out). They had remained up to date on modern cultural fads and fashions, and not become entirely cut adrift in some isolated 'alternative' universe – despite their assertions that they existed in their own little worlds. They all proved to have detailed knowledge of fashions, from 'this season's hair colour' to various 'flavour of the month' pop acts – the proviso being that these things would be frequently criticised and ridiculed. For this reason, the term 'anti-fashion' is unhelpful (although popularly used in academic accounts, such as König, 1973; Wilson, 1985; Davis, 1992) because, although my interviewees were not 'fashionable' in the sense that they shopped on the high street for this season's outfits, neither were they anti-fashion as fashion none the less informed their own appearance, filtered, as it was, through their own personal taste and subcultural background. As Eloise pointed out: *'It's not just about rebelling; it's about my idea of what I find attractive.'* Thornton explains how the mainstream (personified by 'Sharon and Tracy', called townies by the participants) has been 'feminised', thus accounting for its denigration amongst those in subcultures. In contrast, subcultures and those in them are seen to be independent and masculinised in their ability to be independent, non-conformist, and free of burdens such as the family and class (Thornton, 1995: 114–15). This attitude may also account for the participants' use of the term 'girly', which similarly refers to a feminised analogy for all that is conformist and mainstream. Additionally, many of the participants said they simply did not find mainstream fashions attractive; they could not see themselves wearing them because they did not think they looked good – although individual items which could fit into their own *'stock of clothes'* would be bought and adapted.

A second method of ensuring that their appearance was 'alternative' without being vastly out of touch with mainstream fashions was to closely watch the changes in 'alternative' styles, what was being co-opted by mainstream fashions (such as the recent popularity of tongue piercings) and the rise of new subcultures (such as nu-metal), and then they could choose to adapt some of these elements because they were already on the 'inside'. That is, as they were already members of something 'alternative' (no matter how fluid or how often they asserted they had not been, or no longer were, part of a group), they felt able to adopt or adapt new styles (unlike outsiders, such as 'townies'; this was illustrated by their obvious resentment about mainstream fashions subsuming subcultural styles). From this range of options the participants do, however, choose within particular boundaries and contextual limits, such as their age, their job and their families, and these boundaries are both within and outside traditional femininity and within and outside mainstream society.

'The woman I wish to remain' was a category which I adapted from several discourses around clothes that women either maintained or no longer wore (Guy and Banim, 2000; 2001), and which described how the participants saw their maintenance of their appearance. The original five categories assumed a mainstream approach to appearance, which could not adequately be used in an analysis of the ways my interviewees either engaged with their clothes or managed the tensions their appearance created in the 'outside world'. Compromise was a key issue for the participants: they stated they were willing to go only so far and that even if they were to wear something more mainstream (for example, Vash used the example of an item from Top Shop) they would wear it 'differently' because of the way they mixed contemporary, 'alternative' and vintage clothing. Compromising their appearance presented a threat to 'the woman I wish to remain' although several participants said they were willing to 'tone it down' temporarily in order not to offend the people they were with, or if the context really was inappropriate. However, this was not willingly done.

The participants may have appeared to be deliberately drawing attention to their appearance but were often more likely to be attempting to deflect the attention of others. Giddens argues that 'dress is a means of self-display, but also relates directly to concealment/revelation in respect of personal biographies: it connects convention to basic aspects of identity' (1991: 63). In this case the participants did, of course, adhere to many conventions of the feminine body: the very fact that they wore clothes, did their hair and wore make-up ties them to bodily conventions. However, the overall appearance that they deployed drew attention to itself because it was unconventional; in many ways their appearance fitted into Russo's definitions of the grotesque (1995: 14), drawing attention to it because of their tattoos or dyed hair, or their clothes. But the women in this study consciously controlled their appearance to make a spectacle of themselves, an exhibit, and said that they felt this lent them a *'protective layer'* (Gwendolin) or *'armour'* (Delilah); or, as Morgan said, she knew that her appearance would save her from the sexist, negative attention of townie men. This method of drawing attention away from themselves and to their appearance is a way of creating what Giddens calls a 'protective cocoon', fashioned through the appearances and routines that individuals follow in which to feel 'safe' – it is more than just a way to prevent bodily harm but also protects the 'normality' that the individual has created and maintains for herself (1991: 126–9). Whilst attracting attention, many of the participants cheerfully said that they would, and did, look back at people who stared at them; they felt their appearance protected them in ways a more traditional appearance (they said blouses, short skirts and high heels) would not and so felt able to hold the gaze of the potentially hostile observer. 'Men look at women. Women watch themselves being looked at.

This determines not only the relationship of men to women, but the relationship of women to themselves' (Wolf, 1990: 42). Although arguably the participants did not challenge Berger's views on the gaze (in that they were watching themselves being looked at), it is, however, not a traditionally female response in that women are still often expected to modestly/shyly avert their gaze rather than stare back. Morgan's description of her experience of other people's perceptions to her appearance, and her attitude to them, echoed that of many other participants:

> *I see people looking at me in the street and some of them are smiling and that makes me smile and some of them aren't smiling and that makes me smile even more. I think it's funny ... I think a lot of people are challenged by that. Certainly a lot of blokes are, trendy blokes, townies, I get it all the time in town, walking down the street, 'Ooh, look at 'er'. Cos I'm not doing what a lot of people think women should do to make themselves attractive. You know, I am possibly going out of my way to be the opposite of that.*

Not only did the women '*give them something to look at*' (Claudia), they also said that if people were going to look at them it might as well be '*so that I know why they are looking*' (Eloise). They were willing to be friendly and to discuss their tattoos or their piercings with people who were interested and courteous. However, if someone was rude or aggressive, which seemed to be fairly common, the participants drew on a number of different diversionary or reactionary tactics; from being unresponsive and evasive through a '*stony silence*' (Claudia, Bee, Sparkle, Zeb), to arguing back and actually responding by physically fighting back (Kiki, Eloise, Jody and Vash) or, if all else failed, running away (Lara, Eloise, Vash, Kiki). Their bodies did indeed become 'the site of struggle to define beauty' (Tate, 1999: 33) but they were willing to enter into this struggle because they felt their appearance empowered them.

## Women Getting Older

Ussher discusses feminist performance art which:

> showed a performance of a woman continually applying layers of make-up as she sits in front of a mirror. The artists described this as: 'the pain of aging, of losing beauty, the pain of competition with other women. We want to deal with the way women are intimidated by the culture to constantly maintain their beauty and the feeling of desperation and helplessness once this beauty is lost.' (1997: 144)

There were a number of major contradictions when the participants reflected on ageing as 'alternative' women which bring to mind Ussher's description. These were mainly based around their laments that they had 'toned down' their appearance, were aware of the appearance of other women (policing them for wearing clothes and make-up inappropriate for their age), and said that they felt their life (and their appearance) had been better when they were younger. In contrast, they also claimed that they had never felt better, had more confidence at this age and intended to break barriers and challenge assumptions about ageing women as they themselves aged. In Chapter 7, I argued that the women in this study intended to age 'differently' but were increasingly aware of the limiting power of age categories (such as more modest clothing, or more subtle hair styling and make-up). They found that they were increasingly being bound by cultural limitations attached to age – or were simply becoming more aware of them. For example:

[Be] *aware that as your body ages it does change and you own it, it is yours and society has no right to say that we should all be a young Barbie doll. So even though I am very insecure about my body I still have active desires and I am still actively desired so that, to me, is an irony in itself.* (Gemini)

The subject of age unpicked the possibilities of unconventionality, revealing its limitations, and ageing emerged as the primary concern of many of my interviewees. After all, what could signal to us more effectively the constructed nature of the gendered body than the limitations and difficulties faced by the elderly? Overall, the reactions of the participants to the spectre of themselves as elderly women revealed a fear of prevailing negative attitudes. One main example of how their fear manifested itself was their repeated use of the term 'mutton dressed as lamb', using it to describe other women they had watched, or saying that they wished to guard against becoming 'mutton dressed as lamb' themselves. Seven participants mentioned a particular 'mad cat-woman' stereotype (the lonely spinster/widow with many cats) with both fear and pity; four defiantly claimed to wish to become this type of woman. Interestingly, this stereotype does remain one of the few accepted, although ridiculed, options for an elderly woman to live alone, dressing and living unconventionally.

Mainstream representations of ageing women were a preoccupation with several participants, and restrictions of what is inappropriate to women in the mainstream obviously still seeped into the understandings of the participants, despite their wish to remain distanced from traditional forms of femininity. The quest for age-defying creams and exercise regimes continues, and the numbers of women having plastic surgery continues to rise – only one participant said she would like to have cosmetic surgery but most said they used creams or exercised. Several also pointed out that the perceptions about the ceiling on the chronological age of a woman's ability to be attractive has been lengthened, citing the examples of various female celebrities.[5] However, attractive 'older' women are still subject to narrow expectations about what is feminine and sexy, what is acceptable or possible, and have to keep themselves exercised, snipped, polished and preened to present an appropriate female body that fulfils all those expectations. For example, there was considerable media interest in Demi Moore when she appeared in the second Charlie's Angels film (2003). Much of the newspaper coverage, which focused on her body and how much surgery and intensive exercise she had endured to achieve it, stressed the fact that Moore was forty years old (and a mother of three children). My interviewees appeared to be fighting against being intimidated about the possibility of their looks 'fading' and yet were most anxious that their ageing would have the power to compromise their ability to remain alternative – something which they had so far successfully resisted through the delicate balance of the strategies I outlined above. Several pointed out that there would be numerous women with multiple body modifications, as if they hoped that this fact would make it more acceptable and would challenge ideas about what was appropriate for elderly women.

General definitions of subcultures remain too youth-oriented (and, to an extent, too gendered) to contain women such as my participants: for example, although both Thornton (1995) and Muggleton (2000) do 'add in' the experience of young women, the focus remains on teenagers and those in their early twenties. My interviewees acknowledged that subcultures are spaces for teenagers and young adults, a space for them to safely experiment with rebellion and difference. For example, as Claudia states:

*I think as you get older you tend to be like, you know, being able to say stuff the world really. I can cope with not being able to do things. But if you're younger you can't, you're like 'Oh no, I can't possibly!' You see a lot of girls going out together and ... they daren't look different. So I think you accept it more as you get older ... you tend to worry less about what other people think as well.*

But they were also insistent that they could not just grow out of being alternative since this was more than rebellion, it was a way of life. By the time the participants had reached an age where they had finished experimenting, they felt they had drifted away from the more formal, organised/social aspects of the subculture, and this is reflected in the places where they lived, worked and socialised (their 'own little worlds', which existed parallel to mainstream society and from which they would venture as little as possible). Other commitments had drawn their energies away from their appearance: for example, Zeb did not have to time to manage her appearance to the same level any more because she was working; Vash had only relatively recently started to concentrate on her appearance again after the birth of her son; and Diz said she would be less 'extreme' if she were to have children (which echoed the policy Claudia adopted when her daughter was small, saying that people took you more seriously as a mother if you looked 'normal'). So, although the commitment to their appearance may be forced to fluctuate due to life changes, these changes were seen to be only temporary and did not change their overall view of themselves as alternative. Brake suggests that the term 'youth culture' is approached as referring to those who are "youthful" in the sense that they are the domain of the young in outlook rather than merely the chronologically young' (1985: 23). This is an aspect of an alternative identity that some of the participants commented on: they felt younger than they actually were, they felt that they looked younger than they thought they would when they reached this age, or they reported that other people had commented that they did not look their age. Because of its close links with those who are chronologically young, their alternative appearance imbued them with the false confidence of being younger than they were – which may have explained their difficulties in facing up to their ageing.

Finally, I would like to outline a possible study of older and elderly women who go to the very extremes of traditional femininity (an example of this is Barbara Cartland's make-up and wearing of pink), thus actually becoming transgressive in the process. There are many fixed ideas about how women should tone down and be appropriate for their age as they get older and women who go to the extremes of 'fluffy' femininity can arguably be seen to be resisting and rebelling. The tensions lie in the fact that they are resisting through very traditional feminine aspects of appearance, and are possibly unconscious of the effect of the end result. The difficulty would be how to collect such a sample. Would these women define themselves in the ways mentioned above? Where are they? If one could collect the sample a great deal of delicacy would be required, but it would add much to a body of work which often concentrates on how elderly women suffer as they age, for example, accumulating poverty (Gannon, 1999) and being ignored in health studies (Friedan, 1993). Whilst there have been several studies of older women's leisure (for example, Green *et al.*, 1990), only Furman's (1997) account of a beauty shop attempts to study how older women manage beauty and appearance.

## Shifts and Changes

During the time of the research (the latter half of the 1990s) there was a considerable societal shift of the massive expansion in the popularity and availability of the internet. Its growth was rapid and began during the time I was interviewing, facilitated by the creation of internet service providers (ISPs) such as Freeserve. This development is possibly a major limitation to this work in that the internet can be seen as a liberatory and comprehensive communication tool for those who can afford it and yet only two participants (Sparkle and Eloise) mentioned the internet (although it was clear that at least three others did use it). As a source of support and information the internet has surpassed the resources previously available, as none of the plethora of women's magazines on offer address the different and very particular interests and foci of 'alternative' women. As Wolf points out, a magazine's 'function is to provide readers with a comfortable sense of community and pride in their identity ... adornment is a great part of female culture' (1990: 56) and yet the participants would not be able to fit 'comfortably' in the community of mainstream, fashionable, traditionally feminine glossy magazines. The sort of adornment the participants preferred was not generally the same as that featured in the magazines. 'The ideals and fantasies offered to women are points of orientation for the realisation of a gendered self ... To this end, the media have provided the means for promoting desirable images and icons of femininity, because they can be endlessly reproduced and widely consumed ... a particular recipe for femininity' (Craik, 1994: 73). Although widely consumed, this particular recipe is one the participants did not wish to reproduce. Therefore, while only Sparkle mentioned searching for websites (in this case, 'grrl' websites), no other participant mentioned being aware of the myriad of websites about, for example, 'alternative' or 'indie' music and fashions or body modifications. Some time after I interviewed her, Flong contacted me to give me her tattooing studio's new website address and two other participants recently emailed me to say they now had email addresses. What would the impact have been on the interviews and the interviewees had the internet been more widespread when I interviewed them? Arguably, the effect would be minimal but it might have made two differences to methodological matters. Contacting the participants might have been somewhat easier if I could have emailed them instead of constantly trying to catch them in when I rang. Additionally, I could have sent the transcript of their interviews by email – but this is something I do not believe I would have done anyway as I preferred to send them a hard copy.

However, the internet may now complement or facilitate the collection of participants. I did consider trying to advertise for respondents on-line at the beginning of the research (using message boards, instant messages and chatrooms) but the fact that most people did not have access at that time meant that this precluded the internet as a comprehensive form of sampling. Users of messaging and chatrooms might also have responded even though they did not fulfil the requirements of the research (being female, over twenty-five and considering themselves to be resisting traditional types of femininity), thus wasting a considerable amount of time. Or, worse, if I never found out that the response was merely a hoax, the data could have severely undermined the veracity of the entire research. I also considered the possibilities and problems of conducting interviews by email, the rationale being that more women from outside Yorkshire (and, indeed, the UK) would be able to participate in the research. I envisioned their participation as an extended form of narrative where participants replied by writing answers to questions, and concluded that there was no guarantee that the respondent was even either female or 'alternative'. As Selwyn and Robson (1998) point out, the speed and temporary nature of email lend it a 'certain ephemerality which may compromise its effectiveness as a research tool'. The exclusionary nature of this kind of response (that some women may be unable to write fluently or that only particular social groups would be able to own a computer) also made me uncomfortable and I disagree with Selwyn and Robson's assertion that the medium is one which 'sets up a democratisation of exchange'. The drawback of few people having access to the internet has now significantly changed, with an estimated third to a half of the population having regular access (Nua Surveys, 2001). I feel that at least collecting and contacting participants (although not interviewing them remotely) would be much more possible through the profileration of UK feminist and 'grrl', not to mention goth and other 'alternative', resources and sites now available. 'Email's lack of verbal interaction is an obvious limit to its use as an interviewing tool' (Selwyn and Robson, 1998) and for this reason I would still not attempt to conduct any interviews via email.

Feminism, and women in general, were issues which divided the participants, with most of them saying they were not feminists. They appeared to equate the term femininity with the same negativity that they associated with feminism. Both words held the same restrictive connotations for them. Those who did define themselves as feminists were the women who had undertaken some form of further or higher education and saw feminism as an inevitable by-product of being a woman. Their appearance was linked to their feminism but was not only a way to express their politics: it was more an expression of their personalities and feelings about a range of issues connected to, but also apart from, feminism. 'Dress is often itself a political statement ... It can be taken as a mode whereby politics is aestheticised – that is, given an aesthetic expression' (Wilson, 1994: 108), and all of the participants said that their appearance was, at least in part, done for personal pleasure and aesthetic reasons. It was not always about resisting or fighting or challenging something. The term 'grrl' now offers a much less vilified euphemism for modern politicised feminism, primarily through websites and fanzines, often produced by and for girls and young women (Leonard, 1998) (only one participant mentioned the term 'grrl'). Often most of the participants, even those who were feminists, said that they felt they had more in common with 'alternative' men rather than other women in general. A twin study of 'alternative' men may reveal if this evidences an overall attitude which is 'highly cohesive [and] group-centred' (Muggleton, 2000: 162), or is more problematic, revealing more about femininity and its relation to masculinity. In a comparison study of men who continue to 'resist', the question would be, are they also resisting a traditionally gendered appearance? For example, are they seen as less 'transgressive' or rebellious the women of the same age? How do they negotiate resisting aspects of mainstream masculinities such as being a football fan, when football often seems to threaten to saturate the media?

There has been a sea change in the mainstream fashion for body modifications since I finished the interviews. At the time of the interviews, facial and body piercing had become fashionable with *'Joe Bloggs in the street'* (as Flong put it); thus there was a palpable feeling of resentment amongst the participants that this element of their 'alternative' appearance had been co-opted, and a corresponding feeling that they needed to push back the boundaries more and go much further with their own body modifications. Now, in late 2003, the fashion has receded significantly in the mainstream with tongue and belly-button piercings remaining the most common amongst young girls. Eyebrow, nose and lip piercings are now much less visible than they were only a few years ago[6] and this, I imagine, will have come as a great relief to many of the participants, particularly Delilah, Louise, Jody, Lara and Vash, who all mentioned the fashion.

The major findings of my work were the number of conflicts and strategies managed daily by the participants in their efforts to maintain an acceptable (to themselves) degree of femininity whilst also maintaining an alternative appearance, which they perceived as automatically eroding or threatening their femininity. Additionally, I have highlighted how ageing has an impact on alternative women in many similar – but also many different – ways. This is something which is missing from many accounts of both subcultures and ageing, which tend to concentrate, respectively, on young people (primarily teens) and on traditionally feminine women. As the women in my study illustrated, they find themselves increasingly bound by cultural expectations (possible because they never entirely distanced themselves from what was 'in fashion'), and the boundaries which they had attempted to challenge (if not to change) narrow again as they get older. In some ways, the participants are liable to be more negatively affected by the ageing process as their appearance does not hold broad social meaning: an old woman with pink hair and multiple tattoos is more visible and would be seen as more grotesque than an old woman who has retained her own version of traditional femininity. My question at the outset was whether these narratives would illustrate whether or not appearance is a vital component in gendered identities and a way to resist, a 'breaking out of structured obedience ... [an] escape from assigned roles' (Kuhn, 1997: 229), and in some ways it clearly was: the participants felt they had escaped from what they saw as the restrictions of a traditionally feminine appearance. However, they did not see femininity as some overarching and rather menacing orthodoxy but, instead, as something which they had a right to and constantly sought to integrate with their appearance. Their own scattered versions of 'subculture' offered a multiplicitous and paradoxical approach to opposition and 'difference' with no central manifesto and, in some cases, an avowed distancing from female-centred ideas or activities. Thus, the accounts of these women provided more variegated readings of both resistance and femininity.

# Notes

## Chapter 1. Growing Up but Staying 'Freaky': An Introduction

1. Feral Cheryl is a 'hippy ... anti-fashion doll ... [who] needs NO fashion wardrobe ... is 34″ tall with dark hair, a realistic body shape and pubic hair' (accessed 4 September 2001) http://www.feralcheryl.com.au

## Chapter 2. Background Reading

1. The classic, and crudest, example (and negative stereotype) is the woman who 'bats her eyelashes' to get what she wants.

2. Other variations on this theme include the head of the house being called 'the one who wears the trousers' and a pompous or boring person being called a 'stuffed shirt'.

3. Davis also uses the same phrase: 'fashion has in Western society been a quintessential component of the societal machinery – or ruling discourse, as Foucault (1980) would have it – by which women have been kept "in their place" ' (1992: 176).

4. Others, such as Evans and Thornton (1989) and Barnard (1996) accept this definition but I prefer Davis's account because folk or traditional dress does not *respond* to fashion.

5. In the *Guardian Weekend* (8 December 2001) Soueif explains that (in Cairo)

> hijab [is] a long, loose garment topped with a large plain scarf securely fastened so no hair, ears or neck show through ... The full niqab [is] a black hijab outfit with a thick, black cloth over the face and a narrow slit to see through ... [which] says loud and clear: '... I am in opposition to this government'. It takes guts to do this in these days of arbitrary detentions and torture. (2001: 32)

6. Certainly, the women in this study demonstrated many unconscious, paradoxical attitudes to their identities, which are discussed in the empirical chapters.

7. Other terms used to indicate a 'townie' are 'trendies' (although this is now a dated term, it was used by one participant), to reflect contempt for their regard for mainstream fashions, and 'pieheads'. The latter term has quite a broad meaning. It refers to the stereotypical habit of 'townies' to emerge drunk from clubs or pubs, eat take-away food and get into fights, and so signals the user's disdain for this kind of behaviour. It also refers to the fact that 'townies' are not thought (by alternative

people) to be sensitive or reflective enough to be vegetarians/vegans. Both meanings of the term indicate the divisions of behaviour and lifestyle between the two groups whilst relying on rigidly drawn divisions and stereotypes.

8. It can also refer to a thing or occurrence that is markedly unusual or irregular, for example 'freak weather conditions'. More recently, the term has been used to indicate being an enthusiast for something, for example, 'salsa freak' would refer to someone who loves salsa dancing. It is also used to refer to a drug user or addict: 'a speed freak'.

9. Those of the participants in this study who defined themselves as 'alternative' said that the term was, to them, an umbrella term for 'anything which is not conventional'.

## Chapter 3. Negotiating Fluffy Femininities

1. The term lad ('laddism', 'lad culture') to denote a particular type of young man has a recent cultural history of its own and is the subject of some of the scholarship on masculinities (e.g. Segal, 1990; Robinson, 1996). Its offshoot (briefly) was the laddette: hard-drinking, 'un-fluffy' young women and a 'shallow model of gender equality' (Whelehan, 2000: 9). None of the participants said they were laddettes or referred to the term.

2. The dictionary definition of 'fluffy' includes 'fluff, a soft down ... a girl (*coll.*)'. The definition of 'frothy' includes 'froth, foam: chatter, something frivolous or trivial ... empty: unsubstantial', and of 'girl' includes ' a young unmarried woman: a woman irrespective of age: a sweetheart (*coll.*): a maid servant ... *adj.* Girlie, girly (of magazines, photographs, etc.) showing nude or scantily clad young women' (*CED*, 1992).

3. I find this loose definition of 'woman' problematic in that it could equally involve choosing not to 'manage' one's appearance, not having children and having relationships with women or remaining celibate.

4. But the difference between masquerade and 'flashing femininity' is that the latter is done consciously with a particular intent.

## Chapter 4. How To Be a Fairy Princess

1. For example, Rose Princess, Princess Barbie, Dream Wedding, Sugar Plum Princess and Midnight Moon Princess.

2. Several participants described themselves as tomboys, with Claudia saying she was still a tomboy. For example, Gemini said that, although her favourite play was as a fairy princess, her mother dressed her in 'sensible playing clothes' which made her look like a boy, which was echoed in various ways by other participants such as Eloise, Sparkle and Gwendolin.

3. Toni Morrison's novel *The Bluest Eye* (1979) is about just this sort of destructive sense of 'failure' when a little Black girl, Pecola, prays for her eyes to turn blue like her privileged blonde classmates.

4. Apart from clothes shopping, Delilah spent at least £80 a month on a facial and having her hair done. She spent at least an hour and a half a day on her face and hair: in the evening cleansing, toning, plucking her eyebrows; in the morning, doing her hair and make-up.

5. Talking about the paper patterns of the 1960s and 1970s, with three choices of outfit on the front, Lara said her mother's attitude was that Lara could be cut to fit the ideal image of the daughter she wanted! *'I almost see* [my mother] – *she didn't really, its just my imagination – looking at me over the top of one of those patterns with her eyes glittering and thinking 'aaah, well, we'll fit her into this'. Like I was a bolt of cloth to cut to size ...* [she was always] *breathing down my neck, looking into my wardrobe and sighing ... it makes me annoyed just thinking about it.'*

## Chapter 5. Categories of Unconventional

1. 'The "Macaronis" had been fops whose dress had been an exaggeration of frills and brocade, powder and paint ... The role of the dandy implied an intense preoccupation with self and self-presentation ... his devotion to an ideal of dress that sanctified under-statement inaugurated an epoch not of no fashions for men, but of fashions that put cut and fit before ornament, colour and display' (Wilson, 1985: 180).

2. See Chapter 3 for a discussion of how some of the participants in this study adapt some aspects of a Pre-Raphaelite romanticism.

3. As Scarlett O'Hara found, but did not observe, in *Gone With the Wind*: 'A widow had to wear hideous black dresses without even a touch of braid to enliven them, no flower or ribbon or lace or even jewellery, except onyx mourning brooches or necklaces made from the deceased's hair. And the black crêpe veil on her bonnet had to reach her knees, and only after three years of widowhood could it be shortened to shoulder length' (Mitchell, 1974: 134).

4. Social mores or what Veblen (1994) called 'conspicuous consumption', that is, full mourning could be adopted only by those who could afford to do so, thus signalling one's means to do so.

5. A return to 'elegant femininity ... [with] longer, fuller skirts, the waist was small and the shape of the bust was lifted and accentuated, giving the modern hour-glass figure' (Thesander, 1997: 155). The amount of material used to create the look would simply not have been available during the war.

6. For a case-study of punk women, see Evans and Thornton (1989: ch. 2) (several participants said they started out as punks).

7. Every one of the participants quoted in this section were wearing all black on the day of their interview.

8. The idea of comfort as being important to an 'alternative' look despite the obvious discomforts is discussed further in Chapter 6.

9. A full discussion of 'toning down' follows in Chapter 7.

10. There is also, as Davis points out, an important difference between anti-

fashion and fashion indifference in that the former is aware of 'in' fashions and the latter is not and does not care (1992: 161).

11. See Table A1.4 in Appendix 1 and the participant profiles in Appendix 2 for a full list.

12. For example, Foote includes the account of one journalist who 'accused women of wearing shirt collars, and expressed his conviction that women would continue to masculinize their appearance by strapping down their pantaloons and wearing wellingtons. Carrying canes and smoking cigars, he said, could not be far behind' (1989: 149).

13. See Bullough and Bullough (1993: ch. 7), Rolley (1990) writing about Radclyffe Hall and Una Troubridge, Garber (1992: 147–61) on the 'masculine' woman, and Schuyf (1993), which includes 'the politics of wearing trousers', for accounts of how these women resisted ideologies about both women's appearance and sexualities.

14. Vash, Zeb, Miss Pink, Claudia, Bee, Sparkle, Lara and Kiki.

15. All of the following participants specifically stated that their occupations 'allowed' them to dress as they did: Delilah (artist), Miss Pink and Flong (tattoo artists), Claudia (body-piercer), Gwendolin (hairdresser), Louise (artist and youth worker), Eloise (student), Vash (student), Edie (stallholder) and Janet (student).

## Chapter 6. 'More Like Torture than Love'

1. A full list of each participant's body modifications can be found in Table A1.5 in Appendix 1.

2. For example, Chernin (1983), Brownmiller (1984), Wilson (1985), Chapkis (1986) and Wolf (1990) all consider how women experience their bodies.

3. DeMello's work encompasses some non-Western history of tattooing but primarily concentrates on the USA.

4. Her attitude echoed that of a tattooist quoted by DeMello: 'if they're there just for total decoration then it's like a paint job on a car, it doesn't tell you much ... If they don't tell a story that involves you emotionally ... then they're not a valid tattoo' (2000: 193).

5. A 'tie-sign', a phrase first coined by Goffman (1984), provides information about a desired social identity and indicates 'membership' of a (subcultural) group. Generally, tie-signs have only one meaning and can be easily 'read' (for example, the Hamish, Rastafarians and Hare Krishnas all wear/use 'tie-signs' which signify their membership and belonging. The tie-sign is used as a means of expression and marks out members from non-members, and is a conscious decision to denote commitment (Rubinstein, 1995: 208). Body modifications are a conscious effort to signal that the bearer is 'alternative'.

6. Kiki said of the symbol on her hand: *'It means paw. Hand, paw or foot'* and she uses the same symbol to sign her artwork.

7. The post-modern aspect can be applied in this case because of the self-con-

sciousness of their girly and anti-girly stance. That is, a flowery tattoo is both consciously feminine and sending up norms of femininity.

8. An example of this might be the breast cancer awareness campaigns trying to
persuade women to conduct regular breast examinations. A campaign in 2001/2
suggested that a woman might be more willing or able if her partner did it for her!

## Chapter 7. Defying the Crone?

1. However, talking about 'ageing' in such a general way was quite problematic
as 'old age can encompass a span of more than thirty years, and ... the old are not
one homogenous group. They exhibit great variety in the way they live and during
this lengthy period of retirement can experience marked changes' (Ford and
Sinclair, 1987: 3). Because of this I constantly tried to clarify what stage of life the
participants were talking about; for example, middle age, old age and elderly were
all defined differently. Generally, though, the participants seemed to discuss middle
age as anything from 50 to 60, old/er women as retired women (over 60) and
elderly women as being in their late 70s upwards.

2. The Wicked Queen/Stepmother in *Snow White* experienced this when she
asked her mirror who was the fairest of them all: her mirror no longer reflected
back herself but, instead, a younger – and therefore more attractive – version of
herself in her stepdaughter.

3. There have been several studies of the word and its power to chastise and
belittle, for example, Lees, 1993; Sharpe, 1994; and Ussher, 1997.

4. This paradox of taming/maintaining is considered further in 'Reflections and
Conclusions'.

5. See Chapter 6 for Gemini's comments on her attitude to her body.

6. Claudia said that after a certain point it is easier to say how many hours'
worth of tattooing you have on your body than how many tattoos.

7. She had kept a taped diary of her thoughts and experiences and, later, had
written it up. She had also insisted that the hospital give her her womb so that she
could plant it in her garden under a mulberry tree.

8. DeMello talked to a male tattooist who said that in the 1950s only women
who were 'skags' and 'dykes' had tattoos (2000: 63).

## Chapter 8. Reflections and Conclusions

1. And often there is little choice for women who do not wish to buy unscented
or 'plain' soaps and deodorants, especially as the 'male' equivalents are also usually
strongly scented with more 'manly' fragrances.

2. Definitions of 'glamour' include 'a magic spell' (Kramarae and Treichler, 1985:
177) and 'the supposed influence of a charm on the eyes, making them see things
as fairer than they are ... fascination: enchantment: witchery ... groomed beauty
and studied charm ... bewitching, alluring' (*CED*, 1992).

3. The requirements of the study were that the participants were over twenty-five

years old and considered themselves to be resisting traditional femininity. See Appendix 3 for the leaflet with which I originally collected participants.

4. Steele (1997a) points out that hair is still an under-researched area. 'Hair histories' could provide a detailed way to 'map' changing gender roles and contexts.

5. For example, Marilyn Monroe died at the age of thirty-six and was seen to be just about 'over the hill'. In contrast, modern celebrities, such as Pamela Anderson, Gillian Anderson, Lucy Lui and various supermodels (all in their 30s), or Susan Sarandon, Sigourney Weaver and Sharon Stone (in their 40s or 50s), all manage to maintain an extended period of being attractive and sexualised – but still within narrow and rigorous boundaries.

6. To check if my own perception about facial piercings was correct I recently went into three body-piercing studios, two in Leeds and one in Sheffield, to ask whether they had found that the 'fashion' had receded. In all three studios the piercers (two men, one woman) asserted that they were very aware that far fewer townies or students now had facial piercings and that these particular piercings had devolved primarily back to 'true' alternative people and 'freaks' in general.

# Bibliography

Abrams, M. (1959) *The Teenager Consumer*, London: London Press Exchange.

Ainley, R. (ed.) (1998), *New Frontiers of Spaces, Bodies and Gender*, London: Routledge.

Alcott, L.M. (1994), *Little Women*, London: Penguin.

Ash, J. and E. Wilson (eds) (1992), *Chic Thrills: A Fashion Reader*, London: Pandora Press.

Ash, J. and L. Wright (eds) (1988), *Components of Dress. Design, Manufacturing, and Image-making in the Fashion Industry*, London: Routledge.

Atkinson, R. and J. Flint (2001), 'Accessing Hidden and Hard-to-reach Populations: Snowball Research Strategies', *Social Research Update*, 33, summer, Guildford: University of Surrey.

Babad, E.Y., Max Birnbaum and Kenneth D. Benne (1983), *The Social Self: Group Influences on Personal Identity*, London: Sage.

Banerjee, M. and D. Miller, *The Sari*, Oxford: Berg.

Banim, M. and A. Guy (2001) 'Dis/Continued Selves: Why Do Women Keep Clothes They No Longer Wear?', in A. Guy, E. Green and M. Banim(eds), *Through the Wardrobe: Women's Relationships with Their Clothes*, Oxford: Berg.

Banks, I. (2000), *Hair Matters: Beauty, Power and Black Women's Consciousness*, New York: New York University Press.

Barnard, M. (1996), *Fashion as Communication*, London: Routledge.

Beatty, L. (2000), *Lillie Langtry. Manners, Masks and Morals*, London: Vintage.

Bell, J. (1987), *Doing Your Research Project*, Oxford: Open University Press.

Berger, J. (1972), *Ways of Seeing*, London: Penguin.

Berger, P.L. and T. Luckmann (1966), *The Social Construction of Reality*, London: Penguin.

Betterton, R. (ed.) (1987), *Looking On: Images of Femininity in the Visual Arts and Media*, London: Pandora.

Blackman, S.J. (1998), ' "Poxy Cupid!". An Sthnographic and Feminist Account of a Resistant Female Youth Culture: the New Wave Girls', in T. Skelton and G. Valentine (eds), *Cool Places: Geographies of Youth Cultures*, London: Routledge.

Blake, C.F. (2000), 'Foot-binding in Neo-Confucian China and the Appropriation of Female Labor', in L. Schiebinger (ed.), *Feminism and the Body*, Oxford: Oxford University Press.

Borden, I. (2001), *Skateboarding, Space and the City. Architecture and the Body*, Oxford: Berg.

Bordo, Susan R. (1989), 'The Body and the Reproduction of Femininity: A Feminist Appropriation of Foucault', in S. Bordo and A. Jaggar (eds), *Gender/Body/Knowledge: Feminist Reconstructions of Being and Knowing*, New Brunswick, NJ: Rutgers University Press.

—— (1993), *Unbearable Weight. Feminism, Western Culture and the Body*, London: University of California Press.

Bordo, Susan R. and A. Jaggar (eds) (1989), *Gender/Body/Knowledge: Feminist Reconstructions of Being and Knowing*, New Brunswick, NJ: Rutgers University Press.

Bourdieu, P. (1990), *Outline of a Theory of Practice*, Cambridge: Polity Press.

Braidiotti, R. (1996), 'Cyberfeminism with a Difference', *Technoscience*, 29, summer: 9–25.

Brake, M. (1985), *Comparative Youth Culture: The Sociology of Youth Culture and Youth Subcultures in America, Britain and Canada*, London: Routledge.

Breward, C., B. Conekin and C. Cox (eds) (2002), *The Englishness of English Dress*, Oxford: Berg.

Bristow, J. and A.R. Wilson (eds) (1994), *Activating Theory: Lesbian, Gay, Bisexual Politics*, London: Lawrence & Wishart

Brownmiller, S. (1984), *Femininity*, London: Paladin.

Brownmiller, S. (1986) *Against Our Will. Men, Women and Rape.* Harmondsworth: Pelican.

Bruzzi, S. (1997), *Undressing Cinema. Clothing and Identity in the Movies*, London: Routledge.

Bryer, R. (2000), *The History of Hair: Fashion and Fantasy Down the Ages*, London: Philip Wilson.

Bryson, V. (1999), *Feminist Debates. Issues of Theory and Political Practice*, London: Macmillan.

Bullough, V.L. and B. Bullough (1993), *Cross Dressing, Sex and Gender*, Philadelphia: University of Pennsylvania Press.

Burgess, R.G. (1984), *In the Field. An Introduction to Field Research*, London: Routledge.

Burkitt, T. (1991), *Social Selves: Theories of the Social Formation of Personality*, London: Sage.

Burman, B. (ed.) (1999), *The Culture of Sewing. Gender, Consumption and Home Dressmaking*, Oxford: Berg.

Butler, J. (1990), *Gender Trouble. Feminism and the Subversion of Identity*, London: Routledge.

Butler, J. (1993) *Bodies that Matter: On the Discursive Limits of Sex*, London: Routledge.

Bytheway, B. and J. Johnson (1998), 'The Sight of Age' in S. Nettleton and J. Watson (eds), *The Body in Everyday Life*, London: Routledge.

Cahill, S.E. (1989), 'Fashioning Males and Females: Appearance Management and the Social Reproduction of Gender', *Symbolic Interaction*, 12, (2): 281–98.

Cahill, S. and S. Riley (2001), 'Resistances and Reconciliations: Women and Body

Art', in A. Guy, E. Green and M. Banim (eds), *Through the Wardrobe: Women's Relationships with Their Clothes*, Oxford: Berg.

Campbell, B. (1998), *Diana, Princess of Wales. How Sexual Politics Shook the Monarchy*, London: The Women's Press.

Carter, M. (2003), *Fashion Classics from Carlyle to Barthes*, Oxford: Berg.

Cartledge, S. and J. Ryan (eds) (1985), *Sex and Love. New Thoughts on Old Contradictions*, London: The Women's Press.

Carver, T. and V. Mottier (eds) (1998), *Politics of Sexuality*, London: Routledge.

Chambers English Dictionary (CED) (1992), Edinburgh: W. & R. Chambers.

Chapkis, W. (1986), *Beauty Secrets: Women and the Politics of Appearance*, London: The Women's Press.

Charles, N. and F. Hughes-Freeland (eds) (1996), *Practising Feminism: Identity, Difference, Power*, London: Routledge.

Chernin, K. (1983), *Womansize: The Tyranny of Slenderness*, London: The Women's Press.

Clarke, A. and D. Miller (2002), 'Fashion and Anxiety', *Fashion Theory: The Journal of Dress, Body and Culture*, 6 (2): pp.191–214.

Coates, J. (1996), *Women Talk: Conversation Between Women Friends*, Oxford: Blackwell.

Cohen, S. (1979), *Folk Devils and Moral Panics*, London: Basil Blackwell.

Coles, F. (1999), 'Feminine Charms and Outrageous Arms', in J. Price and M. Shildrick (eds), *Feminist Theory and the Body*, Edinburgh: Edinburgh University Press.

Conboy, K., N. Medina and S. Stanbury (eds) (1997), *Writing on the Body. Female Embodiment and Feminist Theory*, New York: Columbia University Press.

Condor, S. (1989), 'Biting into the Future: Social Change and the Social Identity of Women' in S. Skevington and D. Baker (eds), *The Social Identity of Women*, London: Sage.

Connell, R.W. (1987) *Gender and Power*, Cambridge: Polity.

Cordwell, J. and R. Schwartz (eds) (1979), *The Fabrics of Culture: The Anthropology of Clothing and Adornment*, The Hague: Mouton Press.

Corrigan, P. (1979), *Schooling the Smash Street Kids*, London: Macmillan.

Craik, J. (1994), *The Face of Fashion: Cultural Studies in Fashion*, London: Routledge.

Crane, D. (1999), 'Clothing Behavior as Non-Verbal Resistance. Marginal Women and Alternative Dress in the Nineteenth Century', *Fashion Theory: The Journal of Dress, Body and Culture*. 3 (2): pp. 241–68.

Daly, S. and N. Wice (1995), *alt.culture - An A-Z of the 90s: Underground and Online*, London: Fourth Estate/Guardian Books.

Davies, B. (1989), *Frogs and Snails and Feminist Tales. Preschool Children and Gender*, Sydney: Allen & Unwin.

Davis, A. (1988), *Women, Race and Class*, London: The Women's Press.

Davis, F. (1992), *Fashion, Culture and Identity*, Chicago: Chicago University Press.

Davis, K. (ed.) (1997), *Embodied Practices. Feminist Perspectives on the Body*, London: Sage.

de Beauvoir, S. (1997) *The Second Sex*. London: Vintage.

de Groot, J. and M. Maynard (eds) (1993), *Women's Studies for the 90s: Doing Things Differently?* London: Macmillan.

Delano, P.D. (2000), 'Making Up for War: Sexuality and Citizenship in Wartime Culture', *Feminist Studies* (on line), spring (accessed 29–11–00), http://www. inform.umd.edu/EdRes/ReadingRoom/Newsletters/FemStud/

DeMello, M. (2000), *Bodies of Inscription: a Cultural History of the Modern Tattoo Community*, Durham, NC: Duke University Press.

DeMellow, M. and A.B. Govenar (1996), *Pierced Hearts and True Love: a Century of Drawings for Tattoos*, Honolulu, Hawaii; Hardy Marks Publications.

Denzin, N. (1997), *Interpretive Ethnography*, London: Sage.

Douglas, S. (1995), *Where the Girls Are: Growing Up Female with the Mass Media*, London: Penguin.

Douglas, M. (1991), *Purity and Danger*, London: Routledge.

Dryden, C. (1999), *Being Married, Doing Gender*, London: Routledge.

Du Gay, P., J. Evans and P. Redman (eds) (2000), *Identity: A Reader*, London: Sage.

Elkins, R. (1996), 'Career Path of the Male Femaler', in R. Ekins and D. King (eds), *Blending Genders. Social Aspects of Cross-dressing and Sex-changing*, London: Routledge.

—— (1997), *Male Femaling. A Grounded Theory Approach to Cross-dressing and Sex-changing*, London: Routledge.

Ekins, R. and D. King (eds) (1996), *Blending Genders. Social Aspects of Cross-dressing and Sex-changing*, London: Routledge.

El Guindi, F. (1999), *Veil. Modesty, Privacy, Resistance*, Oxford: Berg.

Entwhistle, J. and E. Wilson (eds) (2001), *Body Dressing*, Oxford: Berg.

Evans, C. (1997), 'Dreams That Only Money Can Buy… Or, The Shy Tribe in Flight from Discourse', *Fashion Theory: The Journal of Dress, Body and Culture*, 1 (2): 271–310.

—— (2001), 'The Enchanted Spectacle', *Fashion Theory: The Journal of Dress, Body and Culture*, 5 (3): pp. 271–310.

Evans, C. and M. Thornton (1991), 'Fashion, Representation, Femininity', *Feminist Review*, 38, summer.

—— (1989), *Women and Fashion: A New Look*, London: Quartet Books.

Fairhurst, E. (1998), ' "Growing Old Gracefully" as Opposed to "Mutton Dressed as Lamb": the Social Construction of Recognising Older Women', in S. Nettleton and J. Watson (eds), *The Body in Everyday Life*, London: Routledge.

Finch, J. (1993), ' "It's Great to Have Someone to Talk to": Ethics and Politics of Interviewing Women' (1984), in M. Hammersley (ed.), *Social Research. Philosophy, Politics and Practice*, London: Sage.

Finkelstein, J. (1991), *The Fashioned Self*, Oxford: Polity Press.

—— (1997), 'Chic Outrage and Body Politics', in K. Davis (ed.), *Embodied Practices. Feminist Perspectives on the Body*, London: Sage.

Fischer, L. (1997), 'Sunset Boulevard. Fading Stars', in M. Pearsall (ed.), *The Other Within Us. Feminist Explorations of Women and Aging*, Oxford: Westview Press.

Foote, S. (1989), 'Challenging Gender Symbols', in C.B. Kidwell and V. Steele (eds), *Men and Women: Dressing the Part*, Washington, DC: Smithsonian Institution Press.

Foote Whyte, W. (1943), *Street Corner Society: The Social Structure of an Italian Slum*, Chicago: University of Chicago Press.

Ford, J. and R. Sinclair (1987), *Sixty Years On: Women Talk About Old Age*, London: The Women's Press.

Foster, H.B. and D.C. Johnson (2003), *Wedding Dress Across Cultures*, Oxford: Berg.

Franz, C.E. and A.J. Stewart (eds) (1994), *Women Creating Lives: Identities, Resilience and Resistance*, Oxford: Westview Press.

Friedan, B. (1993), *The Fountain of Age*, London: Jonathan Cape.

Frith, S. (1984), *The Sociology of Youth*, London: Causeway Books.

Furman, F.K. (1997), *Facing the Mirror. Older Women and Beauty Shop Culture*, London: Routledge.

Gaines, J. (1990), 'Fabricating the Female Body', in J. Gaines and C. Herzog (eds), *Fabrications. Costume and the Female Body*, London: Routledge.

Gaines, J. and C. Herzog (eds) (1990), *Fabrications. Costume and the Female Body*, London: Routledge.

Gammon, L. and M. Marshment (eds) (1988), *The Female Gaze. Women as Viewers of Popular Culture*, London: The Women's Press.

Gannon, L.R. (1999), *Women and Aging. Transcending the Myths*, London: Routledge.

—— (2000), 'Psychological Well-being in Aging Women', in J.M. Ussher (ed.), *Women's Health. Contemporary International Perspectives*, Guildford: BPS Books.

Garber, M. (1992), *Vested Interests: Cross-dressing and Cultural Anxiety*, London: Routledge.

Gardner, K. (2002), *Age, Narrative and Migration. The Life Course and Life Histories of Bengali Elders in London*, Oxford: Berg.

Garrison, E.K. (2000), 'U.S. Feminism – Grrrl Style! Youth (Sub)Cultures and the Technologies of the Third Wave', *Feminist Studies* (on line), spring (accessed 29–11–00). http://www.inform.umd.edu/EdRes/ReadingRoom/Newsletters/FemStud/

Gelder, K. and S. Thornton (eds) (1997), *The Subcultures Reader*, London: Routledge.

Giddens, A. (1991), *Modernity and Self-identity. Self and Society in the Late Modern Age*, London: Polity Press.

Gilbert, S.M. and S. Gubar (1986), 'The Queen's Looking Glass', in J. Zipes (ed.), *Don't Bet on the Prince*, Aldershot: Gower.

Glover, D. and C. Kaplan (2000), *Genders*, London: Routledge.

Goffman, E. (1964), *Stigma*, London: Penguin.

—— (1984), *The Presentation of Self in Everyday Life*, London: Penguin.

Gottlieb, J. and G. Wald (1994), 'Smells like Teen Spirit: Riot Grrls, Revolution and Independent Rock' in T. Rose and A. Ross (eds), *Microphone Fiends: Youth Music and Youth Culture*, London: Routledge.

Green, E., S. Hebron and D. Woodward (1990), *Women's Leisure, What Leisure?* London: Macmillan.

Greer, G. (1999), *The Whole Woman*, London: Doubleday.

Gregory, J. and S. Lees (1999), *Policing Sexual Assault*, London: Routledge.

Gregson N. and L. Crewe (2003), *Second-hand Cultures*, Oxford: Berg.

Gregson, N., K. Brooks and L. Crewe (2001), 'Bjorn Again? Rethinking 70s Revivalism through the Reappropriation of 70s Clothing', in *Fashion Theory: The Journal of Dress, Body and Culture*, 5 (1): 3–27.

Griffin, C. (1989), ' "I'm not a Women's Libber, but ...": Feminism, Consciousness and Identity', in S. Skevington and D. Baker (eds), *The Social Identity of Women*, London: Sage.

—— (1993), *Representations of Youth: The Study of Youth and Adolescence in Britain and America*, Oxford: Polity Press.

Grogan, S. (1999), *Body Image. Understanding Body Dissatisfaction in Men, Women and Children*, London: Routledge.

Guy, A. and M. Banim (2000), 'Personal Collections: Women's Clothing use and Identity', *Journal of Gender Studies*, 9 (3), 2000: 13–327.

Guy, A., E. Green and M. Banim (eds) (2001), *Through the Wardrobe: Women's Relationships with Their Clothes*, Oxford: Berg.

Hall, S. and P. du Gay (eds) (1996), *Questions of Cultural Identity*, Oxford: Sage.

Hall, S. and T. Jefferson (eds) (1976), *Resistance Through Rituals: Youth Subcultures in Post-war Britain*, London: Hutchinson.

Hammersley, M. (ed.) (1993), *Social Research. Philosophy, Politics and Practice*, London: Sage.

Hansen, K. Tranberg (2000), 'Other People's Clothes? The International Second-hand Clothing Trade and Dress Practices in Zambia', *Fashion Theory: The Journal of Dress, Body and Culture*, 4 (3): 245–74.

Hardin, M. (1999), 'Mar(k)ing the Objected Body: A Reading of Contemporary Female Tattooing', *Fashion Theory: The Journal of Dress, Body and Culture*, 3 (1): 81–108.

Hawkes, G.L. (1995), 'Dressing-up - Cross-Dressing and Sexual Dissonance', *Journal of Gender Studies*, 4 (3): 261–70

—— (1996), *A Sociology of Sex and Sexuality*, Milton Keynes: Open University Press.

Hebdige, D. (1979), *Subculture: The Meaning of Style*, London: Methuen.

Heimel, C. (1991), *If You Can't Live Without Me Why Aren't You Dead Yet?* London: Fourth Estate.

Hekman, S. (1990), *Gender and Knowledge. Elements of a Postmodern Feminism*, Boston: Northeastern University Press.

Hill Collins, P. (1990), *Black Feminist Thought: Knowledge, Consciousness and the Politics of Empowerment*, London: Routledge.

Hodkinson, P. (2002), *Goth Identity, Style and Subculture*, Oxford: Berg.

Hollander, A. (1993), *Seeing Through Clothes*, Berkeley, CA: University of California Press.

hooks, b. (1990), *Yearning: Race, Gender and Cultural Politics*, Boston: South End Press.

Hollands, R.G. (1995), *Friday Night, Saturday Night: Youth Cultural Identification in the Post-industrial City*, Newcastle upon Tyne: Department of Social Policy, University of Newcastle.

Ingraham, C. (1999), *White Weddings. Romancing Heterosexuality in Popular Culture*, London: Routledge.

Irwin, S. (1995), *Rights of Passage: Social Change and the Transition from Youth to Adulthood*, London: Routledge.

Jackson, S. and S. Scott (eds) (1996), *Feminism and Sexuality. A Reader*, Edinburgh: Edinburgh University Press.

Jeffreys, S. (1996), 'Heterosexuality and the Desire for Gender', in D. Richardson (ed.) *Theorising Heterosexuality. Telling It Straight*, Oxford: Oxford University Press.

Jenkins, R. (1994), *Social Identity*, London: Routledge.

Johnson, K.K.P. and S.J. Lennon (eds) (1999), *Appearance and Power*, Oxford: Berg.

Johnson, K.K.P., S.J. Torntore and J.B. Eicher (2003), *Fashion Foundations. Early Writings on Fashion and Dress*, Oxford: Berg.

Kaiser, S. (1990), *The Social Psychology of Clothing and Personal Adornment*, London: Macmillan.

Kear, A. and D.L. Steinberg (eds) (1999), *Mourning Diana. Nation, Culture and the Performance of Grief*, London: Routledge.

Keenan, W.J.F. (ed.) (2001), *Dressed to Impress. Looking the Part*, Oxford: Berg.

Kellner, D. (1995), *Media Culture*, London: Routledge.

Kidwell, C. B. and V. Steele (eds) (1989), *Men and Women: Dressing the Part*, Washington, DC: Smithsonian Institution Press.

Kirkwood, C. (1993), 'Investing Ourselves: Use of Researcher Personal Response in Femininst Methodology', in J. de Groot and M. Maynard (eds), *Women's Studies for the 90s: Doing Things Differently?*, London: Macmillan.

Kitzinger, J. (1999), 'The Moving Power of Moving Images: Television Constructions of Princess Diana', in T. Walter (ed.), *The Mourning for Diana*, Oxford: Berg.

Klausmann, U., M. Meinzerin and G. Kuhn (eds) (1997), *Women Pirates and the Politics of the Jolly Roger*, Montreal: Black Rose Books.

König, R. (1973), *The Restless Image. A Sociology of Fashion*, London: Allen & Unwin.

Kramarae, C. and P.A. Treichler (1985), *A Feminist Dictionary*, London: Pandora Press.

Kuhn, G. (1997) 'Anarchism and Piracy', in U. Klausmann, M. Meinzerin and G. Kuhn (eds), *Women Pirates and the Politics of the Jolly Roger*, London: Black Rose Books.

Lancaster, W. (1995), *The Department Store: a Social History*, London: Pinter.

Lee, R.M. (1993), *Doing Research on Sensitive Topics*, London: Sage.

Lees, S. (1993), *Sugar and Spice: Sexuality and Adolescent Girls*, London: Penguin.

Leonard, M. (1997), ' "Rebel Girl, Yyou Are the Queen of My World": Feminism, "Subculture" and Grrrl Power' in S. Whiteley (ed.), *Sexing the Groove: Popular Music and Gender*, London: Routledge.

—— (1998), 'Paper Planes: Travelling the New Grrrl Geographies', in T. Skelton and G. Valentine (eds), *Cool Places. Geographies of Youth Cultures*, London: Routledge.

Lehnert, G. (1999), *Fashion. A Concise History*, London: Laurence King.

Leonard, R. and A. Burns (2000), 'The Paradox of Older Women's Health', in J.M. Ussher (ed.), *Women's Health. Contemporary International Perspectives*, Guildford: BPS Books.

Lieberman, M.K. (1986), ' "Some Day My Prince Will Come": Female Acculturation through the Fairy Tale', in J. Zipes, *Don't Bet on the Prince*, Aldershot: Gower.

Lieblich, A. and R. Josselson (1993), *The Narrative Study of Lives: Exploring Identity and Gender*, Thousand Oaks, CA: Sage.

Lyons, A.C. and C. Griffin (2000), 'Representations of Menopause and Women at Midlife', in J.M. Ussher (ed.), *Women's Health. Contemporary International Perspectives*, Guildford: BPS Books.

Macdonald, M. (1995), *Representing Women: Myths of Femininity in the Popular Media*, London: Edward Arnold.

McNay, L. (1992), *Foucault and Feminism. Power, Gender and the Self*, Oxford: Polity Press.

McRobbie, A. (ed.) (1989a), *Zoot Suits and Second-hand Dresses*, London: Macmillan.

—— (1989b) 'Second-hand Dresses and the Role of the Rag Market', in A. McRobbie (ed.), *Zoot Suits and Second-hand Dresses*, London: Macmillan.

—— (1991), *Feminism and Youth Culture. From Jackie to Just Seventeen*, London: Macmillan.

—— (1994a), *Postmodernism and Popular Culture*, London: Routledge.

—— (1994b) 'Shut Up and Dance: Youth Culture and Changing Modes of Femininity', in A. McRobbie, *Postmodernism and Popular Culture*, London: Routledge .

McRobbie, A. and J. Garber (1991), 'Girls and Subcultures', in A. McRobbie, *Feminism and Youth Culture. From Jackie to Just Seventeen*, London: Macmillan.

McRobbie, A. and M. Nava (eds) (1989), *Gender and Generation*, London: Macmillan.

Mansfield, A. and B. McGinn (1993), 'Pumping Irony: The Muscular and the

Feminine', in S. Scott and D. Morgan (eds), *Body Matters. Essays on the Sociology of the Body*, London: Falmer Press.

Mansfield, L. and J. Maguire (1999), 'Active Women, Power Relations and Gendered Identities: Embodied Experiences of Aerobics', in S. Roseneil and J. Seymour (eds), *Practising Identities*, London: Macmillan.

Marsh, J. (1985), *The Pre-Raphaelite Sisterhood*, New York: St Martin's Press.

Marsh, J. (2000), 'But I Want to Fly Too!: Girls and Superhero Play in the Infant Classroom', *Gender and Education*, 12(2): 209–20.

Maushart, S. (1999), *The Mask of Motherhood: How Becoming a Mother Changes Everything and Why we Pretend it Doesn't*, London: Pandora.

Mead, G.H. (1972), *Mind, Self and Society*, Chicago: University of Chicago Press.

Melia, J. (1995), 'An Honest Human Body. Sexuality and the Continuum of Resistance', in *Women's Studies International Forum*, 18 (5/6): 547–57.

Mercer, K. (1987), 'Black Hair/Style Politics', in K. Gelder and S. Thornton (eds), *The Subcultures Reader*, London: Routledge.

Merck, M. (ed.) (1998), *After Diana. Irreverent Elegies*, London: Verso.

Mifflin, M. (2001), *Bodies of Subversion. A Secret History of Women and Tattoo*, New York: Juno Books.

Miller, D. (1998), *A Theory of Shopping*, Oxford: Polity.

Millett, K. (1977), *Sexual Politics*, London: Virago.

Mirza, H.S. (ed.) (1997), *Black British Feminism: A Reader*, London: Routledge.

Mitchell, M. (1974), *Gone With the Wind*, London: Pan Books.

Modleski, T. (ed.) (1986), *Studies in Entertainment: Critical Approaches to Mass Culture*, Bloomington: Indiana University Press.

Morgan, D. (1993), 'You Too Can Have a Body Like Mine: Reflections on the Male Body and Masculinities', in S. Scott and D. Morgan (eds), *Body Matters. Essays on the Sociology of the Body*, London: Falmer Press.

Morrison, T. (1979), *The Bluest Eye*, London: Picador.

Muggleton, D. (2000), *Inside Subculture*, Oxford: Berg.

Mulvey, L. (1988), 'Visual Pleasure and Narrative Cinema', in C. Penley (ed.), *Feminism and Film Theory*, New York: Routledge.

Nettleton, S. and J. Watson (eds) (1998), *The Body in Everyday Life*, London: Routledge.

NUA Surveys (2001), www.nua.ie

Oakley, A. (1981), 'Interviewing Women: A Contradiction in Terms', in H. Roberts (ed.) *Doing Feminist Research*, London: Routledge.

Okely, J. (1996) *Own or Other Culture*. London: Routledge.

Olwig, K.F. and K. Hastrup (eds) (1997), *Siting Culture: The Shifting Anthropological Object*, London: Routledge.

Orbach, S. (1988), *Fat Is a Feminist Issue*, London: Arrow.

Padfield, M. and I. Proctor (1996), 'The Effect of Interviewer's Gender on the Interviewing Process: A Comparative Study', *Sociology*, 30 (2): 355–66.

Parkins, W. (2000), 'Protesting Like a Girl. Embodiment, Dissent and Feminist Agency', *Feminist Theory*, 1 (1): 59–78.

Pearce, L. (1991), *Woman/Image/Text. Readings in Pre-Raphaelite Art and Literature*, Hemel Hempstead: Harvester Wheatsheaf.

Pearsall, M. (ed.) (1997), *The Other Within Us. Feminist Explorations of Women and Aging*, Oxford: Westview Press.

Pierce, S. Szostak (1999), 'Even Further: The Power of Subcultural Style in Techno Culture', in K.K.P. Johnson and S.J. Lennon (eds), *Appearance and Power*, Oxford: Berg.

Plant, S. (1997), *Zeros and Ones: Digital Women and the New Technoculture*, London : Fourth Estate.

Polhemus, T. (1994), *Street Style. From Sidewalk to Catwalk*, London: Thames and Hudson.

—— (1996), *Style Surfing. What to Wear in the 3rd Millennium*, London: Thames & Hudson.

Polhermus, T. and L. Proctor (1978), *Fashion and Anti-Fashion: Anthropology of Clothing and Adornment*, London: Thames & Hydson.

Price, J. and M. Shildrick (eds) (1999), *Feminist Theory and the Body*, Edinburgh: Edinburgh University Press.

Raphael, A. (ed.) (1995), *Never Mind the Bollocks: Women Rewrite Rock*, London: Virago.

Reinharz, S. (1992), *Feminist Methods in Social Research*, Oxford: Oxford University Press.

Reynolds, S. and J. Press (1995), *The Sex Revolts: Rebellion and Rock 'n' Roll*, London: Serpent's Tail.

Ribbens, J. (1989), 'Interviewing – An 'Unnatural' Situation?', *Women's Studies Internation Forum*, 12 (6): 579–92.

Ribbens, J. and R. Edwards (1998), *Feminist Dilemmas in Qualitative Research*, London: Sage.

Rich, A. (1996), 'Compulsory Heterosexuality and Lesbian Existence', in S. Jackson and S. Scott (eds), *Feminism and Sexuality. A Reader*, Edinburgh: Edinburgh University Press.

Richardson, D. (ed.) (1996), *Theorising Heterosexuality. Telling it Straight*, Oxford: Oxford University Press.

Richardson, D. (2000), *Rethinking Sexuality*, Oxford: Sage.

Roberts, H. (ed.) (1981), *Doing Feminist Research*, London: Routledge & Kegan Paul.

Robinson, V. (1996), 'Heterosexuality and Masculinity: Theorizing Male Power or the Male Wounded Psyche?', in D. Richardson (ed.) *Theorizing Heterosexuality. Telling it Straight*, Oxford: Oxford University Press.

Rogers, M.F. (1999), *Barbie Culture*, London: Sage.

Rolley, K. (1990), 'Cutting a Dash: The Dress of Radclyffe Hall and Una Troubridge', *Feminist Review*, 35, summe: 54–66.

Roman, L.G. (1988), 'Intimacy, Labor and Class: Ideologies of Feminine Sexuality in the Punk Slam Dance', in L.G. Roman and L.K. Christian-Smith (eds), *Becoming Feminine. The Politics of Popular Culture*, London: Falmer Press.

Roman, L.G. and L.K. Christian-Smith (eds) (1988), *Becoming Feminine: The Politics of Popular Culture*, London: Falmer Press.

Ross, A. and T. Rose (eds) (1994), *Microphone Fiends: Youth Music and Youth Culture*, London: Routledge.

Roseneil, S. (1996), 'Experience, Consciousness and Identity at Greenham', in N. Charles and F. Hughes-Freeland (eds), *Practising Feminism: Identity, Difference, Power*, London: Routledge.

Roseneil, S. and J. Seymour (eds) (1999), *Practising Identities*, London: Macmillan.

Rosenthal, R. and R. Rosnow (1975), *The Volunteer Subject*, New York: Wiley & Sons.

Rowe, K. (1986), 'Feminism and Fairytales', in J. Zipes (ed.), *Don't Bet on the Prince*, Aldershot: Gower.

Rubinstein, R.P. (1995), *Dress Codes. Meanings and Messages in American Culture*, Oxford: Westview Press.

Russo, M. (1995), *The Female Grotesque. Risk, Excess and Modernity*, London: Routledge.

Schulze, L. (1990), 'On the Muscle', in J. Gaines and C. Herzog (eds), *Fabrications. Costume and the Female Body*, London: Routledge.

Schreier, B.A. (1989), 'Introduction', in C.B. Kidwell and V. Steele (eds), *Men and Women. Dressing the Part*, Washington, DC: Smithsonian Institution Press.

Schuyf, J. (1993), '"Trousers with Flies!!" The Clothing and Subculture of Lesbians', *Textile History*, 24 (1): 61–73.

Sciebinger, L. (ed.) (2000a), *Feminism and the Body*, Oxford: Oxford University Press.

—— (ed.) (2000b), 'Introduction', in L. Sciebinger (ed.), *Feminism and the Body*, Oxford: Oxford University Press.

Scott, J. (1988), *Gender and the Politics of History*, New York: Columbia University Press.

Scott, S. and D. Morgan (eds) (1993*)*, *Body Matters. Essays on the Sociology of the Body*, London: Falmer Press.

Segal, L. (1990*)*, *Slow Motion: Changing Masculinities, Changing Men*, London: Virago.

Selwyn, N. and K. Robson (1998), 'Using E-mail as a Research Tool', *Social Research Update*, 21, summer.

Sharpe, S. (1994), *'Just Like a Girl'. How Girls Learn to be Women. From the 70s to the 90s*, London: Penguin.

Shilling, C.(1993), *The Body and Social Theory*, London: Sage.

Silverman, K. (1986), 'Fragments of a Fashionable Discourse', in T. Modleski (ed.), *Studies of Entertainment. Critical Approaches to Mass Culture*, Bloomington: Indiana University Press.

Skelton, T. and G. Valentine (eds) (1997), *Cool Places. Geographies of Youth Cultures*, London: Routledge.

Smith, D.E. (1988) 'Femininity as Discourse', in L.G. Roman and L.K. Christian-

Smith (eds), *Becoming Feminine. The Politics of Popular Culture*, London: Falmer Press.

Soloman, M. (ed.) (1985), *The Psychology of Fashion*, Lanham, MD: Lexington Books.

Sontag, S. (1997), 'The Double Standard of Aging', in M. Pearsall (ed.), *The Other Within Us. Feminist Explorations of Women and Aging*, Oxford: Westview Press.

Soueif, A. (2001), 'The Language of the Veil', in *The Guardian Weekend*: 15–32.

Stacey, J. (1988), 'Desperately Seeking Difference', in L. Gammon and M. Marshment (eds), *The Female Gaze. Women as Viewers of Popular Culture*, London: The Women's Press.

Stanley, L. and S. Wise (1993), *Breaking Out Again: Feminist Ontology and Epistemology*, London: Routledge.

Steele, V. (1995), *Fetish: Fashion, Sex and Power*, Oxford: Oxford University Press.

—— (ed.) (1997a), Editorial, *Fashion Theory: The Journal of Dress, Body and Culture*, 1 (1): 1–2.

—— (ed.) (1997b), 'Anti-Fashion: The 1970s', *Fashion Theory: The Journal of Dress, Body and Culture*, 1 (3): 279–95.

—— (ed.) (1997c) Editorial, *Fashion Theory: The Journal of Dress, Body and Culture*, 1 (4): 337–8.

Studlar, G. (1990), 'Masochism, Masquerade and the Erotic Metamorphoses of Marlene Dietrich', in I. Gaines and C. Herzog (eds), *Fabrications, Costume and the Female Body*, London: Routledge.

Summers, L. (2001*)*, *Bound to Please. A History of the Victorian Corset*, Oxford: Berg.

Sweetman, P. (1999), 'Marked Bodies, Oppositional Identities? Tattooing, Piercing and the Ambiguity of Resistance', in S. Roseneil and J. Seymour (eds), *Practising Identities*, London: Macmillan.

Tasker, Y. (1993), *Spectacular Bodies. Gender, Genre and the Action Cinema*, London: Routledge.

—— (1998), *Working Girls. Gender and Sexuality in Popular Cinema*, London: Routledge.

Tate, S. (1999), 'Making your Body your Signature: Weight-training and Transgressive Femininities', in S. Roseneil and J. Seymour (eds), *Practising Identities*, London: Macmillan.

Taylor, C. (1989), *Sources of the Self: the Making of the Modern Identity*, Cambridge, MA: Harvard University Press.

Taylor, L. (1983), *Mourning Dress. A Costume and Social History*, London: George Allen & Unwin.

Thesander, M. (1997), *The Feminine Ideal*, London: Reaktion Books.

Thornton, S. (1994), 'Moral Panic, the Media and British Rave Culture', in A. Ross and T. Rose (eds), *Microphone Fiends. Youth Music and Youth Culture*, London: Routledge.

—— (1995), *Club Cultures. Music, Media and Subcultural Capital*, London: Polity Press.

Tseëlon, E. (1995), *The Masque of Femininity*, London: Sage.

Turner, B.S. (1996), *The Body and Society*, London: Sage.

Urla, J. and A.C. Swedlund (2000), 'The Anthropometry of Barbie. Unsettling Ideals of the Feminine Body in Popular Culture', in L. Sciebinger (ed.), *Feminism and the Body*, Oxford: Oxford University Press.

Ussher, J.M. (1997), *Fantasies of Femininity: Reframing the Boundaries of Sex*, London: Penguin Books.

—— (ed.) (2000), *Women's Health. Contemporary International Perspectives*, Guildford: BPS Books.

Veblen, T. (1994), *The Theory of the Leisure Class*, New York: Dover Publications.

Walter, T. (ed.) (1999), *The Mourning for Diana*, Oxford: Berg.

Weeks, K. (1998), *Constituting Feminist Subjects*, Ithaca, NY: Cornell University Press.

Wheaton, B. (2004), *Lifestyle Sport. Consumption, Identity and Difference*, London: Routledge.

Whelehan, I. (2000), *Overloaded. Popular Culture and the Future of Feminism*, London: The Women's Press.

Whiteley, S. (ed.) (1997), *Sexing the Groove: Popular Music and Gender*, London: Routledge.

Widdicombe, S. and R. Wooffitt (1995*)*, *The Language of Youth Subculture: Social Identity in Action*. London: Harvester Wheatsheaf.

Williamson, M. (2001), 'Vampires and Goths: Fandom, Gender and Cult Dress', in W.J.F. Keenan (ed.), *Dressed to Impress. Looking the Part*, Oxford: Berg.

Willis, P. (1977), *Learning to Labour. How Working Class Kids get Working Class Jobs*, Aldershot: Gower.

Willis, P. (1978), *Profane Culture*, London: Routledge.

Wilson, E. (1985), *Adorned in Dreams: Fashion and Modernity*, London: Virago.

—— (1990a), 'Deviant Dress', *Feminist Review*, 35, summer, 67–74.

—— (1990b), 'All the Rage', in J. Gaines and C. Herzog (eds), *Fabrications. Costume and the Female Body*, London: Routledge.

—— (1992), 'Fashion and the Postmodern Body', in J. Ash and E. Wilson (eds), *Chic Thrills. A Fashion Reader*, London: Pandora Press.

—— (1994), 'Is Transgression Transgressive?', in J. Bristow and A.R. Wilson (eds), *Activating Theory: Lesbian, Gay, Bisexual Politics*, London: Lawrence & Wishart.

—— (1998), 'Bohemian Dress and the Heroism of Everyday Life', *Fashion Theory: The Journal of Dress, Body and Culture*, 2 (3): 225–44.

—— (2000), *Bohemians. The Glamorous Outcasts*, London: I.B. Tauris.

Winship, J. (1987), *Inside Women's Magazines*, London: Pandora.

Wolf, D. (ed.) (1996), *Feminist Dilemmas in Fieldwork*, Oxford: Westview Press.

Wolf, N. (1990), *The Beauty Myth*, London: Chatto & Windus.

Woods, P. (1999), *Successful Writing for Qualitative Researchers*, London: Routledge.

Woodward, K. (ed.) (1997), *Identity and Difference*, London: Sage.

Wurtzel, E. (1998), *Bitch. In Praise of Difficult Women*, London: Quartet Books.

Yin, R.K. (1984), *Case Study Research: Design and Methods*, London: Sage.

Young, I.M. (1990), *Throwing Like a Girl and Other Essays in Feminist Philosophy and Social Theory*, Bloomington: Indiana University Press.

Zipes, J. (ed.) (1986), *Don't Bet on the Prince*, Aldershot: Gower.

Zita, J.N. (1997), 'Heresy in the Female Body: the Rhetorics of Menopause', in M. Pearsall (ed.), *The Other Within Us. Feminst Explorations of Women and Aging*, Oxford: Westview Press.

# Appendix 1
# The 'Nuts and Bolts': Methods

> Presenting the research process as orderly, coherent and logically organized has consequences ... Most of us get a nasty shock when we come to do the research ourselves ... The point at which we begin to realize that this 'hygienic research' in which no problems occur, no emotions are involved, is 'research as it is described' and not 'research as it is experienced', is frequently a crucial one.
>
> L. Stanley and S. Wise, *Breaking Out Again*

For reasons outlined in Chapter 1, I feel it is important (not to mention interesting to those of us who enjoy methodological matters) to include the background to the research, the practicalities of actually collecting the data. Therefore, here I reflect on the methods I employed (the 'nuts and bolts' of my approach): my methodological framework, sampling, the interviews, analysis and narrative, and a brief reflection on my own place in (or outside) the research. As I argued in Chapter 1, more empirical research is needed generally in these areas and, by the same token, more transparent discussion of methods because data are not collected simply by waving a magic wand. After all, effective researchers are vital for the continuation of effective research data!

The women in this study are not representative of some kind of 'generalised population'. Their narratives are personal and localised, whilst also drawing out several key themes, which were echoed throughout the interviews and which identified areas of contradiction or concern which the research could focus on. The themes emerged from the women's narratives and, ultimately, were not the ones initially sought by me. 'Through careful examination, and in the telling, we can discover that specific moments in individual lives inform us about both dominance and forms of resistance' (Okely, 1996: 214). The narratives of the women in this study provided ways of locating them within the dominance of 'traditional' feminine norms, and the types of resistance (and acceptance) that they practised within this framework.

## Framework

The methodological frameworks of this study are sociological, qualitative methods. In particular, several feminist methodological articles were helpful. For example, Oakley (1981), in a ground-breaking article, demonstrates how traditional methods have failed to account for the relationship between researcher and participant; Finch (1984) argues for a political approach, where one's feminism is taken into account as part of the research process; Ribbens (1989) examines the friendships and collaborations which can be found in research where women are researching women; and Kirkwood (1993) criticises the lack of the researcher's personal response in traditional methodologies. I also drew on the work of the following, who were invaluable at different stages: Burgess (1984) on fieldwork; Yin (1984) on design and methods; and Woods (1999) on successful writing for qualitative researchers, with advice on everything from overcoming writer's block to structure.

I asked the participants the questions that I did, in relation to the analytical framework, in an effort to 'fill in gaps' and to move forward existing analysis. For example, whilst there have been numerous studies seeking to 'place' girls and young women in subcultures via analyses of how, when and where they participated (McRobbie, 1989a; McRobbie and Nava, 1989), there have been no attempts to analyse how and why adult women continue to dress in the rebellious and often outrageous styles of their youth. Similarly, there are many studies about style and fashion (Soloman, 1985; Evans and Thornton, 1989; Rubinstein, 1995; Breward *et al.*, 2002), about various subcultural or subversive styles and 'anti-fashion' (Steele, 1995; Finkelstein, 1997; Williamson, 2001) and about how previously ignored cultural forms (such as appearance) could, in fact, be repeatedly co-opted by the mainstream until it, again, refashioned itself back into 'alternative' style (Hebdige, 1979). Many of the existing studies originate from backgrounds of history of fashion, art, fashion production and cultural or media studies. This research is multidisciplinary, since it draws upon the work of cultural studies or gender studies (for example, about both the representation and rendition of traditional and unconventional femininities).

Whilst this research is about placing women within (and outside) both dominant ideologies and 'alternative' subcultures, I was seeking replies which might illuminate how and why these women continue to dress as they do, and what the personal meanings of their appearance are – insights into their own constructions of femininities, pleasures and resistance.

## Sampling

I spent some time considering how I would establish access to potential respondents since it was not immediately clear where I could effectively 'collect' data. There was no central register or definite meeting point that I could go to to find participants. So my difficulties could have been in actually finding the women I wanted to interview, that no one would respond, rather than, other types of research which may, for example, have to deal with gatekeepers (which can be anything from ethics committees to day centre-managers). There is a distinction between physical access (that is, the researcher gains entry to the physical setting) and social access (where rapport and consent are a continually negotiated process) (Lee, 1993: 121). At the early stages I was establishing physical access. During the fieldwork stage of my research I was maintaining physical access and establishing social access. At the latter stage of my research up until, and sometimes beyond, sending the copy of the transcript to the participant, I was maintaining social access.

One of the first ways I established access was by making contact with two women, one who owned a tattooing studio and one who ran the piercing studio there. I introduced myself and my research topic to them, and asked if they would be willing to participate. Even when potential interviewees are clear about the scope and aims of the research, the issue of consent is a formal and ongoing process and should not be overlooked at any time – which may sound obvious but should be key: It is important always to give people the opportunity to change their mind about participating. An important way of collecting the sample was the use of 'snowballing', where one woman recommends or introduces another woman, who also becomes a participant. I found that participants were always happy to do this, in fact offered to do it. For example, an extract from my field diary for 14 January 1998 reads: '*Claudia nonchalantly asked Gwendolin if I could interview her whilst I stood there feeling rather fluffy.* '*Sam's doing research about women and their appearance*' she said. To Gwendolin's credit she didn't look me up and down.' My main concern with reaching the sample through the same five sites and one magazine, padded out with some snowballing, was that the sample would overlap to such an extent that the interviews would not produce data varied enough to base my research on. However, as the interviews progressed and themes emerged, this was no longer a worry. Although many of the women I interviewed echoed the words of other participants, this repetition created rich data, questions about and tensions within the narratives: there were issues and paradoxes that were important to the participants. Leaflets were placed in one tattooing studio and two piercing studios in Leeds, and two tattoo studios in Sheffield. The one interviewee in Blackpool was a participant who answered a letter I had sent to a magazine *Diva*, which was published in July 1997. Other women responded to the letter in *Diva*, women from, for example, Scotland, Durham, London, but I did not go to interview them as the travel costs were prohibitive. I believe now that sending a letter to *Diva* was not the wisest choice. I chose *Diva* as one of the few feminist magazines still widely available. Although I received sixteen letters and nine emails as a result of the letter, I had not anticipated that anyone would respond from anywhere other than Yorkshire, which I see now shows inadequate forethought. Women wanted to talk about themselves and their appearance and yet I believed that if I said I was doing the study in Yorkshire potential respondents would be only from Yorkshire. In the end, four participants came from *Diva*, ten from leaflets and six from 'snowballs' (Table A1.1).

**Table A1.1.** Sources for participants.

| Participant | Source |
|-------------|--------|
| Louise | Diva |
| Kiki | Leaflet |
| Sparkle | Leaflet |
| Morgan | Snowball |
| Vash | Leaflet |
| Zeb | Snowball |
| Claudia | Leaflet |
| Jody | Diva |
| Miss Pink | Snowball |
| Gwendolin | Snowball |
| Diz | Snowball |
| Flong | Leaflet |
| Bee | Diva |
| Janet | Diva |
| Delilah | Leaflet |
| Eloise | Leaflet |
| Gemini | Leaflet |
| Edie | Snowball |
| Marilyn | Leaflet |
| Lara | Leaflet |

## Pilot Study

I conducted a small pilot study to test the effectiveness of the interview schedule. 'The purpose of a pilot exercise is to get the bugs out of the instrument so that ... [participants] will experience no difficulties in completing it' (Bell, 1987: 128). It was crucial that I elicited what was of central significance to the participants in the time I had. (The theory may be to go back if an interview fails or if more information is required, but who really wants to ask someone to give up another hour or more of their time? Certain situations demand you are as effective as possible the first time!) Prompts could then be drawn from the list of every question I wanted to ask to construct a much more open interview schedule, for example, 'What do you mean by ...'. These two pilot interviews took place in Sheffield over two days and were simply the first two women who responded and for both interviews I went to the woman's house. Yin advises that 'the pilot case study helps investigators to refine their data collection plans with respect to both the content of the data and the procedures to be followed ... In general, convenience, access, and geographic proximity can be the main criteria for selecting the pilot case' (1984: 80).

I used open questions and the same questions for each participant for data purposes. The first participant was very articulate and clear about what she wished to discuss. It became immediately obvious to me that I had too many questions at this stage and needed far fewer, more generic questions so that the participant could choose her interpretation. For example, several questions asking about different aspects of appearance worked more effectively when condensed into the much broader 'tell me about your appearance'. It also became clear to me that what I would have liked to ask would not necessarily be answered, or even listened to, and shorter, broader, fewer questions would allow for more flexibility. In contrast, the second participant became tongue-tied by the tape recorder (this is discussed further below) and was anxious to answer all the questions I had. I edited the number of questions I asked whilst I was there and found that the fewer things I asked, the more she talked. This was a key lesson I learnt from the pilot study. 'The pilot case ... [is] mainly of value to the investigator' (Yin, 1984: 81), although it should still be seen as a valid part of the overall research project. I learnt that short open questions produced longer answers that seemed to more clearly reflect the participant's own interests and concerns. Additionally, I learnt to give plenty of time to each question and each answer, to keep silent while a participant was considering her answer. Learning not to fidget as the seconds ticked by was a valuable lesson.

## The Interviews

'Interviewing offers researchers access to people's ideas, thoughts, and memories in their own words rather than in the words of the researcher. This asset is particularly important for the study of women because in this way learning from women is an antidote to centuries of ignoring women's ideas altogether or having men speak for women' (Reinharz, 1992: 19). I had four main questions which formed the main framework of the interview schedule and also had a list of prompts and reminders according to the topics the participant talked about (see Appendix 5 for the interview schedule). Although there are many similarities between most of the interviewees, there are also differences: questions left out, asked differently, something ignored by a participant in one interview may have had particular importance for someone else. In comparison, structured interviews use a more rigid framework and take less account of the differences between each participant. Here I was not seeking information about representative trends but, rather, what was of significance to each particular woman on the particular day that I interviewed her, to examine the complex meanings around identity through personal narratives. However, although all the women were very different in aspects of their appearance or personality or beliefs, lots of duplicated themes emerged from the interviews (this is discussed further below).

The methods chosen are suitable for this particular research because semi-structured, in-depth interviews allowed me to explore more fully the experience of women who do not conform to traditionally feminine appearance. In contrast, questionnaires would not have provided an in-depth, personalised account of feelings about appearance and 'self'. If I had used questionnaires, I would not have been able to immediately 'tailor' questions and prompts according to the individual participant. The interview schedule was: 1. Tell me about your appearance. 2. Do you think you resist traditional sorts of 'femininity'? 3. Do you consider yourself part of a subculture or group? 4. How do you place yourself within wider society? I asked these questions for the following reasons:

1. The first question was designed to elicit from the participants their own priorities about their appearance. They were invited to start wherever they liked and construct a narrative about their appearance. Most participants chose to start with their childhood or teen years and charted for me the progress of their appearance, things they had done, things they wanted to do or wished they had done. This provided information about their concerns and anxieties as well as about the pleasures they

experienced. Asking about appearance raised other issues such as ageing. For example, I asked them to describe or name two famous women, one who signified, for them, traditional femininity and one for non-traditional femininity – and then where would the participant see herself on this continuum. To complement this understanding I also asked each participant what she used which was 'traditionally feminine'. This was to assist in 'placing' the participant in relation to her own perceived boundaries of femininity.

2. This question aimed to find out how the participants understood and described femininity; where they placed themselves in relation to different sorts of femininity; and what, if anything, they used which they none the less considered to be a feminine item (for example, perfume). Understanding the participants' own attitudes to both traditional and non-conforming femininities was key to analysing how and why they dress as they do. For example, I asked them for a description of a 'different' femininity, someone or something they would include within their own meaning of the term 'unconventional', to illuminate what other group/s of women she would include within/out the boundaries of acceptability. Some participants mentioned particular famous women; others simply described particular details that they would look for.

3. The third question was to 'place' the participants: did they think they were part of a subculture? Were they too old? This was in light of subcultural theory, which almost without exception overlooks the experiences of those past their 'youth'.

4. If the participants didn't think they were part of a subculture (whether any more or ever), this final question could help me to understand where they did place themselves in a society in which they consciously stated their 'difference' through their appearance.

I hoped to achieve relaxed, friendly interviews where I asked the questions I wanted to ask, listened carefully to the answers so that I could appropriately prompt or clarify any points and hoped not to 'lead' anyone on any answers they gave me. I found that not every woman needed a prompt and if she did it seemed to be because we had just begun and she was still 'feeling her way'. The other questions were quickly interpreted by each participant in whatever way she chose. I was wary of the interview being *too* relaxed and friendly and becoming nothing more than a chat where the 'conversation' veered wildly away from the research and stayed there. Oakley describes traditional interviewing techniques as: 'essentially a conversation ... but it is also, significantly, an instrument of data collection ... The motif of successful interviewing is to be friendly but not too

friendly ... A balance must be struck between the warmth required to gen-
erate 'rapport' and the detachment necessary to see the interviewee as an
object under surveillance' (1981: 33). Oakley is commenting on traditional
(outdated) interview methods and thus needs to draw a marked distinction
between feminist and traditional methods in order to reveal that 'unbiased'
interviews are not possible. My own experience has shown me that no two
interviews will be the same and that, while plans can be made, they must
be flexible enough to accommodate different interviewees. The women I
interviewed were all welcoming but it was also obvious throughout that
this was something 'extra', not just a chat. For example, several women
thanked me for doing research about 'older' women, many said that they
felt excited because they had never been interviewed before, and all of them
told me that they had enjoyed the experience (although I realise this could
just be because they were polite!).

The interviews were 'focused' in that they lasted for a relatively short
period of time (an hour to an hour and a half), had features of a conversation, but were adhering to an interview schedule (Yin, 1984: 89). Researchers should be aware of 'providing for unanticipated events, including
changes in the availability of interviewees as well as changes in the mood
and motivation of the case study investigator' (Yin, 1984: 75). This is
something I encountered at the beginning and again at the end of the interviewing period: 'losing' two potential participants before I had even collected them (summer 1997 and early autumn 1998). Two different women
responded to the leaflet, rang me, expressed great enthusiasm and arranged
an interview but then neither carried through with the interview. I organ-
ised eleven interviews in Sheffield and one in Blackpool over a six-month
period. I transcribed these interviews (four of them several months later)
and began writing up my research findings applying much the same questions as after the pilot study. Two months after this I arranged another two
in Sheffield and the final eight interviews in Leeds. Interviews were taped
with permission and notes made afterwards as soon as possible in a
research diary. The reason for this is that I would make notes about a participant's excitement or agitation in response to particular themes or body
language that had drawn my attention. I also noted what each participant
wore and where we were so that I could more clearly remember everyone
afterwards (for example, I interviewed one participant in her piercing
studio with us both standing throughout, sorting through body jewellery
and drinking tea).

I chose to call the women who are interviewed in this study participants,
rather than subjects, interviewees or respondents, because the term 'participants' more adequately demonstrates their interest and personal invest-

ment in the subject of the study. Reinharz describes participatory research as when participants make decisions about some elements of the study although this can be limited to 'a slight moderation of roles' (1992: 181). I asked all participants to choose their own pseudonym. Asking participants to choose their own pseudonyms can be seen to be a *very* slight moderation of roles and therefore does not make this research participatory in that the participants did not have input into the analysis of data. The reason for deciding to use pseudonyms was primarily that the research was done in and around Sheffield or Leeds and, as with any 'minority' group, lots of the women knew, or knew of, other participants. Also I asked the women to choose names themselves so that they had some choice about their interview 'persona' and most women enjoyed the idea of choosing a pseudonym. The choice of pseudonyms was interesting in its own right; why did women choose particular names? 'Miss Pink', for example, chose hers because of her pride in her long pink hair, 'Gemini' because of her birth sign, 'Claudia' and 'Zeb' for cats. 'Delilah' chose her name because *'I would like to bring the lot down'*, 'Eloise' because *'it's a good goth name'* (the title of a 1986 song by *The Damned*) and 'Kiki' for a favourite artist. See Table A1.2 for a full list of reasons why each woman chose the pseudonym she did.

There was a great reluctance among the participants to be categorised at all but there was a particular aversion to people attempting to label them who were 'outsiders', people who were mainstream, 'townies', people who were not like-minded – participants resisted the idea of being categorised whilst categorising the people who might do so. For example, one woman complained that most people called her a goth although this was not how she categorised herself. With this in mind I asked the women to consider some possible self-appellations. At the beginning of each interview I gave the participant a list of words and asked her to choose one or more words or short phrases to describe herself, or none at all, or to add her own (Table A1.3).

Five interviews took place at the sites where respondents were 'collected' via the leaflet, for example, in the tattooing and piercing studios and in the hairdressing salon. However, if participants wished to be interviewed somewhere else, such as their own home, interviews were conducted there. I usually took up to half an hour before I switched on the tape to make sure I had given the participant the introductory letter and form (see Appendix 4), and to give us time to talk and for the participant to ask any questions about what was going to happen. It was always worth checking that the tape recorder was switched on in suitable conditions. For example, when I interviewed in the tattooing studio, I had to insist that the interviewing

**Table A1.2.** Reasons participants gave for choosing their pseudonym.

| Participant | Reason for pseudonym |
|---|---|
| Louise | Character from a film |
| Kiki | Favourite artist |
| Sparkle | Favourite word |
| Morgan | Always liked the name |
| Vash | Favourite TV character |
| Zeb | Name of cat |
| Claudia | Name of cat |
| Jody | Favourite name |
| Miss Pink | Pink hair |
| Gwendolin | An old nickname |
| Diz | Favourite TV character |
| Flong | From her real initials |
| Bee | First initial of her real name |
| Janet | Middle name |
| Delilah | Favourite character |
| Eloise | Favourite song title |
| Gemini | Birth sign |
| Edie | Always liked the name |
| Marilyn | Favourite movie star |
| Lara | From playstation character |

took place in a back room so that the buzz of the needle did not drown out the words on the tape.

All of the participants I interviewed in their own homes (thirteen in total) treated the interview as a social occasion: five had got out photographs of themselves for me to look at; one escorted me to the sea front; two opened wine and asked me to stay for a meal; everyone with tattoos or piercings offered to show them to me; I was offered biscuits, tea, sandwiches, cake, cigarettes; two showed me poems they had written. I also found that we talked some more when the interview was over. Oakley calls the idea of women interviewing women a contradiction in terms since, she argues, women are more likely to turn an interview into a conversational, social occasion due to their propensity for 'talk':

I found that interviewees very often took the initiative in defining the inter-viewer–interviewee relationship as something which existed beyond the limits of

**Table A1.3. Descriptions of self.**

| Participants | Words Chosen to Describe Themselves |
| --- | --- |
| Louise | 'Not mainstream' |
| Kiki | 'Individual', 'non-conforming', 'not mainstream', 'not traditionally feminine?' |
| Sparkle | 'Unique', 'distinctive', 'comfortable' |
| Morgan | 'Individual' |
| Vash | 'Resisting', 'non-conforming', 'not mainstream', 'not traditionally feminine' |
| Zeb | 'Different', 'resisting', 'not mainstream', 'dressing to signal politics (with a small "p")' |
| Claudia | 'Alternative', 'non-conforming', 'not traditionally feminine' |
| Jody | 'Part of a subculture', 'dressing to signal politics' |
| Miss Pink | 'Individual' |
| Gwendolin | 'Individual' |
| Diz | 'Nothing' |
| Flong | 'Not alternative, just easy going', 'different but only to other people', 'individual, I hope so', 'rebelling in the beginning', 'resisting', 'non-conforming', 'part of the above – not subculture', 'just not fluffy rather than not traditionally feminine' |
| Bee | 'Not outlandish or flaming; a "femme" body with a "butch" attitude; still way out there' |
| Janet | 'Individual', 'not conforming', 'not traditionally feminine' |
| Delilah | 'Angry', 'resisting', 'non-conforming' |
| Eloise | |
| Gemini | 'Different', 'individual', 'anti-fashion', 'non-conforming', 'not mainstream', 'not traditionally feminine' |
| Edie | 'Not traditionally feminine' |
| Marilyn | 'Individual' |
| Lara | 'Different', 'non-conforming', 'alternative', 'individual', 'rebelling', 'resisting', 'not mainstream' |

question-asking and answering. For example, they did not only offer the minimum hospitality of accommodating me in their homes for the duration of the interview: at 92 per cent of the interviews I was offered tea, coffee or some other drink; 14 per cent of the women also offered me a meal on at least one occasion (1981: 45).

There have been other researchers who have written about the hospitality of participants (for example, Finch, 1984; Ribbens, 1989) and the difficulties (as well as the pleasures) that arise from this. Ribbens argues that interviews should be approached as 'particular types of social encounters' as there are no social situations that are not socially constructed and so not 'natural' anyway. She points out that 'social differences have major implications for how people talk to each other and what they say to each other as a result' (1989: 579), meaning that women share the social characteristic of being women and so find common ground on which to relate to each other. However, there are other important considerations, such as differences in class, age, sexuality and ethnicity, which may hinder the automatic provision of a 'gender bridge' to mutual understanding and friendly and/or open communication. In this study there were no significant class, age or ethnicity differences between myself and the participants. Finch admits she was 'startled by the readiness with which the women talked to me' (1993: 167) and I found the same with the women I interviewed. Even the two participants who were shy of the tape recorder were ready and willing to talk before and after I switched the tape on, and equally willing to talk (however stiltedly) when it was on.

Many of the participants were initially rather wary of being taped ('*I hate my voice*' was a common reason) so time to talk beforehand gave me a chance to reassure them that it was not going to be an unpleasant experience and that I could stop and start the tape, we did not have to plough straight through. Since women's words are often undervalued and women's voices and experiences marginalised, I wondered if the reticence to being taped stemmed from this, being unused to someone soliciting their opinions and not only sitting raptly listening but also taping them. Finch notes how many of the women she interviewed 'had found this kind of interview a welcome experience, in contrast with the lack of opportunities to talk about themselves in this way in other circumstances' (1993: 168). Several of the participants also expressed a fear of sounding '*squeaky*' or '*girlish*', which indicated a tension before the interview even began: here were women answering an appeal for participants because they do not subscribe to traditional 'femininity' and yet expressing worry that their voices would be too '*girly*'. Perhaps also the thought of being held hostage by something that was said off the cuff or the thought that they would say something 'wrong' made a small number of the participants markedly unenthusiastic about being taped rather than just listened to. Finch also reported 'some initial anxieties about ... their own "performance" in the interview situation' (1984: 167). One woman found the presence of the tape player particularly intrusive and could barely answer any of my questions or prompts

('*Oh, I've gone completely to pieces*'); another seemed to suffer from a form of stage fright as soon as I switched the tape on ('*I should know this, right?*') and changed from the articulate and bubbly woman who had drunk tea with me in her kitchen to being monosyllabic for the first part of the interview. As Kirkwood points out, women spend a lot of time being the listener (1993: 22). However, in this situation several participants said they felt that they were the expert telling their story.

Such details as how long the interviews lasted and where they took place are the concern of sociological work generally and not the concern only of feminist research, although establishing rapport has been a key element of many studies defined as feminist. 'Contemporary feminist interviewers are apt to report ... whether others were present, if material was recorded as it was obtained, how long the interview lasted, and how the researcher strove to establish rapport" (Reinharz, 1992: 23). When I first began my research, I had thought that 'rapport' was vital so that the participant relaxes and does not talk stiltedly. When I began my interviews, I realised that rapport is important for its own sake. Some level of reciprocity was also necessary, just as in 'normal' conversation, to establish a comfortable and 'safe' environment for the participants to reveal things about themselves, but also so that there is a more natural to and fro between two people talking. So, if someone asked me something about myself, I answered honestly, something which is likely to happen if two people are talking to each other. 'When I was asked questions I would answer them. The practice I followed was to answer all personal questions and questions about the research as fully as was required' (Oakley, 1981: 47). This willingness to be open about myself was a way to overcome some of the concerns about the 'real exploitative potential in the easily established trust between women ... [and is] the only morally defensible way for a feminist to conduct research with women' (Finch, 1993: 174). However, after interviewing one woman in her tattoo studio, I was 'interviewed' by her friends when we came back into the main waiting area. Three men (all tattooists) and two women (of which one was another participant, a tattooist, and another was a body piercer) quizzed *me*, in a friendly way, about what I was doing, why, how, to do what, for whom and for how long.

I initially made assumptions such as that I would just go in and interview someone and then leave after my two hours – which, of course, is what I did do but I had not made any kind of provision for enjoying talking to them, for feeling that some of them felt very lonely and did not want me to leave, and being asked to go out drinking with them, or being invited to a wedding in autumn 1998 ('*You can pretend it's for work and look at everyone's clothes*'); for being invited into their lives and feeling (at first) guilty, as if I were somehow there on false pretences. I felt some anxiety at the apparent unfairness of sweeping in, taking information from people to benefit myself, and then leaving (with a swish of my cloak as I left). I eventually rationalised this in various ways: that participants were fully aware of the scope and nature of our 'chat' (that is, interview), that I travelled to them, that all interviews were painstakingly planned to be convenient to participants, and that they were given records of what had happened in a letter introducing my research, along with a form with their names, date of interview, pseudonym chosen, etc. I also promised a transcript to each participant – explaining that it might take at least several weeks. Transcribing is the protracted and often intensely tedious end of data collection; a revelation not always apparent when one is planning the research, but none the less a good opportunity to hear the whole interview again. I also made clear that for practical reasons (the cost, the time) I did not intend to send a copy of the whole finished thesis to anyone. In these ways I felt that I was being ethically thorough.

The number of participants was appropriate for time and resources available to this study; time for interviewing was over one year and resources were practically non-existent. Thirteen of the interviews took place in Sheffield, South Yorkshire; five in Leeds, West Yorkshire; one in Huddersfield, West Yorkshire; and one in Blackpool, Lancashire. This apparently random division came about because I moved from Sheffield to Leeds during the research. I interviewed twenty women in total. The reason I interviewed twenty women is because, although twenty-two women showed a willingness to be interviewed, only twenty actually arranged and carried out the interview. This process was not a speedy one and participants trickled, rather than flooded, in between June 1997 and September 1998. As late as June and August 2000 two different women contacted me asking if I was still interviewing. I said no but with regret and I still see women that I would like to interview. (However, sometimes you have to know when to stop and sometimes you have to know when to stay stopped.) One had got my number from a leaflet found beneath a pile of magazines in a tattooing studio. Another had asked for my number from her friend who had been a participant. I found this strangely inspiring: it meant that the interest other participants had shown in the research had not just vanished, there was still interest in the subject and there were still women wanting to contribute.

## The Researcher

My interest at the outset stemmed from the lack of writing about women who looked 'different' and who were not teenagers but adults. Although there is existing and valuable literature about girls and women in subcultures (and about fashion generally, both discussed in Chapter 2), there is little work about how this relates to the personal narratives of participating grown-up women. I sought access via face-to-face formal introductions of myself and my research and did not encounter any major problems. On the contrary, the women I approached were always very interested and willing to be interviewed. This may have been partly or wholly due to my own appearance and the ways in which they perceived me because of this, that is, I was not an 'outsider' as such but, in fact, it was very possible that I would be like-minded. My own appearance was similar to that of the women. 'Persons more interested in the topic under investigation are more likely to volunteer ... personal characteristics of the recruiter are likely to affect the subject's probability of volunteering. Recruiters ... likely to obtain higher rates of volunteering ... are female recruiters. This latter relationship is especially modifiable by the sex of the subject and the nature of the research' (Rosenthal and Rosnow, 1975: 197). According to these findings, then, being a woman with similar characteristics to the participants, and having participants who were interested in the research, helped the process of finding volunteers. However, I would also argue that the participants of this study (like the participants of Padfield and Proctor's 1996 study) would have responded with equal enthusiasm to a male interviewer if they thought he was not an 'outsider' and was in some way 'like-minded'.

Researching a group with whom one shares some common experiences or lifestyle or beliefs can offer opportunities, albeit limited, for easier understanding, for example, if only in that slang terms or place names would be recognised without explanation. 'The connection between the research project and the researcher's self frequently takes the form of "starting with one's own experience"... Feminist researchers use [this] strategy ... for many purposes. It defines our research questions, leads us to sources of useful data, gains the trust of others in doing the research, and enables us to partially test our findings' (Reinharz, 1992: 259). Objectivity does not have to mean that the researcher maintains an almost superhuman distance from the participants and then afterwards coolly assesses the data. Objectivity can mean being reflexive and accurate and acknowledging one's subjectivity whilst maintaining a professional, rigorous approach. I would be 'most satisfied by a stance that acknowledges the researcher's position right up front, and that does not think of objectivity and subjectivity as warring with each other, but rather as serving each other' (Reinharz, 1992: 263). This approach was appropriate for this study in view of my similarities to the participants; of course, there would be instances where an exchange of personal information might be less appropriate.

In many ways the women exhibited feelings of pride about their appearance, the aesthetic element of it as well as their resistance, and this affected me in that I felt I had somehow 'lost my way'. One of several profound changes I found in myself was that all the talk of appearance and the conversations I had with the women about the history of their appearance made me reflect on my own 'image'. 'Field research is a learning situation in which researchers have to understand their own actions and activities as well as those of the people they are studying' (Burgess, 1984: 1). I was asked several times if I did this or that, for example, whether I had kept my hair crimpers plugged in twenty-four hours a day to keep my hair ferociously back-combed and crimped when I was younger, and I had done that for perhaps five years. This information seemed to hold some importance for the participants in that, although they almost all avowed their own 'individuality', they were happier and more comfortable knowing that I had some similar experiences, that I was approaching them (and the research) from a background and attitudes which indicated my 'like-mindedness'.

One's identity as a woman therefore provides the entrée into the interview situation ... that does not mean that only interviewers whose life circumstances are exactly the same as their interviewees can conduct successful interviews. It does mean, however, that the interviewer has to be prepared to expose herself to being 'placed' as a woman and to establish that she is willing to be treated accordingly. (Finch, 1993: 173)

So I shared some of the same social characteristics with the women I interviewed; a positive aspect of this is that I was approaching research from 'below' (or 'on the level'!), which can assist in grounding the data by being already familiar with elements of the particular lifestyle. A negative aspect is that I had to rigorously avoid assumptions; this can manifest itself in expectations about replies, and also in questions not asked.

Insights from feminist methodological research have raised questions about the meanings of subjectivity and objectivity and whether the two can be mutually exclusive. An important aspect of research labelled feminist is to endeavour not to allow personal experiences to 'colour' the research whilst recognising that the researcher is in the research. 'Our consciousness is always the medium through which research occurs' (Stanley and Wise, 1993: 164). The researcher is always the 'filter' through which findings are presented; the researcher is inextricably bound to her findings and theories. Despite my own feminism I did not expect or need the participants to feel the same. In fact, as Padfield and Procter also found: 'very few interviewees identified themselves as feminists and a ... proportion expressed reservations about what they defined as "feminism" ' (1996: 359). Therefore, although I am a feminist, this research is feminist 'only in the sense that it is concerned with ... building ... a portrayal of the situation of [some] women' (Stanley and Wise, 1993: 106).

## Analysis

The primary aspect of my approach to analysis was a focus on the contradictions and tensions which were clearly apparent in all of the interviews. So, for example, inconsistencies emerged about ageing; about feminine 'trappings' such as perfume and luxurious underwear; and about the meanings of being 'alternative' versus the realities of placing themselves as 'feminine'. This is in line with other studies such as Tseëlon (1995), who studied how women maintain a traditionally feminine appearance and how they felt 'damned if they did and damned if they didn't', and Fairhurst (1998) and Furman (1997), who both interviewed elderly women. Within this general framework of 'contradictions' are other 'subplots', which are approached in a 'stand-alone' manner in that I explore them as much for themselves alone as for how they fit into the wider framework of contradictions. For example, within the main theme of childhood are the tensions negotiated between being a 'girly' girl and being a tomboy and how this has implications even in adulthood. My own understandings of these issues comes from examining the interviews as a series of short stories, what Denzin calls 'slices', as well as looking at them as one long story or narrative: '[Qualitative interviewing can] produce particular, situated understandings ... These understandings are based on glimpses and slices of the culture in action' (1997: 8).

I considered how the participants talked about particular things and why they might do so in particular ways, that is, how they expressed themselves in response to certain cues. Denzin suggests the participant's narrative is itself not an exact, minutely noted rendition of the details of their life but rather that: 'every transcription is a re-telling – a new telling of a previously heard, now newly heard voice. Similarly, each telling by a speaker is a new telling, a new event in the history of the event being recounted' (1997: 43). So, whilst I could listen, understand and attempt to analyse the things the participants told me, I had to take everything they said at face value. My analysis of their narratives was to listen and remember the words they used, the subjects they brought up and elaborated on, ways of speaking (for example, laughter or stammering over a word or phrase) and body language. I also used Goffman's (1964) ideas about the 'front' people create through their surroundings. I took their narratives to be 'truth' (for example, did the overall meaning *radically* change if one participant told me she had dyed her hair at thirteen when, in fact, it was sixteen?) and instead focused on the content. As Giddens argues, 'a person with a reasonably stable sense of self-identity has a feeling of biographical continuity which she is able to grasp reflexively and, to a greater or lesser degree, communicate to other people' (1991: 53–4).

Issues about class, ethnicity and sexuality were generally not stated explicitly. Two women identified themselves as lesbians, although their narratives did not feature their sexuality as a primary theme. For all the women who did not mention their sexuality, it was possible to infer that they were heterosexual through what they said about relationships, attractiveness and sex. All the participants were white women and at no time did anyone say anything about 'alternative' styles being primarily, if not exclusively, a white phenomenon. Several participants owned their own businesses although the implication (whether stated openly or not) was that this had been a way to continue dressing as they did. Several participants were unemployed or students, and the remainder worked full- or part-time (see Appendix 2). Despite these variations, only one participant described her financial situation ('well off'). For the rest, their income was not mentioned at all. Nor did they refer to their backgrounds as being 'working-class' or 'middle-class', although it was perhaps possible to infer this from what they said about where they lived or other information about their families. However, I am wary of making any assumptions or suppositions about sexuality or class background, since my questions had not prompted this information in concrete terms.

Qualitative research traditionally sees data collection, analysis and writing up as tasks which occur simultaneously rather than one after the other. This was true of this study despite periods of inactivity. Identifying and evaluating the themes of a study need to be ongoing: during data collection to find the 'gaps' as well as during analysis, and still during final writing. Woods recommends studying the data repeatedly in order to identify themes; there may be one particular theme (or several) which rise above all the detail, or no sense may be drawn from anything it may seem like a collection of random opinions. However, just one insight or connection commonly leads to others (Woods, 1999: 42). This repeated study of the interviews meant that I could hold much of them in my head and could clearly remember fairly long quotes from interviews. So much of what someone has said is rarely consigned to memory in such detail – particularly when there are so many people saying so much! Olwig and Hastrup refer to dealing with and remembering so many words as their 'head-notes' (1997: 94) and this is arguably a by-product of the research process.

## The Participants

In Appendix 2 I provide a list of participant profiles. Additionally, here I provide some biographical background and descriptive information in order to 'introduce' the participants. I have chosen this information simply to illustrate recurring points about the women and not to attempt to make any general points about them as a group.

Out of twenty participants:

- twelve were in their thirties;
- two were in their forties;
- six were in their late twenties;

- all of them were white women;

- six had one or more children;
- eleven mentioned having cats;
- other pets (for example, dogs or rats) were mentioned six times;

- ten said that they were vegetarians;

- six had graduated with degrees (Gemini, Jody, Kiki, Lara, Sparkle, Zeb);
- nine had some other sort of professional qualification (Bee, Claudia, Delilah, Flong, Gwendolin, Jody, Louise, Miss Pink, Morgan);

- sixteen lived with partners, of which one was married;
- two were divorced;
- four lived alone;

- one participant (Bee) described herself as a performance artist;
- six owned their own businesses: two were tattooists (Flong, Miss Pink), one was a body piercer (Claudia), one was an artist (Delilah), another ran an 'alternative' clothing stall (Edie), and one was one of three people who had set up a drystone-walling business (Morgan);

- four were mature students (Jody, Vash, Kiki, Sparkle);
- three were unemployed (Janet, Marilyn and Eloise);
- seven worked full- or part-time (Jody, Gwendolin, Lara, Gemini, Vash, Diz, Louise).

**Table A1.4.**   Physical characteristics

|  | *Hair* | *Piercings* | *Tattoos* |
|---|---|---|---|
| Bee | Short purple | 10 ears | 2 |
| Claudia | Long black and blue | 1 body, 7 facial + ears | Multiple |
| Delilah | Long pink and yellow | 13 ears, 7 facial, 2 body | 10 |
| Diz | Very short hair | 12 ears, 1 body, 4 facial | 1 |
| Edie | Short hair | None | None |
| Eloise | Long bright red | 4 facial, 20 ears | 1 |
| Flong | Long black and white-blonde | 3 facial, 21 ears | 6 |
| Gemini | Medium bob | 2 body + ears | 3 |
| Gwendolin | Long bright orange | 3 facial, 2 body + ears | 3 |
| Janet | Very short hair | None | None |
| Jody | Short hair | 3 body, 2 facial + ears | 2 |
| Kiki | Long dreadlocks | 6 facial, 6 body + ears | 6 |
| Lara | Long black and purple | 2 facial, 4 body + ears | 5 |
| Louise | Very short hair | Multiple | Multiple |
| Marilyn | Short bob | None | None |
| Miss Pink | Long bright pink | 2 facial, 3 body + ears | 5 |
| Morgan | Very short hair | 6 facial, 6 body + ears | 6 |
| Sparkle | Long blue | Multiple facial, body + ears | 10 |
| Zeb | Long black | 2 facial, 20 + ears | 1 |
| Vash | Short black and blue | 3 facial + ears | 1 |

Although all the participants claimed to be individualists throughout their interviews, most of them shared particular characteristics, such as multiple tattooing and piercing and brightly dyed hair (for example, eleven said that they wore only black and fourteen said that they wore *only* boots (i.e. not shoes). In order to understand how much of a commitment this type of appearance can be it became necessary to have a breakdown of the amount of time and money one or more participants spent in a typical month. I contacted four of the participants who had said they were happy to contribute further at a later date. Of these four, two, Delilah and Vash, agreed to draw up a 'diary' of a typical month. Delilah's was done in July 2000 and I went to collect the diary in August, and Vash later rang to say she did not have time to do it (ironically, she had not realised how much she would have to write down and so how time-consuming it would be). However, as with her approach to all aspects of the interview, Delilah applied herself to her 'appearance diary' with enthusiasm and produced a detailed record of her activities and expenditure in a typical month. I tabled some examples of Delilah's diary entries, editing entries which were generally lengthy and so digesting entries for four weeks, and these are discussed in Chapter 4.

## Conclusion

Some of the main points of the research process were as follows.

I feel that one of the strengths of this study was that my relationship with the participants worked well; I was similar enough (to them) for them to feel able to talk to me, and yet different enough (from them) for them to trust that I was doing something 'serious'. For this reason, interviewing worked particularly well, as it provided opportunities for a range of subjects and issues to be discussed that less flexible methods of data collection might not have been able to accommodate. Another strength was the range of data produced in the narratives and the ways they tied in with and moved alongside, existing work.

Some weaknesses which I have since reflected on include one of the ways I accessed the participants: I feel it was a waste of my time to send a letter to a national magazine; with hindsight, I should have realised that many of the responses would be from too far away for me to go to and I think I was carried away with the excitement of finding my first participants. This research is not an exhaustive study of 'difference' and 'resistance'; all twenty participants were white women between the ages of twenty-seven and forty-nine years old, and no issues of sexuality, ethnicity or class are discussed here. Amongst the most obvious limitations of this research study were the time-scale and the budget, both of which were limited.

This study was begun initially in 1996, so this has meant that some early drafts felt stale when I returned to them, necessitating more rewriting than might otherwise have been needed. An anxiety connected to this was that other studies would emerge which covered the same area. However, although other studies have been published which were about women and their relationships to clothes (for example, Guy *et al.*, 2001), there are still none which deal specifically with the main themes of this study.

This research has taught me that ideas about rapport need not be ago-nised over. As Reinharz points out: 'it would be unfortunate if we were to introduce self-imposed limits to our research possibilities because of the notion of rapport ... Rather [researchers] who do research with people should consider rapport to be a fortunate outcome of some projects rather than a precondition of all research relationships' (1992: 266).

I found that some research relationships cannot be successfully 'made to fit' the subject area of the research since people will always have their own agendas. I have discovered the joys of successfully interviewing someone; the disappointments of a stilted or cancelled interview; the necessary tedium of transcribing interviews (each interview took approximately five hours to transcribe); and the boredom and the excitement of identifying themes and critical analysis.

In this appendix, I have examined why and how I approached the plan-ning of the research, and I have considered the interviews and the interview data. I have attempted to be as transparent as possible about my approach, my concerns, the difficulties and successes I encountered, and how these elements coagulated into the themes and analysis of the research.

# Appendix 2: Participant Profiles

Ages are at time of interview.

At the interview each participant was asked how she would describe herself and was asked to choose from a list of words. If she felt that none of the words applied to her, she could either add her own or choose not to have any.

'Bee': performance artist, age 38, Canadian, lives with partner and foster-children in own house, *'not outlandish or flaming; a "femme" body with a "butch" attitude; still way out there'*.

'Claudia': body piercer, age 37, one daughter, lives in own house with partner and cat, *'alternative'*, *'non-conforming'*, *'not traditionally feminine'*.

'Delilah': freelance artist, age 36, single by choice, lives in own house, *'angry'*, *'resisting'*, *'non-conforming'*.

'Diz': works in a factory, age 27, lives with husband and dogs and cat in own house, would like to have children, *'nothing'*.

'Edie': runs an 'alternative' clothing stall, age 39, has three children, lives with partner and four cats in own home, *'not traditionally feminine'*.

'Eloise' : currently unemployed, age 31, lives with cats and rats in rented flat, suffers from ME, *'unconventional'*.

'Flong': tattooist, age 31, lives with partner and cats in own house, *'not alternative, just easygoing'*, *'different but only to other people'*, *'individual, I hope so'*, *'rebelling in the beginning'*, *'resisting'*, *'non-conforming'*, *'part of the above – not subculture', 'just not fluffy rather than not traditionally feminine'.*

'Gemini': magistrate and district development officer for educational charity, age 48, lives with daughter and cats in own house, *'different'*, *'individual'*, *'anti-fashion'*, *'non-conforming'*, *'not mainstream'*, *'not traditionally feminine'*.

'Gwendolin': hairdresser, age 28, lives with partner (who currently works away) in own house, *'individual'*.

'Janet': unemployed, age 31, lives with partner and dog and cat in rented house, *'individual'*, *'not conforming'*, *'not traditionally feminine'*.

'Jody': mature student and care worker, age 33, divorced, lives with cat in own house, *'part of a subculture'*, *'dressing to signal politics'*.

'Kiki': mature art student, age 29, lives in a shared rented house, 'individual', *'non-conforming'*, *'not mainstream'*, *'?not traditionally feminine?'*.

'Lara': civil servant, age 31, lives alone in own house, *'different'*, *'non-conforming'*, *'alternative'*, *'individual'*, *'rebelling'*, *'resisting'*, *'not mainstream'*.

'Louise': youth worker and artist, age 40, lives in own house, *'not mainstream'*.

'Marilyn': age 27, lives with small son in rented flat, 'individual'.

'Miss Pink': tattooist, age 27, lives with fiancé in rented house, *'individual'*.

'Morgan': drystone-waller, age 30, in a relationship, lives with cats, rats, and chinchillas in rented flat, *'individual'*.

'Sparkle': mature postgraduate student, age 27, American, lives with partner and cats in rented flat, *'unique'*, *'distinctive'*, *'comfortable'*.

'Vash': mature student, age 37, lives with son and partner and cats in rented maisonette, *'resisting'*, *'non-conforming'*, *'not mainstream'*, *'not traditionally feminine'*.

'Zeb': researcher in health service, age 34, lives with husband and cats in own house, *'different'*, *'resisting'*, *'not mainstream'*, *'dressing to signal politics (with a small "p")'*.

**ARE YOU A WOMAN WHO
CONSIDERS HERSELF TO BE
NOT CONFORMING TO THE
POPULAR IDEALS OF
'FEMININITY'
THROUGH YOUR CLOTHES AND
APPEARANCE?**

**For example, IS YOUR STYLE/CLOTHING
TRADITIONALLY THOUGHT TO BE
'UNFEMININE' OR 'DIFFERENT'?**

**or, ARE YOU TATTOOED AND/OR
PIERCED?
DO YOU CONSIDER
YOURSELF TO BE 'ALTERNATIVE'
RATHER THAN MAINSTREAM?**

Would you be interested in participating in research?

I am a woman doing research about adult women (over 25) who dress and present themselves in ways which resist how a woman 'should' look. I am seeking women who are willing to volunteer for confidential, informal interviews/chats (which will take between 1 and 2 hours).

The interviews will take place as soon as possible in and around Leeds (at a place to suit you).

If you would like to know more (*without* obligation to end up being interviewed) please phone me:
Sam (0114) 222 XXXX
(this is an answerphone but I will get back to you very quickly)

# *Appendix 4*
## *Letter and Forms Given to Participants at the Interview*

[Note: this letter was given to participants on University headed paper.]

Samantha Holland
home: (0113) xxxxxxx
work: (0114) xxxxxxx
S.Holland@xxxx.ac.uk

**INTRODUCTION TO RESEARCH STUDY FOR PARTICIPANTS.**

(Provisional) Title:
'*Damned by their garb*'?
Women, Appearance and 'Alternative' Femininities

I am looking at the relationship between women and their clothing/appearance.

The study is for PhD research. The end result should be about 75,000 words of original work. End of registration is initially August 2001.

The interview is **ENTIRELY CONFIDENTIAL**. I will send you a copy of the interview as soon as I have transcribed it. When I start using the interview transcript as data your identity will be anonymous – I will be using pseudonyms for all participants (which you'll have chosen yourself).

If there is ANYTHING you would like to comment or elaborate on, or clarify, you are welcome to ring me (my no. is above). This could then be added as a footnote or postscript to the original transcript.

## Participant Details    <u>**CONFIDENTIAL**</u>

**Name:**

**Address:**

**Age:**

**Tele:**

**Pseudonym:**

**Date of interview:**

Are you willing to be telephoned, if necessary, at a later date to answer any more questions which might arise? (this could take the form of a second interview or a telephone call).   **Yes/No**
(*If you say yes now it <u>doesn't</u> mean you have to agree if I do contact you at a later date.*)

Would you be willing to take part in a focus/discussion group (with perhaps 4–6 other participants) in about a year's time? This is a tentative idea at this stage but would take approximately 1–2 hours and would be to check my interpretations of the data generated by the interviews (this would be done through participants' comments on my analysis).   **Yes/No**
(*Again, saying yes now does <u>not</u> mean that you will be expected to participate if a focus group is arranged.*)

---

Transcript sent:

Please choose a word or words (or no words, or add your own) to self-select.

Do you consider yourself/your appearance to be ... ?

- Alternative
- Different
- Individual
- Rebelling
- Anti-fashion
- Resisting
- Non-conforming
- Not mainstream
- Part of a subculture
- Dressing to signal politics
- Not traditionally feminine
- Unconventional

# Appendix 5
# Interview Schedule

## Themes/Questions

Tell me about your appearance – a history of your appearance.
Do you consider yourself as resisting traditional sorts of 'femininity'?
if so, how?
If no, would other people think so?
Do you consider yourself part of a subculture or group?
How do you place yourself within wider society?

## Prompts?

YOUR definitions of femininity.
Social conventions of age.
Social constraints – e.g. Families, motherhood, jobs, etc.
Politics/sexuality – just getting dressed up or for social change?
Who else would you include in unconventionality?
Who is traditionally feminine.
Sliding scale of 'differentness' – where/how do you feel more or less 'yourself'?
What contexts are different? E.g. social events, etc. How/would you compromise?
Body language/posture.
How far appearance linked to feelings of self-worth?
How do groups work? E.g. gatekeepers, particular places, etc.
Forms of migration – areas where like-minded people gather/live.

# Index